# LINDSAY HASSETT
### ◆ ONE OF A KIND ◆

## JACK McHARG

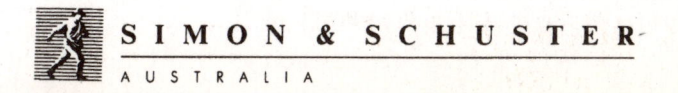

**SIMON & SCHUSTER**
AUSTRALIA

LINDSAY HASSETT: ONE OF A KIND

First published in Australia and New Zealand in 1998 by
Simon & Schuster Australia
20 Barcoo Street, East Roseville NSW 2069

A Viacom Company
Sydney  New York  London  Toronto  Tokyo  Singapore

© Jack McHarg 1998

All rights reserved. No part of this publication may be reproduced,
stored in a retrieval system, or transmitted, in any form or by any
means, electronic, mechanical, photocopying, recording or otherwise,
without the prior permission of the publisher in writing.

National Library of Australia
Cataloguing-in-Publication data

McHarg, Jack.
Lindsay Hassett : one of a kind.

Bibliography.
Includes index.
ISBN 0 7318 0726 X.

1. Hassett, Lindsay. 2. Cricket – Australia – Biography.
3. Cricket players – Australia – Biography. I. Title.

796.358092

Cover and book design: Anna Soo Design
Set in 10/13pt New Baskerville
Printed & Bound by the Griffin Press Pty Ltd

10 9 8 7 6 5 4 3 2 1

# FOREWORD

It must have given Jack McHarg great pleasure writing this book on Lindsay Hassett. Why? Simply because Lindsay is — was — such a wonderful and appealing personality. To write about him is to share the pleasures of a man who had everything and gave immense pleasure to his countless friends and fans.

Lindsay was small in physique but a giant in all things that mattered. There was not a petty bone in his body. He was mischievous, humorous, always saw the bright side of things but could, nevertheless, be as serious as necessary when the occasion demanded.

He was a superb athlete who could have played VFL football for Geelong, winning as he did two best and fairest awards in the amateur A-grade competition. He was reputed to be a better tennis player than his brother, Harry, who made the Davis Cup Squad. He was a single-figure golfer and A-grade standard at squash.

Lindsay's cricket, of course, speaks for itself, yet he has never been fully appreciated, mainly because World War II robbed him of his best years. While he had been a scintillating stroke player prewar, necessity turned him into a rather more dour player in his later years. That necessity was to the benefit of his team, especially to the younger players in his team. This book amply illustrates this role that Lindsay played. It is the first time I have seen, in print, this appreciation of his considerable contribution to the sides he captained, although I have known it for years.

He was not an opening batsman, but on many occasions he stood in at the sacrifice of his own performances. If a wicket fell early, he would go in at number three. If the start was good, he would send the younger player to the wicket. His total unselfishness has all too often been overlooked, as have the benefits his actions had on the success of the team. It is pleasing that at last someone has written of the selflessness of Lindsay Hassett — a man among men, at home equally with royalty, prime ministers and us more menial mortals.

It has been a pleasure to read this tribute and an honour to write the foreword to a book on so outstanding a character and so close a personal friend.

IAN JOHNSON

# CONTENTS

| | | |
|---|---|---|
| Foreword | | iii |
| **Chapter 1** | Getting to know Lindsay | 1 |
| **Chapter 2** | A man of varied gifts | 12 |
| **Chapter 3** | At school and beyond | 21 |
| **Chapter 4** | A notable debut — England 1938 | 31 |
| **Chapter 5** | Prelude to the Victory Tests | 47 |
| **Chapter 6** | The Australian Services team | 56 |
| **Chapter 7** | A few short ones from Lindsay | 70 |
| **Chapter 8** | The Tests of 1946–47 | 76 |
| **Chapter 9** | Australian summer with the Indians — 1947–48 | 87 |
| **Chapter 10** | Bradman's understudy — 1948 | 110 |
| **Chapter 11** | A drubbing for the Springboks — South Africa 1949–50 | 122 |
| **Chapter 12** | Freddy Brown's Englishmen — 1950–51 | 130 |
| **Chapter 13** | John Goddard's West Indians — 1951–52 | 141 |
| **Chapter 14** | The Springboks surprise Australia — 1952–53 | 148 |
| **Chapter 15** | Cricketing swan song — England 1953 | 158 |
| **Chapter 16** | Matching wits with Menzies | 179 |
| **Chapter 17** | Some thoughts on Lindsay | 186 |
| **Chapter 18** | 'Fade-out' | 197 |
| Statistics | | 204 |
| Author's note | | 212 |
| Bibliography | | 214 |
| Index | | 215 |

## CHAPTER 1
# GETTING TO KNOW LINDSAY

Neville Cardus, who is to cricket journalism what Shakespeare is to drama, tells of meeting Lindsay Hassett one hot night in Adelaide after the little man had bored spectators witless during the afternoon with a strokeless innings of 68 against a perspiring but fairly innocuous England attack. Cardus, who'd frequently seen Hassett bat with the grace and timing of Kippax or McCabe, asked him, 'Are you, too, forgetting how to hit the ball? Are you joining the Cricketers' Union of Universal Borers? Good heavens, Lindsay, what's the matter with you?' Poker-faced and inscrutable, Lindsay instantly replied, 'Wore Out! Just plain wore out'.

In his first-class career, which extended from 1933 to 1954, with a lengthy interruption owing to the war, Hassett was two batsmen. Prior to 1939, he was the swift-footed, elegant scourge of all bowlers (including the great O'Reilly as often as not), with that delicacy of touch which comes from perfect timing and an instant perception of where the feet should be placed to deal effectively with the delivery about to be received. War, the Victory Tests and the exhausting schedule insisted upon by the Board of Control — which required players, some of whom had been absent from home for anything up to five years, to cap their efforts with appearances in all Australian states — were the catalysts for the change. Captaincy, following the vice-captaincy of the national side, gave Lindsay a different perception of batting at the international level. In international games, he appeared to see himself as the sheet anchor. His batting became safe to the point of being boring and he was unrecognisable as the player of ten years previously. In other games, Lindsay reverted to true type, with dazzling strokes, placed to perfection, and with much of the best of Jackson, McCabe and Kippax brought together in his small frame.

Few would place Lindsay in the first half-dozen of Australian batsmen — Don Bradman, Victor Trumper, Charlie Macartney, Stan McCabe, Bill Ponsford and Greg Chappell fill these places — yet on overall first-class figures, Hassett pushes hard: 16,890 runs at 58.24. In scoring these runs, Hassett notched 59 centuries and 74 half-centuries from 322 innings.

These figures represent a score above 50 in every 2.42 innings. Greg Chappell's tally, similarly calculated, shows a half-century every 2.9 innings, Trumper 3.1, Macartney 3.5, McCabe 2.7 and Ponsford 2.6. The incredible Bradman, at 1.8, must be placed in a separate class, but Hassett, perhaps surprisingly, outstrips the others. It's also worth noting that, at the time of his retirement, Hassett's 59 first-class centuries were second only to Bradman's 117. Greg Chappell, with 74, Harvey, with 67, and Border, with 70, have subsequently overtaken Lindsay, all from many more visits to the crease.

In test cricket, Harvey, at 48.4, has slightly the better average — Hassett is at 46.56, while Chappell moves ahead at 53.86. As Test match captain, Lindsay won 14 of the 24 matches in which he was in charge, with 14 wins, 6 draws and 4 losses. Chappell, from 46 matches, won 20, drew 13 and lost 13. Border was skipper in no less than 93 Tests, winning 32, losing 22, drawing 38 and tieing 1.

These brief statistics suggest that Lindsay Hassett deserves consideration when candidates for the cricket Hall of Fame are assessed. His career, particularly in Tests, did not really begin until 1946, when World War II hostilities ceased. Lindsay was then 32 years old. Before 1939, Lindsay played only in the four Tests of the 1938 series in England. Today, many top players are 'doing an O'Reilly' with their boots and quitting at age 32 or soon after.

As the youngest of nine children, six boys and three girls, born to the Hassetts in Geelong, it was inevitable that Lindsay would draw the short straw when the more menial cricketing tasks were allocated by his brothers. When not engaged in backyard cricket, the boys would occasionally repair to the St Augustine's grounds opposite. Lindsay, as the most junior and smallest, would be made long-stop, with the promise that if he did the job properly and without whingeing, he'd get two innings when his seniors had finished. However, this reward was more often honoured in the breach rather than in the observance.

Hassett's years at The Geelong College were eventful. He followed older brothers Vin and Dick, and it would be true to say that this Catholic trio left more than a mark on their Protestant school. How not only Lindsay, but also the other two, came to be there seems to be the subject of some difference of opinion.

In September 1996, Ted, the senior surviving member of the original nine Hassett children, told me with both clarity and conviction that it happened as follows. Frank Rolland (later Sir Frank), principal of The Geelong College and a headmaster of note, was friendly with Edward Hassett, the boys' father, and it had come to his notice that young Lindsay was displaying exceptional elegance in his handling of a cricket bat at the tender age of ten. Lindsay and brothers Vin and Dick were at the time attending Geelong Central School to the satisfaction of all, except that the school was to close in the near future. Rolland put it to Hassett Senior that he would be pleased to offer Lindsay a scholarship to The Geelong College. Edward Hassett accepted the offer gratefully with the proviso, no doubt agreeable to Rolland, that if Lindsay went to the college on a scholarship, Edward would send Vin and Dick there at his own expense. Ted Hassett, was certain this story is true, but Vin and Dick, both in their eighties, doubt its authenticity. However, they are both a little vague when giving alternative reasons, although the name of a beloved family doctor crops up as a possible benefactor and underwriter of the enterprise.

The late Miss Adele Hassett thought that the reasons for sending the three boys to The Geelong College were of a more conventional nature. She believed that the proximity of the college to the Hassett home, together with the absence of any Catholic school in Geelong, were vital considerations.

Ted Hassett died in early 1997, aged 98, and it was not possible to pursue matters with him. Therefore, in the absence of any definite alternative, it seems reasonable to accept Ted's version. The boys' attendance at The Geelong College is not vital to the story of Lindsay Hassett, but it is interesting if only because of the sometimes fierce religious sectarianism that marred our history in the decades between the two world wars.

Not all of Edward Hassett's six boys were sporting champions, but at least four of them are well remembered for various sporting exploits. Edward Hassett, a partner in the Geelong real estate firm of Hendy and Leary, certainly did his bit to encourage his sons. Backyard cricket, with Dad participating when possible, was the order of the day outside school hours or during holidays. Edward would at times turn 'nasty', these occasions usually coinciding with the smashing of a large frosted glass window adjacent to the pitch. At such times, play would be suspended indefinitely — the period depending on when Dad felt like putting his arm over again.

The window 'problem' received the concentrated attention of the three main cricket activists and a happy conjunction of minds eventually produced the solution. A generation ahead of their time, Vin, Dick and Lindsay hit on the idea of louvres. Although they didn't call them 'louvres', the fitting of glass strips instead of the large pane simultaneously solved the problems of expense and unwelcome disruption of play in one dramatic stroke of genius. Broken panes could now be simply replaced from the stock thoughtfully kept close by and purchased at a fraction of the earlier oppressive cost. The batsman guilty of smashing one of the strips was obliged to replace it and replenish the stock at his own expense.

There was one disastrous and completely unallowed-for happening which engulfed the young cricketers, creating a financial crisis and leading to arguments over whether the blame should be sheeted home to the main perpetrator or accepted collectively as a catastrophe that could have happened to anyone. On the day in question, the boys were practising, using a stump only as the bat (à la Bradman). The window, now louvred, as well as being adjacent to the pitch, was approximately at right angles to the batsman on the offside. Dick Hassett, wielding the stump, accidentally lost his grip and the 'bat' flew almost vertically in a gentle parabola towards the window, hitting it and smashing all the louvres in one deadly stroke. This brought proceedings to a sudden stop and you might easily have heard the jaws dropping as the magnitude of the disaster registered. Dad (far from impressed, but appreciating the unusual nature of the misfortune), subsidised the boys in replacing the dozen or so glass strips.

'Tests' were played, usually between Lindsay and Vin, the spin of a coin determining who would be Australia and who would be the unlucky loser, England. Teams comprised the cricketers of the twenties: Collins, Macartney, Taylor and Co. for Australia, Hobbs, Sutcliffe, Tate and Strudwick for 'the Poms'. Scoring was an intricate but fair system, equipment basic (the bat was frequently of galvanised-iron material) and arguments were frequent and fierce.

It seems that at this stage of his life, early teens, Lindsay was quiet to the point of introspection. He blossomed at The Geelong College to become the complex but, on the whole, outgoing character familiar to cricket lovers and teammates. He acquired, or cultivated, the priceless ability to get away with behaviour which, in most other people, would have been regarded as outrageous. And it was all done with the mischievous eyes of a leprechaun framed within an otherwise poker face. E. W. Swanton, an unreserved admirer of Hassett, writing of the postmatch speeches after England recovered the Ashes in 1953, recorded the following exchange between Robert (Walter) Robins of the Marylebone Cricket Club (MCC) and the vanquished Australian skipper who'd just completed a gracious speech accepting defeat.

Robins: 'Well done, Lindsay. You couldn't have said it better.'

Hassett: 'Yes, not bad I thought myself, considering Lockie threw us out.'

The touchy thing about this one-liner is that the bowling action of Tony Lock, a main contributor to England's 1953 victory with 5–45 in Australia's second innings, had long been the subject of much discussion among cricketers of all countries. If Bob Simpson or Allan Border, for instance, had made the remark, one can only guess at the repercussions, both immediately and in the next editions of the English dailies. Hassett said it with a grin and everybody laughed.

An inveterate night person, Hassett had a rooted objection to going to bed before morning's early hours. Whether on tour or at home, he liked to stay up late. On tour, this attribute, which many would have termed a failing, made him less than universally popular as a room-mate.

Autographing photos of himself in India with the services team, Lindsay noticed that in one print he was sporting a very marked five o'clock shadow on his chin. Under his signature he wrote, 'Always use Gillette blades'. One can imagine the puzzlement with which some Hindu in Bangalore or bearded Sikh in Peshawar would wrestle with the intent of this injunction, unless, of course, the ubiquitous Mr Gillette had cast his net in these places!

Hassett liked to win and would do his best to do so, in his roles both as batsman and captain. When all hope of winning was lost, as in the fifth Test match at Melbourne in 1951, with his sense of the ridiculous and the good theatre the absurd could often produce, he delighted the Melbourne crowd with an unrehearsed bit of nonsense. The crowd, almost to a man, both in Melbourne and elsewhere in Australia, was highly delighted that 'the Poms' had broken the postwar drought and were about to inflict an overdue and quite severe defeat on Australia. Set 95 to win, Washbrook and Simpson both departed quickly, and the maestro, Hutton, and the brilliant but luckless (on that tour) Compton, were in at the death. Only three or four runs were required and it seemed that these would be obtained in one more over. Bradman or

Border would probably have called on Lindwall or McDermott to mount a final assault so that a maiden over might be bowled, a wicket might fall or a thunderstorm, earthquake or other act of God might terminate proceedings and the match would be drawn. Bradman was not noted for generosity to opponents and 'A.B.', for all his sterling qualities, was not really a bundle of fun at any time.

Hassett cast his mind back to his youth, when his leg breaks were such as might classify him as an all-rounder in The Geelong College Eleven, and called for the ball. Cardus tells the story: 'Hassett solemnly set his field, moving men here and there to an inch. And just before he began his run, as though seized by inspiration, he suddenly rubbed the old ball vigorously on his thigh then doubled up laughing at the gorgeous joke that had come to him'.

Lest you should deduce from this that Lindsay Hassett set no store on winning, let me hasten to correct any such impression. He could be as tough as any holder of the Australian captaincy, within the rules, ethics and spirit of what he believed to be a great game. He would have deplored the tactics of Douglas Jardine in the bodyline series, just as he deplored the sledging and abuse that crept into cricket, tacitly and frequently actively encouraged by the captains of the period, during his time as commentator with the Australian Broadcasting Commission.

Ian Johnson, one-time Australian captain and colleague of Hassett's at club, state and international level, probably knew him better than anyone else. In an appreciation in the *Age* after Lindsay died, Johnson recalls an incident during the Durban Test in South Africa in 1949–50. Australia had been dismissed cheaply and trailed the home-team by about 236 runs in the first innings. The home-team openers had increased this lead and wickets were desperately needed. 'Jack Nel hit a ball from me,' says Ian, 'wide of Hassett at mid-on and set off for a short single. Lindsay picked up the ball and threw it to me, whereupon I took off the bails with Nel short of his ground. As Nel was leaving the field, Lindsay said to me, "I think I got in his way, didn't I?" I told him I hadn't noticed. But he wasn't sure and asked the umpire if Nel could be called back — which he was.' Johnson goes on to say that, although Hassett played hard, he would never take the semblance of an unfair advantage.

Having accused Bradman of parsimony in the matter of generosity to opponents, it's fair that he should be given credit for laudatory remarks about his erstwhile vice-captain and colleague, written in *Farewell to Cricket* some years before Lindsay died. The Don said, 'A great player and valuable lieutenant as vice-captain. Extremely sound knowledge of game and tactics. Beautiful strokeplayer when in the mood — could take charge in crises, and willing to risk wicket in the interests of the team or the match. Sound defence made him at home under almost any conditions.'

This is praise indeed from Bradman, who also, upon Lindsay's death, acknowledged the little man's complete loyalty when acting as vice-captain. He might have added that the Hassett personality was a perfect link between the rather reserved captain and the rank and file.

At 165 cm (5'6"), Hassett was among the shortest of short batsmen, including Charles Bannerman, and there is an arguable theory that diminutive batsmen have some natural advantage. In support of this theory, there are some redoubtable players — Bradman, Harvey, Walters, Border, Macartney, McCabe and Syd Gregory come to mind. Gregory was possibly a centimetre shorter than Hassett. All those named, with the exception of Border, were strokeplayers of distinction and crowd-pleasers, as was the prewar Lindsay Hassett. All are Australians, which is curious because the same shortness of stature does not prevail nearly so frequently with top-line Englishmen. One thinks of Hammond and Woolley, both very big men and both superb strokeplayers, or Hobbs, the greatest English all-wicket player, who was built on fairly generous lines, as were Hutton, Compton, Cowdrey, May, Graveney and Charles Barnett, who scored 98 before lunch in the Nottingham Test of 1938. Barnett is the only Englishman to get close to the elite Australian trio who notched centuries before lunch, Bradman and Macartney at number three in the batting order not even gaining the extra minute or two enjoyed by Barnett and Trumper, who both batted at number one. Quickness of footwork would be the natural gift of small men. On the other hand, reach and power would seem balancing factors in those of more generous build. Really, there doesn't seem to be much in it. Suffice it to say that Lindsay Hassett, up to 1939, and even after the war in games other than Tests, had the feet of a dancing master. This, coupled with exquisite timing, put him into the class of Stan McCabe, who was the best exponent of pure batsmanship I have seen.

In comparing heights, it's fair to say that the 'shortish' Australians mentioned above were all of stockier build than Lindsay. His frame was lean from boyhood through to mature age and this probably overemphasised his perceived lack of inches. However, back to back with

Bradman or McCabe, for instance, the height difference would appear minimal.

Lindsay idolised Stan McCabe. He wrote to me once that McCabe was the finest sportsman ever to grace a cricket field and most cricketers would go along with that. On the Australia Day Sheffield Shield match between New South Wales and Victoria in Sydney, the annual grudge fixture not unlike the Roses matches at Old Trafford or Bramall Lane, Lindsay would be a regular visitor at the McCabe house overlooking the harbour at Beauty Point, Mosman. Bill O'Reilly, Ian Johnson and Bill Johnston would also frequently accompany him and there would be some carousing and lots of baiting of O'Reilly, known as 'Tiger', particularly if Lindsay or anyone had given him some stick during the day. Bill O'Reilly was well able to look after himself in jousts with Lindsay on or off the field, but sometimes found himself manoeuvred in argument into supporting a position he'd started off opposing. Hassett's tongue and brain were almost as nimble as his feet.

The Hassett name, office and personality failed to impress one of the great men of this century, Winston Churchill. Cricket was too slow for Churchill — indeed, apart from polo, very little is recorded about his sporting activities. As Dick Whitington records the occasion, the Australians in 1953, playing in a match in the south of England, were invited to spend Sunday at Blenheim Palace. The occupier of this slightly ostentatious pile of eighteenth-century masonry, the incumbent Duke of Marlborough, a Churchill, had extended the invitation, which was accepted by the Australians with pleasure and some excitement, particularly when they were told 'Winnie' would be there. Winston, brooding in solitary state, was informed by an aide that Lindsay Hassett, the Australian touring cricket team's captain, a great contributor to the 'bonds of Empire' was at the palace and the aide felt that Sir Winston might like to meet him. Winston did not reply and remained sunk in reverie. Wrongly interpreting the silence as at least qualified assent, the aide separated Lindsay from the refreshments marquee and ushered him into Churchill's presence. After the introduction, there was a long and, for Lindsay Hassett, nervewracking silence. After several minutes, the great man slowly raised his head from its contemplation of the floor and growled, 'How are you?', shook hands and resumed his previous posture.

At the other extreme, Lindsay was extremely adept at handling crowds, friendly or hostile. There's the story of his borrowing a policeman's helmet after dropping Washbrook twice at deep fine leg from Lindwall's bowling — a couple of sitters which at first provoked the Lancastrian crowd into catcalls roughly equivalent to the 'get a bag' of Sydney Hill of happy memory. With Hassett holding the helmet in front of him to ensure that a third catch didn't go begging, the crowd's jeers quickly turned to laughter, although Ray Lindwall was not noticeably joining in the fun. In 1953, responding as captain to the mayor's welcoming speech before a large gathering in front of the Blackpool Town Hall, Lindsay's opening remark was, 'Never in my life have I seen so many ugly men'. This shocked his listeners into a stunned silence for a couple of seconds, after which rumblings of dissent wafted up the town hall steps from the aggrieved listeners, with an occasional unseemly 'Boo' from the threepenny seats. Lindsay quickly parried the incipient unpleasantness with a deft deflection worthy of his best batting days: 'And never have I seen so many beautiful women'. Half the audience, the female half, became his slaves for life, and the men, bathing in reflected glory, quickly overlooked the earlier insult.

Serious rioting had broken out in Calcutta, which was then part of Bengal and under the governor-generalship of R. G. Casey, an Australian of distinction later to become governor-general of his own country. Several people were killed in the riots, rooted in the grim and desperate poverty of the city's citizens, and the scene at Eden Gardens where the Australian Services team was engaged in a cricket match against the Eastern Zone, became ugly when the rioters demanded that the two teams line the pitch and observe two minutes' silence as a mark of sympathy for the rioters who had lost their lives. At Mr Casey's request, the cricketers agreed to do this. This did not stop a line of demonstrators marching on to the field. Hassett was standing at the far end of the pitch as a noisy and angry band closed in on him. Hassett, with admirable coolness, approached the leaders and asked casually, 'Has anyone got a cigarette?'. This bland request seemed to take the tension out of the situation and, as Dick Whitington says, he 'never saw so many people fumbling in their pockets at the same time'. Whitington goes on to state that cigarette and match were both finally located and Lindsay lit up. However, the rioters stayed on the field, some asking for autographs. Hassett would not agree unless the rioters promised to leave the field. They did not do so and eventually both teams walked off. There was no alternative. Lunch was taken, comparative peace was restored and play resumed. Hassett's casual coolness and apparent goodwill very likely prevented an ugly situation escalating into something worse.

It is appropriate, before closing this chapter, to say something about the late Edward (Ted) Hassett, second-born of the nine Hassett children, 'a man worth knowing' as Bill O'Reilly would say. I met him only once, but the afternoon spent with him in his unit in a retirement village will take some erasing from my memory. He was 97 years old with 98 closing on him swiftly (he died soon after his 98th birthday). Among other things, he told me, with much relish, how it was that Lindsay learnt to 'pick' a bosie by watching the ball's rotation in flight. Ted maintained that his mother, Frances, joined the boys in their backyard cricket, resplendent in a long-sleeved black dress with frilly lace around the wrists. According to Ted, she was a handy bowler well equipped with both leg break and bosie, the identity of both kept invisible at the moment of delivery by the frilly lace. This sharpened the batsman's keenness to discern the type of spin on the ball between frills and bat. Ted maintained that this basic training from an unlikely source helped Lindsay in his later unique contests with Bill O'Reilly that so intrigued the public in 1940.

Vin Hassett was interested in my visit to Ted and quizzed me a little on what we had discussed. He asked whether Ted had told me the story about the bosie. I acknowledged that he had and that I'd enjoyed it immensely. 'That's fine,' said Vin, 'but it's bloody rubbish!'. He went on to say that their mother's knowledge of cricket could be comfortably recorded on the back of a postage stamp and still leave space for a margin. 'We took Mum to the cricket one day,' said Vin, getting into his stride, 'to see Lindsay bat at the Melbourne Cricket Ground (MCG). On being seated, Mum looked around the ground and enquired sharply, "Where's the gully? It all looks level to me".'

I was not going to include these stories, but they harm nobody and in my mind's eye, I see that great old man, Ted Hassett at 97, as acute in the 'grey-cells' department as people half his age, now playing his harp in the heavenly orchestra and getting a kick out of his oft-repeated story while he was among us, and also probably at Vin's subsequent rejoinder about their mother.

Vin added that Ted was reluctant to allow the truth to intervene and spoil a good yarn. The beauty of Ted's story is that it led to an even better one about Frances Hassett and her complaint about the absence of a gully at the MCG.

Actually, Lindsay himself attributed his ability to detect O'Reilly's bosie to the fact that close study of the Tiger's action suggested strongly that, when he bowled the bosie, he tended to drop his left shoulder and to toss the delivery slightly higher and a little more slowly than his leg break.

And on that note, Chapter 1 may draw to a close, probably not too soon, some might say.

## CHAPTER 2
# A MAN OF VARIED GIFTS

In common with many cricketing wives, Tessa Hassett (née Davis) had a considerable influence on her husband's career. The same may be said of Molly O'Reilly, Edna McCabe, Judith Morris, Jessie Bradman and many others. All these ladies were, from time to time, left to care for home and children while their husbands were absent on cricketing tours, both overseas and domestic. In more recent times, with the proliferation of tours and one-day matches, the strains on marriages must be even more severe.

The Hassett 'connection' goes back to early childhood — Tess was only seven when she first met Lindsay. This important event took place, not altogether surprisingly, at a cricket match in Geelong at Queen's Park. The participants who brought Master Hassett and Miss Davis together were engaged in a local derby in which Lindsay's older brother, Ted, and Tess's father were playing in the same team. The occasion, of little significance to the two youngsters at the time, proved to be fundamental in their later lives. They saw each other from time to time and the attachment and affection grew in the orderly fashion of earlier generations until it was understood that marriage would be the ultimate goal. Hitler's war caused the postponement of wedding plans and the couple did not marry until Lindsay returned from the Middle East in 1942. They wed on 9th May that year. Shortly afterwards, Lindsay was despatched to New Guinea, where he remained for the next eighteen months or so.

Tess and Lindsay had two lively daughters — Margaret in 1943 and Anna in 1949. The couple's first home was a house in Toorak, Melbourne, which they rented until 1949 when they moved to Hampton. Anna was born shortly before Lindsay took off with his team for a tour of South Africa.

At the end of the Victory Tests, which took Lindsay and his happy band around England, then India and finally home, they were required to make a tour of the Australian states. This was a fairly demanding finale and was not greeted with enthusiasm by the players but was probably of some publicity value when Lindsay eventually acquired a sports shop in Swanston Street. This important milestone in Lindsay's career was greatly assisted by Stan McCabe, who subsidised his friend's £200 deferred pay from the Army with £600 of his own money. This unconditional act of generosity was typical of McCabe. Lindsay gladly helped Arthur Morris a few years later when Arthur had the heartbreaking duty of taking his terminally ill first wife home to Britain to see her family.

McCabe's 'loan' could comfortably be repaid from the profits of a burgeoning business a couple of years later. Lindsay posted Stan a cheque for the principal plus interest at the going rate for the period of the loan. Stan promptly returned the interest.

In 1956, when Lindsay's active cricketing days were behind him, the family moved to Beaumaris on Port Phillip Bay, where they stayed until the early 1970s when the final move to Batehaven was made. They lived there happily, Lindsay enjoying golf and fishing, and for some years working with Alan McGilvray on the ABC cricket circuit. He enjoyed commentating, hitting it off well with 'Mac' and giving pleasure to thousands who appreciated his deep knowledge and understanding of cricket at all levels. As the years passed, the travelling became a little more tiring and the decline in behaviour of cricketers perhaps rather less to his taste. With some regrets, he gave it up in 1982.

Tess found the Batehaven district much to her liking and made many friends, a factor important in her decision to stay there after Lindsay's death in June 1993. Their first stop in Batehaven was a comfortable cottage which, as time passed, became a little too large for their needs. Tess had her eye on the group of villas being constructed a little further to the south, though still in Batehaven, with idyllic views across a charming bay. During construction, Tess was known to enter into hyperbole in voicing her determination to gain possession of a villa and hang the consequences.

Lindsay's sports store extended its operations over the years with outlets in Geelong, Frankston, Ballarat and the larger shopping centres in Melbourne's suburbs. It was Lindsay's custom, once a new enterprise became viable, to appoint a manager. Results were, on the whole, satisfactory and gave Lindsay time to pursue other interests.

Tess did not always accompany Lindsay on tours, nor was she a regular companion at cricket functions unless Lindsay was keen for her to accompany him. This did not stop her from having solid friendships with many of the cricketers and their wives — the McCabes and O'Reillys have been mentioned, and Ian Johnson, Bill Johnston, Arthur Morris and Keith Miller, with their respective spouses, were well known and welcome. One of the advantages of moving away from the Melbourne district, however, was the relief from the continuous cricketing visitors, many of whom were acquaintances rather than friends. With the Bradmans, Tess was fond of Jessie but found Don a little aloof or reserved as many others have done. She confirms Bradman's assessment of Lindsay's unswerving loyalty to him as vice-captain and says that Lindsay would not criticise him at any time.

Mischief was never long absent from Lindsay's mind and Tess recalls a weekend spent at Ushers Hotel in Sydney shortly after their marriage. She was doing her best at dinner to play the part of a matron in the marriage stakes, to deflect the curiosity of other diners. Lindsay quickly undermined this stratagem by leaning across the table and asking her, very audibly, 'Do you take sugar in your tea?'. 'I could have killed him,' says Tess.

In 1956, the Australians under Ian Johnson were badly defeated in the Ashes series, the main destroyer being Jim Laker, who took 19 of the 20 wickets in the Old Trafford (Manchester) Test. Lindsay had an assignment to report on the Tests for the London *Evening Standard* and Tess accompanied him on the trip to England. While the cricket was disappointing from the Australian point of view, she enjoyed the trip and did some sightseeing and caught up with friends. She flew back ahead of Lindsay who followed a little later. The team broke up into groups in England and made trips to various places, meeting up again in Rome. From there they travelled to Pakistan and India. They played one Test in Pakistan and in a three-Test series, defeated India twice and drew once.

Tess recalls that Lindsay had his tonsils removed early in the tour of South Africa, a job not particularly well done by the surgeon on site and requiring a reprise later in Australia. Chappie Dwyer, manager and Lindsay's 'partner in crime' on that happy tour, with rare appreciation of the captain's needs, smuggled a bottle of whisky into him. This particular act of charity would not have been well regarded by the nursing or medical staff had they known of it. The merits of Scotch whisky are acknowledged and widely appreciated, but the benefit to a post-tonsillectomy throat must be considered doubtful. Perhaps the South African surgeon was not so much at fault. Perhaps the fiery impact of whisky on a tender throat caused later problems! Nevertheless, Lindsay played in all Tests and acquitted himself well.

Lindsay played for the South Melbourne Club throughout his career and is naturally one of their favourite sons. His association lasted from 1930 until 1963, when the club committee accepted his resignation. He had been a member of the committee since 1947. His cricket with the club was restricted by state and national commitments, but, despite this, he still played 108 matches in the club's First Eleven, scoring 4,076 runs at 41.1 and, with the ball, ambushing 18 unfortunate batsmen at 29.8 apiece. For the club, there were twelve centuries, including 108 at Yallourn in 1950–51 made in 42 minutes. It's fair to add that about 1930 he made seven ducks in a row. He was still living in Geelong at the time of these disasters and as each match lasted two Saturdays, Ian Johnson notes that, at 200 km per trip, he travelled 1,400 km without scoring a run. The club was in a bind as to what should be done with a man who'd failed to score in seven innings, but finally despatched him to the Colts Eleven for rehabilitation. Lindsay told Ian, 'I reckon I was plumb lbw first ball, but the umpire was kind and said "not out". Then I was dropped twice before I scored and three more times before I reached 30.' Ian Johnson adds that Lindsay didn't mention that he went on to score 150.

The change in Lindsay Hassett's batting has mystified people of various ages and interests. His career may, for convenience, be divided into prewar and postwar. In January 1940, just four months after the outbreak of war, Hassett was in perhaps the most brilliant phase of his career. He scored 122 in both innings of a match against New South Wales and followed it in a March match for War Funds with a dazzling 136 made in 132 minutes for 'The Rest' against New South Wales. During the war, first in the Middle East and later in the Victory Tests, Hassett stuck to his basic, aggressive batting style. On the resumption of Test cricket in 1946 and, disregarding his one innings for 19 in the solitary match against New Zealand, Hassett was unrecognisable as the prewar cavalier except for one thing — the feet and bat were always still in the correct places. Some have attributed the change to the effects of five years' war service, others to Hassett's new responsibilities, first as vice-captain then captain of the national side. These arguments may be rebutted in part because Hassett's newly adopted caution did not extend to his batting in matches other than Tests. He could still be the quick-footed, fluent strokemaker of years gone by in many Sheffield Shield games. This would seem to knock the war theory on the head and leave us with the 'responsibility' hypothesis. Cardus put it succinctly:

*Hassett was born to natural elegance and boldness as a batsman. He found himself caught after 1939 in a tremendous transition both in cricket and world environment. Nothing could have signified more emphatically his resources, as a man of character and cricketer of innate flexible skill, than his adaptation to an altered scheme of things, a changed and less individually enterprising view of Test cricket, a view putting value primarily on security and teamwork. He never lost lightness of touch, but, for the cause's sake, he controlled himself, bat in hand, often seeming to hide himself behind it, over after over.*

Years later, when working as a commentator for the ABC, Lindsay expressed some regret at having allowed responsibility to restrict his stroke play, and he warned Norman O'Neill, beside him in the broadcasting box, against something similar happening to him.

Hassett's basic batting technique did not change. Even during his 'stodgy' period, he was interesting because of the correctness of his play. One always sensed the latent power suppressed by the exigencies of captaincy in Test cricket. He always appeared to have time to spare in making his strokes, whether they were defensive or attacking. He was neither predominantly front-foot nor back-foot in his play, but adhered generally to the principle that the front-foot stroke should be played when the ball could be met on the half volley or close to it. Charles Fry coined the phrase 'play back or drive' and Australians have adhered to this principle much more than the English, who have struck endless difficulty with the forward lunge, back foot anchored to the crease. Hassett, in his heyday, was the classical exponent of Fry's rather elementary but neglected doctrine. Bradman, McCabe, Jackson, Morris and a score of others rarely played forward unless they knew they would make firm contact with the ball. Having made the decision, they carried out the Fry injunction and drove. Few players were the equal of Lindsay Hassett in their judgment of length, timing and placement, all achieved with a minimum of effort and no brutality. Bradman was a murderer of bowlers: Hassett, like McCabe, seemed slightly apologetic when putting them elegantly to the sword. This trait was not especially on view when he was facing O'Reilly, who, like Shane Warne today, presented batsmen with their greatest challenges.

In his obituary on Lindsay, Ian Johnson recalled the occasion in 1950–51 when New South Wales played Victoria in Melbourne. The 'Blues' boasted four fast bowlers at the time — Lindwall, Miller,

Davidson and Walker. Alan Walker was a dual international in rugby and cricket. He bowled left-hand and was incredibly fast. There was some lingering resentment on Lindwall's part at having been omitted from a Test in South Africa, while Walker was nursing a grudge at not having been invited to play in any Test at all. Lindsay knew that the quartet was 'gunning' for him, Miller and Davidson having agreed to go along with the plan.

Lindsay came in early when the bowlers were fresh. Ian Johnson says the attack was ferocious from all four. Hassett stood his ground, hooking, cutting, ducking and weaving, and finished with 179. When finally out, Johnson asked how he felt going out to bat knowing that those four were after him. 'Ian,' he replied, 'I've never known what being in a cold sweat meant before.' This was probably the match when Hassett enquired politely of the umpire: 'When does bowling become intimidatory?'. The occasion reflected little credit on the bowlers concerned.

As part of his social repertoire, Lindsay had his 'Blackbird Song'. This rather childish bit of nonsense was generally well received at social gatherings, particularly when restraints had been mellowed by generous imbibing of the grape. This defused a difficult situation at a function given by the Pakistan High Commissioner during the Indian tour of Australia in 1947–48. The tour took place just after the partition of India and Pakistan, and the Indian team contained a combination of players from both countries, with a majority of Indians who were Hindus. There was naturally some tension in the team. This led to reluctance on the Indians' part to attend the Pakistan High Commissioner's reception. The gathering was not a social success, with the Indians and some of the Australians leaving at the first opportunity, until only Lindsay, Keith Miller and Ian Johnson were left. While the dauntless three were saying their farewells to the rather strained commissioner and his wife, Lindsay whipped a handkerchief out of his pocket, Keith and Ian followed suit plus the commissioner and his wife, who no doubt took the view that if you can't lick 'em, join 'em.

With handkerchiefs over the shoulder, everybody joined Hassett in the 'Blackbird Song', with actions. Mr and Mrs Commissioner picked up the words and actions without difficulty. The song would start with the familiar opening nursery line. 'The king was in his counting house', and proceed normally until the last line, which Lindsay had brought up to date:

'And down came a bloody, great blackbird
And down came a bloody, great blackbird,
And bit off her nose.'

The last bit was done with handkerchiefs waving and knees bent to the ground. It may not have made the hit parade, still less the 'top 40', but it brightened up the evening for the commissioner even though there were only three guests left. Probably only Lindsay Hassett could have carried it off.

Arthur Morris remembers, and the late Ted Hassett confirmed, an occasion in the Hassett's Beaumaris home when he, with Ted and Ian Peebles, former England leg spinner, were visiting. After some liquid refreshment, Lindsay said, 'Let's go down to the Sandringham Club'. This watering hole was close by and was a favourite of Lindsay's. 'I'll just fetch my tobacco,' added Lindsay, 'and we'll go.' While he was out of the room, Peebles said to Morris, 'I've had enough. I don't want to go to the Sandringham Club'. Arthur, who knew his former captain pretty well, having played in about 30 Test matches with him, many under his direction, drained his beer, took a deep breath and said, 'If the little bloke says we're going to the Sandringham Club, that's where we're going'. He'd seen it all before, too, not only at Sandringham, but in Sydney, London, Cape Town and points to port and starboard. This example illustrates that size and determination with authority are not necessarily ill matched, and will usually carry the day.

Ian Johnson's contribution to cricket, both on and off the field, has been understated. He was a very useful all-round cricketer who worried the great Hutton more than any spinner other than O'Reilly and was a reliable late middle-order batsman. In 45 Tests, he took 109 wickets at 29.2 and scored 1,000 runs at 18.5. His slip fielding was first-class. He captained Australia 17 times for 7 wins, 5 losses and 5 draws, despite jibes from commentators and some players. As captain in the West Indies in 1955, he did much, with his two co-selectors, Arthur Morris and Keith Miller, to mend a few fences with the local people — fences pulled down by a stand-offish MCC side which had toured the previous summer.

In 1957, Ian wrote a very readable book entitled *Cricket at the Crossroads*, in which he dealt at some length with the future of Test cricket. Like his friend Lindsay, Ian was surprised and disappointed to discover that the blazers issued to the Australian side to tour New Zealand in 1946 were not of the traditional design. Instead of the coat of arms, the pocket sported an Australian Board of Control monogram. The older players who'd represented Australia previously, such as Hassett, O'Reilly and Bill Brown, the captain, understandably took a dim view of this piece of board parsimony and insensitivity.

In 1956, when Ian Johnson was captain of the ill-fated Australian touring team, he became friendly with Group Captain Leonard Cheshire, VC., DSO plus 2 bars, DFC and bar. Cheshire's peacetime activities won him only a little less fame than he had earned in bomber command. He had devoted his life to setting up homes for the sick and poor, both in England and India. The Australians felt privileged to lend their names to a ball in London, which was to be a fundraising function for Cheshire's homes. The ball was called The Kangaroo Hop and a song with the same title was written for the occasion. Cheshire, Johnson and Hassett (who had been reporting the Tests for a London daily) were invited to sing. Cheshire was then to dance to the tune with ballerina Belita. The song went over so well that Belita complained that she'd been upstaged! Tess Hassett was present and, when the trio was announced, she made herself as inconspicuous as possible in a remote corner of the ballroom — in other words, she feared the worst and was not anxious to be identified as connected with any of the balladeers. However, afterwards she stated: 'It wasn't good, but it wasn't as bad as I expected'.

More than once, Lindsay came close to giving up cricket for good. There was the occasion previously noted when he had seven ducks in a row for South Melbourne. He was young then and could probably have made quite a name for himself at Australian football or tennis. The second occasion was when John Goddard's 1951–52 West Indies team was in Australia and Lindsay had failed dismally in the first Test match, falling twice to Ramadhin. In the second Test at Sydney, he was dropped early in his innings by wicket-keeper Walcott, but then went on to score 132 and 46 not out in the second innings. He told Johnson after the match that had Walcott held the catch, he would have made himself unavailable for the remaining Tests.

We're told that Lindsay was a relaxed figure when at the crease, chewing non-stop even while the ball was in the air. This may have been generally so, but one doubts that it would have applied when Doug Wright was operating. Wright was potentially as great a leg spinner as any. He bowled at O'Reilly's pace from a long, less than rhythmical run, with a hop at the halfway point, and spun the ball probably more than

O'Reilly. He captured Hassett's wicket twelve times in all. Wright's trouble was control or the lack of it. The striker could usually count on a couple of loose deliveries per over which could be punished. O'Reilly, on the other hand, had fantastic control of length as well as spin and pace. However, if anyone can be said to have been Lindsay Hassett's 'nemesis', Doug Wright would come closest. Alec Bedser was said to have a hex on Arthur Morris, but this is arguable — both were openers in their respective fields so it might be expected that Morris might fall to Bedser with some regularity. Wright tended to find the edge of Lindsay's bat for a slip catch. In his later years, Bedser had a slight hex on Bradman, having him caught at leg gully several times. This was almost certainly a case of the years catching up. In his prewar days, Bradman would have scorned the legside uppish flick which saw him fall in 1948 and would instead have forced Bedser through mid-wicket. For all that, Bradman believed Bedser to be a better bowler than Tate, a view which hurt Tate a little and would not have the majority of supporters.

Returning to settle in Melbourne after the war, Lindsay found that his membership of the Melbourne Cricket Club had lapsed during his absence and it took eleven years before he was reinstated. The MCG these days has done Lindsay proud, as indeed it should. Within the numerous halls and chambers of that vast stadium, there is a 'Lindsay Hassett Room', which can be used for appropriate functions and is the main venue for the Lindsay Hassett Club — an organisation largely devoted to the promotion and welfare of young cricketers in Victoria. The club meets regularly and is usually addressed by a speaker. It was formed in 1990 and its meeting room is located in the Great Southern Stand. On 14 February 1997, in 36°C shade temperature, the club held a gathering on the ground itself. Tables were laid out in a heart-shape (it being St Valentine's Day) and it was estimated that 1,400 people attended. Lindsay would have been proud.

With Jack Ryder and the two Bills — Woodfull and Ponsford — Lindsay ranks highly among Victoria's famous sons.

## CHAPTER 3
# AT SCHOOL AND BEYOND

The circumstances by which the three youngest Hassett boys finished their schooling at The Geelong College have been touched on in Chapter 1. All three boys started there at the same time because their previous school had closed, but they were in different forms — Dick, born in 1910, was the senior, Vin, born in 1912, was next, followed by Lindsay, born in 1913. The college produced some good cricketers in addition to the Hassett boys — Jack Iverson, Ian Redpath and Paul Sheahan were all international alumni of the college, which is set in spectacular surroundings and boasts many fine buildings.

The college has recently become co-educational. Paul Sheahan returned as Principal until 1995 when he was appointed to the top job at Melbourne Grammar School. The present Principal is Dr Pauline Turner.

In the May 1924 issue of the school journal, *Ad Astra*, there's a reference to Lindsay's performance in the season just concluded — 11 innings, 3 not out, 341 runs, highest score 60 not out, average 42.6. He was only ten years old at the time. It's worth noting, too, that he sent 58 young hopefuls packing with the ball in the same season, including a hat trick. This performance probably sowed the seed of his lifelong opinion of himself as a bowler of note.

Lindsay appeared in some practice games late in the 1927–28 season when he was fourteen years old. By 1928, he was starting to blossom, first in practice games with scores of 63, 43 and 72. Later, in serious games, there was a 47 against Geelong Grammar, 10 and 36 against Wesley and 4–65 in the same match. Vin was also featuring prominently in this season. Lindsay's first football write-up occurs in the winter of the same year and he is frequently mentioned for good play. His prowess at tennis is also noted as winner of the Under-Sixteens final.

From 1928 onwards, Lindsay's cricketing skills increased markedly season by season. In the 1929 season (remembering that school cricketing years are split by the winter — the 1929 season would begin on resumption of school after the Christmas holidays, be interrupted by football until about October, and finish when Christmas holidays began in mid-December), he scored 72 and 38 not out against Wesley ('attacked bowling'), and 12 and 57 not out against Melbourne Grammar ('a fine innings'), with Vin notching 111 in the same game. Against Scotch College, Lindsay had 24 and 52 and incredibly, 4–93. Lindsay won the batting average with 65.2 — Vin was captain this year, Lindsay his deputy. Lindsay also figures regularly in the football match reports as 'one of the best players'.

By 1930, Lindsay was captain of the school cricket team and reports of the game include some harsh criticism of the college's fielding. Against Geelong Grammar, Lindsay made 118 not out in quick time. Heavy scoring against Scotch saw the college beaten, bad catching and fielding earning some scathing criticism. Scotch made 472 in reply to the college's 7–389, with Lindsay's mate Matt Wright scoring 189, a record at the school. In the next match against Xavier, the college was among the runs again with 8–355, of which Lindsay scored 147 in what was described by the journal reporter as 'a mixture of bright and slow play'. Lindsay's average for the season was 117.33 and he was described as a 'very able captain'. He was again to the fore in football.

Throughout 1931 and 1932, Lindsay continued to score consistently and usually attractively, although if the needs of the side required it, he could adopt a sheet-anchor–type role. He continued to pick up wickets regularly and won a cricket ball throwing competition with a throw of 88 metres (96 yards). His tennis skills developed and he continued to earn good reports at football, where he usually played as rover.

The season of 1931–32 was notable in Australian cricket because it marked the first time a West Indian team visited our shores. They played five Test matches and were clearly outplayed throughout the tour until the closing stages when they beat New South Wales convincingly and followed with a 30-run victory in the final Test at Sydney. Having lost the first four Tests by large margins, the two wins at the Sydney Cricket Ground were both surprising and encouraging to a team of learners with an unbalanced bowling attack who were largely dependent on the performances of a few outstanding players. Among these were George Headley, a player worthy of a place among the greats of any age, and Leary Constantine, an electrifying all-rounder who bowled fast, hit with tremendous power and was a sensational catcher and fielder with a bullet-like throw from anywhere on the field. The team had four fast bowlers of uneven quality with only two spinners of moderate penetration.

Early in the tour, a match between the West Indians and a Victorian Country side was arranged at Corio Oval, Geelong. Among those chosen was Lindsay Hassett, aged seventeen years and five months and still attending The Geelong College. The match was fully covered by the *Geelong Advertiser* and some periods of play were broadcast. The Country lads won the toss on a fine day and put together the respectable total of 327. Lindsay Hassett, coming in at number five, carried his bat for 147 in a display that has been, and will be, long remembered in the Geelong district. The match report says:

> At times Hassett was subdued, but towards the close of the day's play he treated the crowd to an excellent display of hitting, taking 17 in one over from Constantine: 2, 4, 4, 2, 4, 1. He richly deserved the plaudits of the crowd when he left the ground, and the applause of the West Indies players when he reached his century. Hassett's innings occupied 283 minutes and was described as 'flawless'.

Although the tourists would have regarded this as a warm-up game, Constantine cut loose in the West Indies' second innings, scoring 80 in better than even time with twelve fours and a six. The visitors had suffered the indignity of having to follow on, having been dismissed for 222 in their first innings. The second innings was aimed at providing entertainment for the crowd, an objective achieved largely thanks to the efforts of Messrs Constantine and Martin (57). None of the others distinguished themselves and at the close of play the visitors were 8–216, a lead of 111. The match ended in a draw.

In 1932, against Geelong Grammar, Lindsay broke the 1930 record of 189 scored by Matt Wright. Lindsay made 196 and was dismissed only when forcing the pace in the latter part of his innings. Soon afterwards he broke his own record with a punishing 245 against Scotch. In the match against Grammar, the college inflicted a heavy defeat on their opponents, scoring 311 and dismissing Grammar for 110 and 32, with Lindsay Hassett, 'the destroyer', taking 8 wickets in the second innings. Wickets were still coming his way with surprising regularity and, as captain, star batsman and useful bowler, he would have been candidate for 'man of the match' awards if those fripparies had existed in the 1930s.

In football, Lindsay was consistently among the major goal-kickers with three or four per match, and was listed as the best player in three games and runner-up in two. He was also captain.

In its farewell profile of Lindsay Hassett, the college journal listed his achievements: Prefect 1931–32, Captain Shannon House 1931–32, First Eleven 1929–1932, Captain cricket 1930–32, First Eighteen 1929–32, Captain football 1930–32, School Tennis Champion 1930–32 and Public Schools Singles Champion 1931–32.

Special mention was made in the profile regarding his captaincy and the record 245 against Scotch when it seems that he scored very nearly off every ball, with 31 fours and 1 six. His figures for the 1932 season would not shame Donald Bradman, who lacked Lindsay's good fortune as far as schooling is concerned, though no figures for comparative purposes are available. Lindsay's figures were: 7 innings, 1 not out, 644 runs, average 107.3.

In June 1938, *Pegasus* (the college journal) included a special article to mark Lindsay's selection in the 1938 Australian side to go to England. It noted his performances in both academic and sporting pursuits during his years at the college and wished him well in the future.

All four of Geelong College's future internationals acquitted themselves well when the time came. Jack Iverson, who did not make the school's First Eleven, achieved a shortlived but dramatic spin impact on Test cricket in the late 1940s and early 1950s, at the age of 35. A mystery bowler, he flicked the ball from the second finger of his very large hand and discovered that the direction of the ball after pitching could be governed by the direction in which his thumb pointed at the moment of delivery. This caused a great deal of alarm and despondency in 1950–51 when England was in Australia, culminating in a 6–27 haul in the Sydney Test, his victims including Hutton, Washbrook and Simpson, none of whom had a clue. Ian Redpath scored 4,737 Test runs at an average of 43.45, and Paul Sheahan 1,594 runs at 33.91, quitting cricket for teaching at the age of 28.

All three Hassett boys did well at The Geelong College, Dick, Vin and Lindsay figuring in cricket, football and tennis. An elder brother, Harry, born in 1905 and not a college boy, made quite a name for himself in tennis and trained with the Davis Cup squad of the mid-to-late 1920s. Ted, second-born of the family (1889), had a club foot, a serious handicap which, with great determination, he largely overcame. He took part in sport and his brothers recall that he worked and practised with his disabled foot until he could kick a football with it. Ted was a civil engineer and did a lot of work on the Great Ocean Road and on the open-cut coal mine at Yallourn, Victoria. He recalled the mortification of the lads from Xavier College (the Catholic College) when Lindsay and Vin, seen as a couple of apostates, if not worse, put together a partnership of 100 plus in one of Vin's later games for The Geelong College. To make matters worse, Vin's second name is 'Xavier'!

While Ted's inclination not to let truth ruin a good story should be kept in mind, the following tale is too good not to pass on. According to Ted, Stan McCabe, Lindsay Hassett and Bill O'Reilly were given a few days off at the conclusion of the 1938 tour of England. They agreed that it would be remiss of them not to take advantage of the time by paying a visit to the Emerald Isle, home of their forebears. The plan was to make a start in Dublin and hitchhike across the southern half of Ireland towards Galway Bay. Harmless enough one might say, even laudable, to pay one's respects to the land of one's ancestors. Yet the journey was to be interrupted, for whatever time it took, when they came upon a hotel owned or managed by a McCabe, Hassett or O'Reilly. McCabes and Hassetts were fairly numerous in towns and villages along the route, and the trio, on announcing themselves to the publican, adding that they'd just beaten the English at cricket, were given the red-carpet treatment. Food and drink were laid on and a right-royal time was had by all, with browsing, sluicing and revelry far into the night. Conditioned to this sort of treatment, the party was shocked when, at the first 'O'Reilly' pub, they were quickly shown the door. The publican knew nothing about cricket and his wife was English anyway, so would they please leave, closing the door behind them. Stan and Lindsay made the most of this unforgivable O'Reilly treatment and made the Tiger's life a misery for the rest of the trip. Worse than that, they kept throwing the insult up at him for years and warned any of their friends who were planning a visit to Ireland to avoid any O'Reilly establishment like the plague. According to Ted, this never failed to raise the Tiger's hackles. (It is fair to add that the truth of this story has never been tested to my knowledge and Bill O'Reilly never mentioned it to me.)

The years 1933 to 1939 were a mixture of difficulty and success for Lindsay. Like many before and after him, he headed for the South Melbourne Club. No less than six Australian Test captains have been launched by the people at South Melbourne — Blackham, Armstrong, Harry Trott, Woodfull, Hassett and Johnson. Despite his school reputation and his century while still at school, for Victorian Country against George Grant's West Indians in 1930–31, Lindsay had the succession of ducks mentioned earlier in his first outings with the club. Yet regardless of this run of outs, he was still selected to play for Victoria against South Australia in February 1933. It was his misfortune to run into Clarrie Grimmett in this match and Clarrie trapped him leg before wicket with his top spinner for 4. In the second innings, off spinner Philip Lee had him caught at the wicket for 9. A month later, against Tasmania, Lindsay did little better, leg before for 12 and caught for nil. Following these failures, he was not seen in the Victorian side again until the 1935–36 season. There'd been a bit of a drought at South Melbourne as well.

Lindsay came back to the Victorian side for the Boxing Day match in Melbourne in 1935. Bill O'Reilly and the other New South Wales Internationals were absent on tour in South Africa under the captaincy of Victor Richardson. Lindsay was once again out of luck — Alan McGilvray had him for 12 in the first innings and Ted White in the second knock for 4. However, the wheel was starting to turn for Lindsay. In the return match at the Sydney Cricket Ground, on Australia Day 1936, he was out for 21 in the first innings and fell again to White in the second for a very welcome and respectable 51. He followed this with 49 against Queensland and 73 and 2 against South Australia. Tim Wall had him in the first innings and Frank Ward in the second. Wall was a fastish right-hand bowler with a beautiful outswinger and in February 1933 he took 10–36 on a perfect Sydney wicket against New South Wales at full strength — Bill Brown, Jack Fingleton, Bradman and McCabe are a reasonable quartet to start with. Frank Ward was preferred to Grimmett for the 1938 tour of England, a disastrous selection still stoutly defended by Bradman who was one of the selectors at the time.

Lindsay failed against Queensland, but scored an attractive 82 in Melbourne in December 1936 against New South Wales. O'Reilly and McCabe, although home from South Africa, did not play in this match and Lindsay cemented his state spot with 71 not out in the second innings. All was going well at this stage — Lindsay was 'on a roll' as the modern expression has it. He made 93 and 56 not out against Queensland, which had a talented medium-paced off spinner, Ron Oxenham, at age 46 still able to deceive batsmen with skilful changes of flight and pace. He had Lindsay Hassett caught at the wicket by Don Tallon, whose international entry was still nine years off. Lindsay had a good double of 58 and 68 in the Australia Day match at Sydney, followed by 54 against the touring MCC team of George 'Gubby' Allen, when he would have first fallen under the watchful eye of Neville Cardus who, no doubt, made a mental note of the young man's grace and elegance. In this particular innings, Lindsay was caught by Lesley Ames at the wicket off Voce, joint villain with Larwood in the bodyline rumpus four years previously.

Late in 1937, Lindsay played for Victoria against a New Zealand side returning from a tour of England and made a lively unbeaten 127 in the second innings. Another 90 in Brisbane set the stage for his biggest trial to date — an encounter with Bill O'Reilly, widely seen as the best bowler in the world at that time. At least the match would be played on Lindsay's own patch. The New South Wales team was at full strength so the match would be played in the 'no holds barred' tradition of these encounters. Bill O'Reilly, in his book *Cricket Conquest*, after noting Lindsay's dourness in the 1948 Tests with which the book deals, lapses into a little nostalgia regarding Hassett's prewar ability. 'Hassett gave promise of being one of the most graceful strokemakers that Australia has produced. He had fluent control of every stroke in the game and this, with his cheekiness, made him a bowler's enemy.' In parentheses, it could be added that anyone from Bradman to Ironmonger who appeared on the ground with a bat in his hand when O'Reilly was in the opposition, was 'a bowler's enemy'. Bill goes on to recall their first encounter in that match at the MCG in December 1937. 'He appeared with a bat almost as big as himself and defied the New South Wales attack for hours whilst he got Victoria out of a spot of bother, and he collected 81 runs in doing so. I asked him several times whether he had a shot in his locker and informed me that he was saving them up for a later day.'

Ted and Dick Hassett watched this innings, which lasted more than five hours. Dick, who played for the state a few times, was a handy all-rounder. His leg spinners impressed no less a person than Jack Hobbs. Watching his brother battling with a rampant O'Reilly, who was becoming more frustrated over by over, Dick commented that Lindsay was playing Bill so well that he must be picking the Tiger's deadliest delivery, 'the wrong'un', the nightmare ball to all batsmen of the time. Stan McCabe, the New South Wales captain, told Lindsay that at the tea adjournment, an angry O'Reilly hurled his cap into the dressing room and thundered to his assembled team-mates, 'Nobody has ever kept me out like that little bastard'. It seems likely that this innings won Lindsay a spot in the 1938 team to England.

Continuing from O'Reilly's book, the 'later date' mentioned by Lindsay in his marathon innings dawned in January 1940, some time after the England tourists returned. The scene was Sydney, the occasion one of the last official Sheffield Shield games played before the competition was suspended by the war. I'll let the Tiger tell the story:

> *When Hassett came to the wicket he jokingly asked me, who had been a fellow crony on tour, to go easy until he got a sight of the ball. I immediately told him that all friendship ceased as soon as we got on to the cricket field, and proceeded to operate on him. He had rather a hectic period until lunchtime came. At lunch he came over to me and said, 'I'm going to get stuck into you this afternoon, Tiger'. Going back on to the field, he soon proved to me that those were no idle words. He picked my wrong'un better than any batsman I have bowled against and each time that I bowled it, he stepped down the pitch and plastered it high and dry over the leg-side field. I believe he put several of them right over the fence. From that day onward, whenever the Hillites at Sydney wanted to take a rise out of me, they would call: 'Go easy there, Tiger, or we'll send for Lindsay Hassett'.*

It's fair to say that although O'Reilly took hidings in both innings, he did claim Lindsay's wicket in the first innings for 122 while 'Ginty' Lush got him in the second for the same score and New South Wales won despite everything. O'Reilly's match figures were 5–78 from 22 overs and 3–79 off 19 in the second innings.

Just to finish Bill O'Reilly's reminiscing, he went on to make the unlikely remark (for O'Reilly) that the prewar Hassett was a batsman from whom it was a pleasure 'to take a licking'. I venture to say that no batsman who confronted or played with the Tiger would believe he ever took pleasure from a 'licking'. To hit him for four was usually a mistake — the colour would rise, the arms flail and he'd stretch every sinew to avenge the insult, the insolence. New lambs to the slaughter would usually be advised not to hit him for four, 'it only makes him angry'. A rare and lovable man, the Tiger — everybody's friend until he walked through the pavilion gate.

To take up the story from the time of Lindsay's first meeting with Bill O'Reilly when he played the tedious but valuable innings of 81, Lindsay said that he learnt more in five hours than he had in his life to that point. His position in the state side was now assured and he proceeded to register good and consistent scores against all comers — 104 and 73 against Queensland, 56 and 0 against New South Wales in December 1938, 211 not out against South Australia and heavy scoring throughout 1939. In a match played for War Funds in March 1940, Lindsay made 136 in 132 minutes for 'the Rest' against New South Wales.

When assessing Lindsay Hassett's progress from a batting 'perhapser' early in his first-class career to the reliable standard he reached by 1937 and onwards, it is appropriate to consider the type and quality of much of the bowling he had to confront. There was Clarrie Grimmett, possibly the finest of all pure leg spinners of the orthodox type, now, in 1997, under challenge from Shane Warne, a challenge by no means yet resolved. Grimmett in South Africa in 1935–36 took 44 Test wickets at 14 apiece, a feat unsurpassed in a five Test series until Jim Laker took 49 in 1956. Then there was Bill O'Reilly, of whom little more need be said here; 'Chuck' Fleetwood-Smith, a left-hand wrist spinner of uncanny gifts whom O'Reilly considered potentially the best ever; Ron Oxenham, a very good bowler of assorted changes of pace and spin; Frank Ward, preferred to Grimmett in 1936 after the latter's epic feat in South Africa; Ted White, a good quality left-hand orthodox finger spinner; Hughie Chilvers of New South Wales, rated by O'Reilly as 'the best leg spinner never to play for Australia'; and the redoubtable Cecil Pepper. All the above-mentioned required different measures if they were to be countered. O'Reilly advised Jack Ledward of Victoria to try playing back rather than pushing forward when facing him. Bradman always gave colleagues the same advice. Lindsay Hassett was taught the correct technique of back play and he employed it successfully at times, but not against the O'Reilly wrong'un, which was tossed higher. Having mentally registered this in a split second, the brain passed the message to the feet in a trice and these moved quickly down the pitch to hit the high bouncing bosie, the end for many batsmen, high into the outfield. No other batsmen, not even Bradman, could do it.

Lindsay Hassett was 25 years old when he was selected to tour England in 1938. Under the captaincy of Don Bradman, with Stan McCabe his deputy, the side had some incipient problems. The batting was strong enough, built around the experienced nucleus of Bradman, McCabe, Brown and Chipperfield, and much was expected of Barnes (absent owing to injury for most of the tour), Badcock, Fingleton and Hassett. The omission of Tallon as first wicket-keeper was widely criticised, but Ward for Grimmett proved decisive and put a heavy load on O'Reilly and Fleetwood-Smith. It was expected that White, an orthodox medium-paced left-hander, would be suited to English wickets but, in the event, he did not obtain a Test match berth. McCormick had genuine pace but was injury-prone, and the inclusion of Waite ahead of another genuine all-rounder in Lush, who could bowl really fast, was questionable. Hassett could hardly be left out with consistent performances throughout 1937, including his five-hour frustration of O'Reilly at Melbourne a few months before, and he was looking forward to a successful tour. Lindsay was a popular figure in Australian cricket, got on well with both the captain and vice-captain, and was on the friendliest terms with his state colleagues, 'Chuck' Fleetwood-Smith, Ernie McCormick and Ben Barnett. Five of the team shared his Irish ancestry — McCabe, Fingleton, O'Reilly, Fleetwood-Smith and Barnes. The Catholics had more than put behind them the previous sectarian reluctance of Australian administrators to treat them as equals with the Protestant community in the matter of selection for national sides.

## CHAPTER 4
# A NOTABLE DEBUT — ENGLAND 1938

Cricket in 1938 was much different from today's game. There were fewer Tests, no limited-over games, no commercial sponsorship, fewer fast bowlers and 'seamers' with correspondingly more spinners, both wrist and finger. Pitches were not covered and batsmen had to take their chance of a wet or 'sticky' wicket, the latter type usually found in Australia, being virtually unplayable as the sun dried out a saturated strip of turf. There was no television, which meant no jumping on and hugging each other, features that are standard in these more enlightened days. It was expected that 20 overs should be bowled in an hour and at 3 runs per over, this yielded a run per minute. 'Sledging' was unheard of, although batsman and bowler occasionally exchanged the occasional glare or pleasantry. All cricketers were amateurs — except in England, where the old custom of amateurs (gentlemen) and professionals (players) still existed.

Bowlers had been helped significantly by a modification or extension of the lbw rule. The amended law provided that the batsman could be given out if the ball would have hit the wicket, so long as the batsman was struck in front of the stumps, even if the ball had pitched outside the line of the off stump and whether or not the batsman was attempting a stroke. This amendment is still in force.

The bowling of persistent and systematic fast, short-pitched balls would now allow the umpire to issue a warning to the bowler, presumably to 'cool it'.

This, then, was the cricket scene when Lindsay Hassett, aged 25, 167 cm (5'6") tall and weighing 64 kilos (10 stone), undertook his first tour abroad. It is worth noting that the height difference between Hassett and Bradman was minimal. Don was of more solid build than Lindsay and the latter's slight frame led some to overemphasise his shortness. The six-week voyage enabled Lindsay to get to know some players whose acquaintance he'd made only in the occasional interstate match. The voyage was to be broken at Perth and Colombo. Two games were played in Tasmania before sailing across the Great Australian Bight. Lindsay made a bright 75 in the Hobart fixture and, at Perth, he was caught for

29 off the bowling of Zimbulis. Neither Tasmania nor Western Australia had as yet been admitted to the Sheffield Shield competition. He loosened up in Colombo with a lively 116.

Arriving in England in the middle of a chilly April, the players had a couple of weeks in which to become acclimatised. Spring in England is very beautiful, as the homesick Browning noted in his poem, 'Home Thoughts from Abroad'. It is also changeable, with the mercury seldom getting much beyond the high 50s and low 60s Fahrenheit (about 15°C). Practice wickets at Lord's were made available and were well utilised until the first game, played as it had been on previous tours, in the shadow of the cathedral at the lovely Worcester ground. The Australians had learnt on arrival in England that Walter Hammond had announced his retirement from cricket's professional ranks and had secured a position in a tyre company, thus making it known that, if required, he would be eligible as an amateur for the England captaincy. The prestige of the man, as well as his pre-eminence as a batsman, made it virtually certain that he'd get the job.

Bradman won the toss at Worcester and elected to bat. Lindsay Hassett made 43 in good style, falling to Reg Perks, a medium-paced 'seamer' of the type found in most county teams. Perks, over a 25-year first-class career, took 2,233 wickets but played in only two Tests. The Don who'd scored 236 in 1930 and 206 in 1934, went a little better on this occasion with 258. The man's deeds defy all logic. Poor Ernie McCormick had a nightmare initiation in his first appearance on English turf before an English crowd. He bowled 19 no-balls in his first three-over spell and 35 in all during the two Worcester innings. In his third over, he'd already galloped to the stumps six times to deliver three legal balls. Walking back to the head of his run, he was joined by Lindsay, who'd strolled over from mid-on to join Ernie on his miserable walk back to his mark. The two Victorians were friends of long standing and shared a passion for snooker. Ernie broke off talking to himself to glance up and, seeing his mate, enquired in a voice choking with mingled frustration and emotion, 'How many balls to finish this bloody over, mate?'. Hassett, unblinking, replied, 'Ernie, only three more to finish the reds, then you can start on the coloureds'. Ernie's face broke into a grin and he finished the over.

During the lunch break on the first day after Ernie's nervewracking three-over spell, a friendly English gentleman was quietly doing his best to commiserate and comfort Ernie. Without batting an eye, Ernie thanked the gentleman and assured him that he knew he'd be okay if bowling in the afternoon as 'the umpire's hoarse'. Ernie McCormick had used the snooker reference to Bill O'Reilly when a hard-hitting tail-end South African batsman named Arthur Langton took the bat out on O'Reilly in a match towards the end of Australia's 1935–36 tour of the 'Union'. Sixes flowed in profusion, with a couple of deliveries belted out of the ground and lost. When the second ball proved irretrievable, McCormick sauntered over to a not-too-impressed O'Reilly and said, 'That's the last of the reds, Tiger. Now you can start on the coloureds'.

McCormick was a great asset to any touring party, despite the injuries, wides and no-balls which were generally problems. He had a great sense of humour and was especially valuable in times of adversity. As far as his bowling is concerned, Wisden nominated him 'the most overrated bowler ever to come to this country'. On the street, or in public places, if Ernie ignored greetings, a team-mate would explain that repeated shouts of 'no-ball' and 'wide' had affected his hearing.

Following Barnes's accident at Gibraltar when he broke his wrist, the Board of Control, predictable and parsimonious as always, had refused Bradman's request for a substitute player. This was a severe deprivation for the team, for Sid Barnes was that rarity, a genuine all-rounder, albeit still in an early stage of his development. Apart from his batting, which in a few years was to label him one of cricket's most difficult players to dislodge, he could bowl useful leg spinners (mainly 'straight' breaks), was an outstanding close-in fieldsman and a more than adequate standby wicket-keeper.

Against a moderate Oxford University attack at The Parks, Lindsay had some splendid practice in the middle with 146 in his usual effortless style, delighting spectators and students alike. He was finding English pitches to his liking and his innings was described as 'fluent', with no less than 24 fours. Batting with Stan McCabe (110 in 105 minutes) would have given much pleasure to Lindsay. It would be hard to pair two more elegant and effortless strokemakers in any era of the game's history. Totalling 7–679, Australia won by an innings and 487, the University managing only 117 and 75, being completely bamboozled by Fleetwood-Smith's bizarre antics with the ball. He took 5–28 and 4–31.

Moving on to Leicester, there was more heavy scoring with Lindsay having to be run out after making 148 in 200 minutes, Badcock (198) and Chipperfield (104 not out) in a total of 5–590 declared. Frank Ward despatched the county for 212 and 215. McCormick's no-ball count was only fifteen in the match and he took 6–115 with blistering pace administered in three- or four-over spells. Australia again won — by an innings and 163 runs.

By the time the Australians reached the delightful ground known as 'Fenners', which historically has provided a wicket that most batsmen would happily carry with them around the world, Lindsay was perhaps thinking that batting in England was a piece of cake. This happy feeling was reinforced as the Cambridge lads sweated and strained until Bradman mercifully closed the innings at 5–708. Lindsay Hassett was the principal contributor to this almost indecent score with 220 not out, Bradman (137), Badcock (186) and Fingleton (111) adding to the students' misery. Lindsay's 220 was his first double century and contained 35 fours. A minor drought was to follow, however. Australia won by an innings and 425 runs.

It was a thrill for Lindsay to be selected to play at Lord's and the MCC chose a fairly strong side to provide the tourists with their first real test. Seasoned players such as Robins, Farnes and Wyatt were joined by two of England's youngest, brightest and best in Bill Edrich and Denis Compton. Winning the toss, Bradman elected to bat on a grey London day and played what, even for him, was a remarkable innings of 278 in under six hours with 1 six and 32 fours. Lindsay soaked up the unique Lord's atmosphere and, with Bradman, added 162 before being caught at the wicket for 57 trying to cut Compton. MCC were unimpressive, the veteran Wyatt top-scoring with 84 not out in a total of 214 in reply to Australia's 502 and suffering the indignity of having to follow on. They were 1–87 when rain terminated proceedings.

At this stage, Hassett had been out four times and had seen 614 runs accumulate without a great deal of worry, and perhaps thoughts of seeking a contract as a professional with one of the English counties may have flashed across his brain. It is not known whether or not he expressed disappointment when Bradman informed him that he could rest from the next game, which was to be played at Northampton. At all events, he was pleased that Bill Brown, who'd been having a rather lean time, struck form and, in scoring 194, gave the Northampton spectators and players a lesson in elegant play for opening batsmen. The Australians again won easily.

The hallowed turf of Kennington Oval, home ground of the Surrey Club where John Berry Hobbs made a fair percentage of his 194 first-class centuries, was the scene of the next match. The Australians again scored heavily. Bradman, after an uncharacteristic 2 at Northampton, was back in the runs, content this time with a modest 143 out of 528. Hassett made 56 and O'Reilly took 8–104. After Surrey made 271, Bradman incurred some crowd anger by batting again, explaining that some of his team were sore and stiff. He made a fairly meaningless closure at 2–232, which gave Surrey two and a half hours to make 489 for a win. The match report indicated that Lindsay had blossomed after a slow start and was deceived by a clever change of pace by the county seam bowler, Berry.

Hassett didn't get a bat against Hampshire at the pleasant Southampton ground. It was notable for another century by Bradman which, for the second time, gave him his thousandth run by the end of May. Closing the innings at 1–320, the Hampshire people had very little idea of the mysteries of Bill O'Reilly, who took 6–65 out of a total of 157. Rain shortened the game to a draw.

The Middlesex match was played at the Oval, some other fixture being allotted to Lord's and, on a wet pitch, the Australians showed their usual vulnerability. Bradman made 5 and Lindsay was leg before for 29 to Jim Sims, a leg spinner, who toured Australia in 1936–37. Chipperfield once again showed some wet wicket ability with a top score of 32. Middlesex did little better, McCormick being dangerous in the conditions and finishing with 6–58. In Australia's second innings, Bradman made a generous gesture in closing at 2–114 to give Edrich the chance of getting his 1,000 runs by the end of May, which he duly accomplished.

The match against Gloucestershire was robbed of much interest due to the absence of Walter Hammond, who was engaged in the Test trial at Lord's. Hammond, despite being dropped four times, made 107 and appeared certain to gain the England captaincy. Meanwhile, at Gloucester, in a low-scoring game, again in the wet, Australia won by 10 wickets. Hassett was out for 29 in the first innings to the bowling of Sinfield, an off spinner, and did not bat in the second. Australia won by 10 wickets, O'Reilly having 11 wickets in the match.

The MCC selectors chose a squad of thirteen for the Test and appointed Hammond as captain. Leyland, Allen, Bowes and Goddard were unfit. Hutton, Barnett, Edrich, Paynter, Compton, Hardstaff, Ames, Clay, Pope, Verity, Wright and Farnes, with Hammond, were in the squad.

While these deliberations were proceeding at Lord's, the Australians were engaged in a game against Essex on a rain-affected pitch at Southend. In a low-scoring match, Australia scored 145 and 153, Lindsay being bowled by Farnes for 26 in the first innings and fell to the same bowler for 4 in the second. Farnes was a fast bowler who operated from a short run. He lost his life in the war. Essex could reply with only 114 and 87, Australia winning by 97 runs. Bill Brown was top scorer in the match with 55.

Trent Bridge, Nottingham, was the venue for the Test match. It boasted a batsman's wicket for any sort of match and excelled itself in the strip prepared for the present engagement. There was a minor sensation when Lord Hawke, a pillar of the MCC and Yorkshire Club, returned his match tickets. He had stated in 1924 that he prayed that no professional would ever lead England. This could not have been encouraging for Walter Hammond despite his Lordship issuing a statement denying that Hammond's appointment had anything to do with his action.

There was a good spirit between the two teams, who were staying at the same hotel. Bradman and Hammond dined together and Compton chatted until late with O'Reilly, Hassett and Fleetwood-Smith. Australia played three spinners, O'Reilly, Ward and Fleetwood-Smith, and the batting looked strong enough, all those chosen having shown some form in the early tour games — Fingleton, Brown, Bradman, McCabe, Hassett and Badcock were the six, and Barnett and McCormick made the Eleven with the spinners.

Winning the toss, Hammond sent Barnett and Hutton to get things moving. They certainly complied with the captain's instructions, England being a healthy 0-162 at lunch. Barnett was dropped at mid-off by Bradman on 30 and Hutton saw a ball roll onto the stumps without dislodging the bails. Barnett was 98 at the adjournment, 'an innings played on the rim of mortality', said Cardus. Hutton scored an even 100 in his first Test against Australia and was then leg before wicket to Fleetwood-Smith. Barnett was bowled by McCormick for 126 and then O'Reilly, fortunately in view of what was to happen, despatched Edrich for 5 and Hammond clean bowled for 26, 'by art, beautiful, skilful and deceitful', said Cardus, who, after early doubts, had come to an appreciation of the great bowler's skill.

Thereafter the England innings proceeded at a fair pace with heavy scoring from Paynter, 216 not out, and Compton 102. At 3.30 p.m. on day two, the innings ended at 8–658, which suggested some fairly dismal bowling figures — O'Reilly 3–164, Ward 0–142, Fleetwood-Smith 4–153.

The Australian innings was distinguished by Stan McCabe's historic 232. This has been so beautifully described by Cardus that further comment is superfluous. Stan made 232 out of 411 with not much help from the others. Lindsay miscued an attempted drive off a Wright leg break and was caught at slip — Hassett caught Hammond, bowled Wright 1. Following on, Brown and Bradman seized gratefully the lifeline thrown by McCabe and batted their side into a draw. Lindsay improved on his first innings effort — caught Compton, bowled Verity 2. This resulted from a reflex prod at a sharply rising Verity delivery — the ball ballooning gently forward to Compton at silly point.

In this innings, Bradman demonstrated his many-sided greatness. A naturally attacking batsman, he could, when circumstances required, drop the anchor, bat out time and save a match. In this Trent Bridge innings he was at the crease for 365 minutes and was still in occupation when the game ended in an honourable draw. Stan McCabe, a far more graceful player, could not have done that, even though his first-innings masterpiece laid the foundation upon which his captain and Bill Brown were able to save the match despite trailing by 247 runs on the first innings. Australia were 6–427 at the close, 180 runs ahead and, given an extra day, with three spin bowlers to operate on a fifth-day pitch, might conceivably have won. The match will be long remembered for McCabe's innings, the third remarkable effort of his eight-year international career, none of which resulted in an Australian victory.

Lindsay had a rest against the Gentlemen of England at Lord's. Bradman and Badcock scored centuries and Fleetwood-Smith took 7–44 in the Gentlemen's second innings total of 149. Australia won by 282 runs.

At Old Trafford, Hassett was back in the runs with 118 in quick time. He and Badcock added 182 in 150 minutes before Hassett was bowled by a little-known trundler named Nutter. There was some resentment when Brown and Fingleton used the second innings for batting practice, and after Cardus (a Lancastrian from way back) had a word with Bradman, the Don went in after lunch and made 100 in 73 minutes to the crowd's delight — another example of Bradman's genius with the bat. The match was drawn.

The highlight of an English cricketing summer is the Test match at Lord's, usually played in June. The 1938 match did not produce a result, but was the occasion of a majestic innings of 240 by Hammond. England again won the toss and after McCormick, in a spell of searing, erratic pace, removed the first three batsmen with only 31 runs on the board, Hammond and Paynter put some steel into the innings until O'Reilly had Paynter leg before for 99. Compton quickly followed for six, leg before to O'Reilly like his predecessor.

Hammond was 210 at stumps, England 5–409. His innings was chanceless and possibly the best of his many efforts against Australia. There have been few finer English players than Walter Hammond. This innings lasted 367 minutes and included 32 fours, mainly drives off either foot, forward or back. The England innings closed at 494. Bradman failed, McCabe made 38 in 30 minutes and Hassett helped Brown put on 124 runs in 100 minutes. Lindsay's contribution was 56 with 6 fours from admirable effortless strokes until he was leg before to Wellard, a fastish bowler who had replaced Sinfield. Later, Bill Brown got some unexpected help from Bill O'Reilly in a hurry — 42 in 45 minutes with 5 fours and 2 sixes off successive balls from Verity. The pair added a welcome 85 runs and Australia were out for 422. Brown batted throughout for 206 in an innings described as 'a masterpiece of concentration and strategy'.

Rain curtailed play by three hours and England closed their second innings at about 3 p.m. on the final day at 8–242, giving Australia the optimistic task of making 315 runs in 165 minutes. Bradman was 102 not out in two hours and Lindsay made a brisk 42 in his best fashion. After hitting a no-ball from Doug Wright for 6, the bowler replied with a 'spitting' leg break which left Hassett pushing hopelessly and listening to the death rattle as the off stump fell back in some disarray. At the close, Australia were 6–204 and the match was again drawn.

At this stage of the season, about around the end of June, Lindsay Hassett occupied the fourth position in the averages of all players, English and Australian. Bradman was, not unexpectedly, number one with 1,588 runs at 144.36, followed by Hammond with 1,742 runs at 82.09, Brown with 1,304 at 81.5 and Hassett with 1,020 at 72.85. This was a creditable performance for a young man on his first tour of England. Fleetwood-Smith shaded O'Reilly in the bowling. Both had 56 wickets, Fleetwood at 16.63, O'Reilly at 17.73. Verity had 77 wickets at 17.10.

The Australians travelled to Bramall Lane, Sheffield, to take on the formidable Yorkshiremen and avoided probable defeat owing to the intervention of rain. Hassett held the side together in the first innings

## A NOTABLE DEBUT — ENGLAND 1938

total of 222 with 94 made in two hours and including 12 fours and 2 sixes. He was leg before to Verity. In reply, Yorkshire reached 205, Waite having a day out with the ball — 7–101. In the second innings, Verity got among the Australians on the damp strip and saw them off for 132. Bradman made 42 and Hassett 17, again leg before to Verity. This left Yorkshire only 150 to win and when the rain intervened, they were 3–83.

Lindsay, a practical joker from school days, captured a scruffy-looking goat out on the Grindleford Hills in the neighbouring county of Derbyshire and planted it in the bedroom occupied by Stan McCabe and Bill O'Reilly. This prank was not greeted with unrestrained glee by the occupants and Bill, in particular, expressed his displeasure with some vigour and a marvellous flow of invective, both Australian and Celtic. It also led to a general securing of doors in the future, which rather foiled Lindsay's plans for the next night when he returned with a hedgehog.

The Old Trafford Test was washed out without a ball bowled. This was a pity for the locals who pride themselves on their cricket and cricketers — MacLaren, Tyldesley and Spooner to name three. The Australians sat about playing cards or reading, hoping vainly for a break in the weather.

Bradman cabled the Board of Control asking that his wife be allowed to join him at the end of the tour and at his own expense. The Board, with that unfailing delicacy of touch, sensitivity and appreciation of their captain's deeds in England, refused. Bradman, was understandably angry and threatened to quit international cricket for good. There was a sharp collective intake of breath when this piece of news was passed on and the Board's edict was not only overturned but permission was extended to all players if they so desired.

Hassett had a spell in the Warwickshire game where Brown, 101, and Bradman, 135, saw Australia to 394, more than enough to account for the Warwicks. Another innings win was the result.

At Nottingham, where Harold Larwood used to launch his thunderbolts and his partner in crime, Bill Voce, was still putting his arm over, the Australians were all out for 243. Lindsay Hassett was leg before to Voce for 2. On a damp strip, the Nottinghamshire players could manage only 147, O'Reilly putting insoluble problems to the locals with 5–39. Batting again, Bradman and Hassett had a partnership of 216 in 140 minutes. The match report surprisingly states that Hassett, with 124, was the more aggressive of the two. Bradman made 144 and was content to see his partner assume the dominant role. The Don closed the innings at 4–453 which would have discouraged many better sides than

Notts. They showed little capacity to come to terms with Fleetwood-Smith's 'chinamen' and were out for 137. This left them several hundred short. Perhaps as a reward for his fine innings, Bradman tossed the ball to Hassett to open the bowling in the Notts second innings. His first ball was so far off line that it would have been called a 'wide' if the batsman, Keeton, hadn't reached out and snicked it, to be caught at slip. Hassett bowled seven overs this day, including four maiden overs, and had the respectable figures of 1–4. He made the most of these figures, which confirmed his long-held view that Australia, by neglect, had perhaps robbed itself of an antipodean Tate or Bedser.

There are, I believe, only two survivors of the fourth Test match played at the Headingley Ground, Leeds, in July 1938 — Bradman and Brown. Most of the players of both sides in that match would rate it the best, most nail-biting encounter of their experience. There were no big scores — Bradman, 103, in one of his very greatest innings for Australia and Hammond a fiery 76. Fitting no doubt, that a great match should be marked by the world's two best batsmen.

England batted first and, in the absence of Hutton on his own ground, Edrich and Barnett opened. Edrich, who had terrible problems with O'Reilly, was bowled for 12 by a bosie which hit the stumps via Edrich's pads. Hardstaff didn't help matters by getting himself run out for 4 and Barnett and Hammond were in occupation at the lunch adjournment with England 2–62. O'Reilly's figures at lunch were 14-11-4-1, but he'd blotted his copybook by dropping Barnett at 9 'without hesitation', said Cardus sardonically, 'an easy and lovely catch'. At 142, O'Reilly coaxed Hammond forward and confounded him with a top spinner that fizzed and bowled him emphatically. Compton soon followed, bowled by an O'Reilly leg break, a delivery some thought had been dropped from his repertoire. This left England at 6–172 and O'Reilly and Fleetwood-Smith got rid of the tail despite some resistance from Verity and Wright. O'Reilly finished with 5–66 from 34 overs, all but Price and Bowes in the top order.

On the second day, in atrocious light and with rain threatening, Bradman declined to appeal, preferring bad light and a good pitch to good light and a rain-affected pitch. Doug Wright again accounted for Lindsay Hassett with a well-flighted leg break, which Lindsay had to play at but on which he couldn't manage to get more than the bat's edge. That was enough for Hammond, a bigger man than Mark Taylor and almost as good at slip, smiling grimly as he waved Hassett goodbye at 13.

♦ A NOTABLE DEBUT — ENGLAND 1938 ♦

At 242 all out, Australia had little to cheer about with the prospect of confronting Farnes, Wright and Verity in the gloom on a fourth-day pitch. However, England batted badly and the spinners did the rest. In this innings, Hardstaff, batting at number three, was unwise enough to hit O'Reilly for 4, followed by another 4 from a no-ball from the same bowler. Ralph Barker, in his book, *Ten Great Bowlers*, recalls how O'Reilly reacted to these insults. Barker says that O'Reilly was livid as he called for the ball and, eyes blazing, arms gyrating, he charged in to bowl the fastest leg break anyone had ever seen. Poor Hardstaff! He pushed myopically as this sinful delivery flashed past his groping bat and crashed into the off stump. As he departed, Hardstaff walked past umpire Chester and enquired, 'What chance have you got against a ball like that?'.

With England all out for a dismal 123, Australia started after lunch needing 105 to win. It was in this innings that Hassett came of age as a Test-match batsman. In poor light and, as Fingleton wrote, smelling 'death in the rain laden wind', Brown, Bradman and McCabe out and Wright bowling beautifully, Hassett hit bravely for 33 made in 30 minutes with 5 fours. This put the issue beyond doubt and when Hassett was out (again to Wright) at 91, Badcock and Barnett knocked off the remaining runs.

The win was timely in view of what was to happen at the Oval in a few weeks' time. As holders of the Ashes, Australia would retain them following the Leeds win, irrespective of how the fifth Test turned out.

At Taunton, the Australians took on Somerset, a relaxing fixture after the Headingley tension. Although Lindsay managed only 31, Don Bradman made 202 in 225 minutes and Stan McCabe had a welcome return to form with a brisk 56 not out. The Australians closed at 4–464, Badcock again scoring heavily with 110. One of the mysteries of the tour was Badcock's string of failures in the Tests despite heavy scoring in other games. When Somerset batted, Fleetwood-Smith carried too many guns for them and the best they could do was 110 and 136, Australia winning by an innings and 218 runs.

Against Glamorgan, rain ruined what promised to be an interesting game. Lindsay was 26 not out when the weather intervened.

A couple of games were played in Scotland, one at Dundee and one at Glasgow. Neither was of first-class status nor was a later game at Durham where the Australians again won by an innings, O'Reilly and Fleetwood-Smith both taking 10 wickets in the match.

In the return game against Surrey, leading up to the Test, rain was again the main player, although Stan McCabe got some useful practice with 67 — Lindsay was leg before for 11 in Australia's total of 297. Moving to the lovely ground at Canterbury, Hassett was given a rest against Kent. Sid Barnes was fit again and made a good 94, but the one and only Frank Woolley adorned the match with an effortless 81 in the second innings, Kent having been asked to follow on. His 81 came in 66 minutes out of 109, with one six, one five and thirteen fours. Woolley was 51 years old at this stage. He made 58,969 first-class runs with 145 centuries and took 2,068 wickets. His place among the immortals must always be secure. For the record, Australia scored 479 and 0–7, Kent 108 and 377, Australia winning by 10 wickets.

The fifth Test match of 1938 played at Kennington Oval, London, is engraved on the hearts of those Australians still living who remember the match. The curator, 'Bosser' Martin, was determined to produce a wicket better than that enjoyed by batsmen at Trent Bridge. As the game was to be played to a finish, he was given a free hand by the authorities who, no doubt, hoped fate would favour Hammond when the coin was spun. Umpire Chester remarked that it reminded him of a strip of velvet and O'Reilly swore that it smelt of 'cowyard confetti'. England stacked the team with seven batsmen and Bradman did the same. The pity was that only five of Bradman's seven could bat. The captain himself and Fingleton were both injured in the field and took no further part. McCormick was unfit and the Australians took the field on this graveyard with two recognised bowlers plus part-timers Waite, Barnes and McCabe. Cardus described the wicket as 'ridiculous' and hinted darkly that 'more would be heard of it'. Not much of any note has been heard up to the present.

Hutton and Edrich survived the pace onslaught of Waite and McCabe after Hammond won the toss. McCabe remarked to umpire Chester after completing his first over, 'Frank, they'll get a thousand'. They indeed may have done so had not Hammond been sure Bradman couldn't bat and closed the innings. O'Reilly quickly disposed of poor Edrich leg before for 12 to give him his hundredth wicket in his nineteenth Test against England. Leyland had returned to the England side and as O'Reilly saw him coming through the gate, he growled, 'It's that Yorkshire bastard again'. The 'Yorkshire bastard' went on to score 187 and defied all efforts to remove him until he was run out. Barnett missed one of the costliest stumping chances in cricket history off O'Reilly when Hutton was 41 and O'Reilly informed Chester that he'd shoot the groundsman if he could find a gun.

At the close, England was 1–347, Hutton 160 in six hours, Leyland 156 in just over five hours. The bowlers could not be accused of slowing the game down. No less than 131 overs were bowled, an average of 22 per hour or 50 per cent more than today's heroes manage in the same time. O'Reilly had 1–79 from 35 overs and Leyland confided to Hutton that he had O'Reilly taped, adding that 'he knows it'. Leyland did indeed shield Hutton from O'Reilly and everyone was glad to see the left-hander depart after adding 382 in even time with Hutton. England was 2–434 at lunch on day two, Hutton having proceeded on his calm, unruffled way to 191.

Fingleton tore a muscle during the afternoon session and took no further part in the match. Play was very slow — 'like a cathedral being built', said Tom Valentine in his report. There was some relief when Fleetwood-Smith had Hammond leg before for 59 and when O'Reilly bowled Paynter a run later, joy was unconfined but only briefly, although Compton quickly followed. The scoreboard now showed England 5–555 when Joe Hardstaff appeared. Hutton was well over 200 by now and O'Reilly, who was flat on his back trying to encourage a little zest into his weary bones, heard Hutton say to Hardstaff, 'Will you take O'Reilly? I'm having trouble with him'. Hardstaff, who had a few scores to settle with O'Reilly, politely declined, adding it was 'his turn to have a bit of fun with the Aussies'. He carried this out to the letter with 169 not out made in 326 minutes from 400 balls.

Hutton reached 300 at 6.17 p.m. in 662 minutes from 718 balls and as the Australians plodded their weary way towards the pavilion, rest and sustenance, England's total stood at 5–634, with Hardstaff at 40. Next morning, after 739 minutes, Hutton passed Bradman's 334 made at Leeds in 1930. The Australians congratulated Hutton, with the exception of O'Reilly, who improved the shining minutes by resting. Bradman's 334 eight years before had occupied 383 minutes against an attack comprising Larwood, Tate, Geary, Tyldesley and Hammond.

At 2.30 p.m., on 364, Hutton lifted a drive off O'Reilly and was caught by Hassett at mid-off. He'd faced 847 balls, occupied the crease for thirteen hours and seventeen minutes and struck 35 fours. As a test of concentration and endurance it could not be criticised, but as a spectacle it was less than rivetting. Cardus commented that a new game had been invented 'using the implements of cricket'. Arthur Wood, a wicket-keeper from Yorkshire substituting for Ames, made a lively 53 and shrugged off his colleagues' congratulations: 'I'm at my best in a crisis'. Bradman had twisted his ankle in a hole dug by other bowlers, while attempting to field a drive off his own bowling. He was carried off and took no further part in the match. This was sufficient to convince Hammond that there was little risk in a closure and he called them in at 7–903. The Australians fielded well and Hutton much later remarked that 'O'Reilly was still boring in right to the end' — 85-26-178-3. The church bells at Hutton's hometown, Pudsey, chimed 364 times.

The Australian team's two innings reflected a degree of hopelessness, understandable perhaps, but a little short of what is expected in a Test match. Bill Brown batted with a degree of elegance and defiance for 69 and Lindsay Hassett made an aggressive 42 before being caught at long-on attempting a big hit. The fact that Australia's 201 runs were made in 166 minutes suggests that something akin to a carnival atmosphere prevailed. Bill Bowes, the tall, bespectacled fast bowler from Yorkshire, did most of the damage with 5–49. Barnes took the match batting honours for Australia, if honours they were, with well-made scores of 41 and 33. His absence from the team's earlier matches may have been a serious factor in Australia's overall performances in the Tests. Barnes was a strokeplayer of some distinction at this time when he was just 22 years old. He later forsook aggression for rock-like defence and was recognised as one of the most difficult batsmen to remove.

Apart from Barnes and Barnett, Australia's second innings was a debacle, only four of the nine available batsmen reaching double figures. Farnes took 4–63 and Australia was all out for 123, giving England their biggest victory ever — an innings and 579 runs. This made the English victory by 675 runs at Brisbane in 1928 look like a comparatively close encounter.

Cardus's last word on this painful Test was that 'there should never be a wicket like the Oval wicket again'. Bill O'Reilly and 'Chuck' Fleetwood-Smith would have said 'hear hear' to that.

The tour was now winding down, the business part largely relegated to history, though with the hiding at the Oval lying dormant but unforgotten in the minds of those who'd been on the wrong end of it, particularly the computer-like mind of Donald George Bradman. In the postwar series in which he was engaged, he wrought terrible vengeance for the indignities suffered.

The battle-weary Australians went down to Hove, where Maurice Tate and Arthur Gilligan toiled manfully over many years. Lindsay Hassett

## A NOTABLE DEBUT — ENGLAND 1938

made a dazzling 74 in Australia's first innings of 336 and followed with 56 in the second innings made in 65 minutes. He was batting now in his best fashion, stroking the ball effortlessly to all parts of the field. He reminded people of Kippax of the velvet bat at his graceful best, but there were traces of Jackson and McCabe visible if you cared to cast your mind back. These four men shared a perfection of timing that made batting look the easiest of pursuits. Ian Johnson, writing of Stan McCabe, once said that he bowled what he thought was a good delivery which Stan played, it seemed, defensively off the back foot. Johnson said he turned to walk back to bowl the next delivery, waiting for the ball to be returned to him from cover or mid-off. To his surprise it came back from the boundary at extra cover. That was what Lindsay Hassett's batting was like in those prewar days.

For Sussex, a punishing batsman named Bartlett mauled the Australians to the tune of 157 made in 125 minutes with fours and sixes in rich profusion. Frank Ward took his share of stick but finished with 6–184, the Sussex side making 453. In their second innings, needing 184 to win, the county was 2–53 when time ran out.

The 'Festival' matches followed. The first of these, at Blackpool, against a strong England Eleven was won by the tourists by 10 wickets. In a low-scoring match, Australia scored 174, Hassett not bothering the scorers, and 0–88. Their opponents were bundled out by Ward and O'Reilly for 132 and 99. Amar Singh, an Indian all-rounder of note, bowled fast-medium off a short run and both swung and cut the ball either way as well. His services were lost to the Lancashire League where he had an awesome reputation. In this game against the Australians he took 6–84. Amar Singh died of pneumonia at the age of 30.

At Folkestone, another strong English Eleven turned out. Woolley, Fagg, Paynter, Compton and Ames were a solid nucleus. Batting first, Australia made 390, Barnes 91. England replied with 223 and Australia, batting again, raised the crowd's ire by prolonging the closure until a score of 327 was reached for the loss of 7 wickets. This reduced the match to a farce and acting captain Stan McCabe had to explain that the list of injuries was so long that he was not prepared to risk any more.

Another 'Festival' match against Leveson-Gower's team followed at Scarborough. There was again some acrimony directed at the Australians, who eventually lost by 10 wickets. Hassett did not play in this match, but Barnes with 90 and McCabe with 56 contributed well in their side's first innings of 306. The opposition replied with 363, with

Hardstaff (108) and Hutton (73) scoring heavily. Bowes skittled the tourists for 102 and England knocked off the 46 runs needed without loss. The Australians were accused of timewasting at one stage and 'bad sportsmanship' was mentioned. Stan McCabe straightened things out with Wyatt, the opposing captain, and peace was restored. However, there was evident Australian resentment at the series of so-called 'Festival' matches at the end of a long tour with the 'festival' nature of the games invisible to the naked eye.

After some relaxing games in Ulster and Eire, the Australian cricketers turned homewards. Tom Valentine, who wrote an account of the tour, chose his composite side from the Test players engaged during the season. In a rather controversial line-up, he chose Hutton, Brown, Bradman (captain), Hammond, Paynter, McCabe, Ames, Verity, O'Reilly, Farnes, Bowes.

Of the four Australians, Stan McCabe's inclusion rested on his Nottingham innings. Of the other Australian batsmen, Fingleton, Hassett and Badcock could scarcely be preferred to any Englishmen. Ames instead of Barnett probably rested on the former's better batting qualifications. Of our bowlers, only Fleetwood-Smith might have mounted a challenge to any Englishman, but for him to have replaced Verity would certainly not have been justified.

So it boils down to the fact that Australia had triumphed over a rising England side by the grace of Bradman as captain and O'Reilly as the best bowler on either side.

Lindsay Hassett's Test figures, although not sensational, were marked by some courageous batting when danger loomed, 4 matches, 8 innings, highest score 56, 199 runs, a 24.87 average.

Only three Australians who played in three or more Tests averaged over 40 — Bradman, Brown and McCabe. Five Englishmen fell into this category. Of the bowlers, O'Reilly had the most wickets of either team despite a very heavy workload: 263-78-610-22-27.73. Verity had a better average, 25.28, from 14 wickets.

Hassett's tour performance was highly creditable and he finished third behind Bradman and Brown: 24 – 32 (3 not out) – 1589 – 220 HS – 54.79 with 5 centuries and 6 fifties.

The side was lucky to have halved the rubber and, but for Bradman, almost certainly would have lost both rubber and Ashes. On the other hand, had Grimmett been chosen, the results might have favoured the Australians more. Certainly Bill O'Reilly thought so.

# CHAPTER 5
# PRELUDE TO THE VICTORY TESTS

The year 1938, which marked Lindsay Hassett's introduction to international cricket, had a wider and more sinister significance. The increasing menace of Hitler troubled Europeans, although many could not accept the likelihood of a second world war. But after the occupation of Austria, followed by much of Czechoslovakia, the ominous turn of events could not be ignored.

The Australian cricketers, homeward-bound, found these matters of peripheral concern. Their thoughts were concentrated on returning to wives and families, and a possible war in Europe rested comfortably enough in the backs of their minds. There was still cricket to be played as the 1938–39 season was getting under way at club and district level when they stepped ashore. However, as that last peacetime season drew to its close, the likelihood of a European war steadily increased and, by September 1939, the fuse was lit, air-raid trenches were dug in cities across Europe and, despite warnings, the worst happened.

Lindsay Hassett was working in a Geelong accountant's office where, by a lucky coincidence, a young and attractive Tessa Davis was also employed. The two had had occasional contact since that day in Geelong when they'd first met. Lindsay made a start at studying the arcane mysteries of accountancy, but didn't get far with it when war intervened. After the war, he had other matters on his mind and accountancy was never really in the race. Those who knew him at that time found that, although his early tendency towards introspection had faded with the years, he was still rather reserved at heart despite the great qualities of comradeship, courage, modesty and wit, all of which he had in abundance, together with a complete lack of cant and hypocrisy. Dick Whitington quotes Keith Miller, who played cricket with or against him, as saying, 'I have known Lindsay Hassett and been close to him for a long time, but I'm not quite certain whether I really know him'. For my part, as one who knew him slightly in his later years, I can say only that I found him considerate, polite, witty and knowledgeable about many things apart from cricket.

After war broke out in 1939, there was a long period of inactivity on the part of the declared combatants which came to be known as 'The Phoney War'. In Australia, cricket continued on through the summer, Hassett scored centuries in each innings of a Shield match against New South Wales and people relaxed a little from the nervous excitement of September 1939. Then came Norway and the over-running of the Low Countries and France, and the British Empire found itself alone, virtually without arms and awaiting the next shock.

At about this time, Arthur Lindsay Hassett, aged 26, decided it was time to do something. He joined up, was given the regimental number of VX38843 in the 2–2 A.A. (Anti-aircraft) Regiment of the second Australian Imperial Forces (AIF), based at Puckapunyal, Victoria. Hassett was a difficult man for the quarter master to fit out with a uniform and so on and it seems that the end result was big enough to cover Warwick Armstrong or Lisle Nagle, or both in a pinch. However, there were compensations. Lindsay's long-time friend, George Schofield, was there sporting a lance corporal's stripe and soon Lindsay was sent off to learn how to drive army vehicles. Alec Hurwood and Ted White were also at Puckapunyal. Hurwood, a medium-paced bowler from Queensland, had been a member of Woodfull's 1930 team to England while White had been with Lindsay on the 1938 tour.

Lindsay was allocated to Number 4 Battery of the regiment and was joined by quite a number of Geelong recruits who'd been members of the city's militia anti-aircraft unit before the war.

Lindsay and friends sailed early in 1941 aboard the *Mauretania* as part of a convoy that included the *Queen Mary* and *Aquitania*. The speed of these ships enabled them to sail mostly without escorts. British action against the enemy was concentrated mainly in the Middle East, where successful actions had been fought against the Italians. To the dismay of the troops aboard the *Mauretania*, where they were billeted in comparative comfort, once in Bombay they were transferred to a very dirty Dutch ship, the *S S Westerland*. She had arrived in Bombay carrying a load of French legionnaires from Dakar in Africa. There was no canteen, the food was awful and the water undrinkable. However, there was a redeeming feature. Lindsay and a few mates decided to make an inspection of the hold where, to their delight, they found crates of Chinese beer called *ewo*. Although the beer, in theory, was there for the crew's consumption, this minor obstacle was quickly disposed of, as was the beer. Empties, crates and straw packing were ditched overboard.

The ship's crew, naturally put out by this act of piracy, made a fuss and the regiment's Commanding Officer imposed a levy of sixpence (five cents) per head to be deducted from all members of the regiment to cover the cost. Lindsay and his mates were well satisfied with the outcome and stated that they'd never been so full at so small a cost. They saw the episode as a ringing endorsement of the old army proverb that 'time spent in reconnaissance is seldom wasted'.

The convoy made for Suez where the troops disembarked and continued by train to El Kantara and across the Sinai Desert to Haifa in Palestine, which was to be their base.

A number of matches was arranged when service conditions permitted and Australia had a good spread of talent available in various AIF units. In addition to White and Hassett, Albert Cheetham was part of the Tobruk garrison and was released from time to time. He'd played for Balmain in the Sydney District competition and was showing promise in the New South Wales side when war cut short his progress. Rayford Robinson, from the Gordon Club, was there, a genuinely 'brilliant' player on his day, in the best sense of that hackneyed word. Bradman once said to Neville Cardus, 'You'll forget about me when you see Ray Robinson bat'. Tragically, Ray had personal problems that limited his effectiveness for much of the time. Bill O'Reilly, who felt the weight of Robinson's bat in a club game, rated him highly. Jack Rymill was another who'd played interstate cricket. Dick Whitington, opening batsman for South Australia and prolific cricket writer, was also there.

Lindsay narrowly escaped trouble in Haifa when he and some mates masqueraded as officers to gain entry to a club that bore the sign 'Officers Only'. The Provost Marshal apprehended and evicted them and reported them to the unit. Fortunately, 4 Battery was posted to another location and the Provost Marshal was transferred to the desert and the matter dropped.

At Alexandria, the AIF team, captained by Hassett, defeated a South African forces team. The AIF made 201, Hassett 7, Cheetham 58, and dismissed the Springboks for 171, Wade 59. In the second innings, Hassett redeemed himself with a brilliant 101 not out. South Africa did better in the second innings with 223, but this was insufficient to avert defeat by 6 wickets.

Walter Wade from Natal was a wicket-keeper and batsman of note and younger brother of Herbert Wade, who, in 1935 against the Australians, appealed against the light as fielding captain because he feared for the safety of his fieldsmen as McCabe cut and drove in the

Johannesburg murk in the second of his three remarkable innings.

In a later game against the New Zealand forces at Maadi, Hassett again failed with the bat, scoring only 19, but his side put the cleaner through the Kiwis, 161 and 5–173 against 159 and 77. White and Hurwood took all but one wicket in the match. Hassett starred in the second innings with 102 not out.

In a match played at the Gezira Club in Cairo, the Australians had a game against a side skippered by Freddy Brown and including Bill Bowes. Hammond had been due to play, but was called away on duty. The Australians made 337 and those present were privileged to see a classy 117 from the bat of Ray Robinson. Hassett made 39 and spent some time in the middle admiring the run-a-minute elegance of Robinson. The Club Eleven could manage only 124 and 132 and were defeated by an innings and 81.

Hard upon this game, the side had to confront the more serious aspects of war. German troops had now arrived in the Western Desert and life had become much more difficult. Cheetham returned to Tobruk, Hassett and Co. to Haifa and some to join the Eighth Army, which suffered severe misfortunes until the Battle of El Alamein nearly fifteen months later. The war was soon to assume a far more menacing aspect after the entry of Japan in December 1941. Early successes and advances to Australia's near north led to the recall home of the 6th and 7th Australian Divisions. Number 4 Battery of Hassett's regiment left Haifa and boarded ship at Suez on the *Strathallan*, which was originally due to proceed to Singapore. By February 1942, however, Singapore was under threat and was, in a matter of days, to fall to the Japanese with the imprisonment of almost the entire 8th Australian Division. Diverted to Bombay, the Australians eventually sailed for Australia via Colombo.

In Fremantle, Lindsay was quickly in breach of Kings Regulations and its offshoot, 'Australian Military Regulations and Orders', by absenting himself from fire piquet. He joined his mates in Perth, returning slightly under the weather, and was greeted by the orderly officer of the day who charged him with being 'absent without leave while on duty'. Lindsay's climb up the army promotion ladder to lance corporal was put on hold as a result of this escapade and, in addition, he was fined £20 and confined to barracks (i.e. no leave) for 28 days.

Eventually, Lindsay made it to Melbourne and his marriage to Tessa Davis was speedily arranged, with George Schofield acting as best man. After some escapades of a non-regimental nature in Sydney with his disreputable mates, in which dentists, taxi drivers, Stan McCabe and the New South Wales Cricketers Club were involved, Lindsay and a lot of other Australian soldiers, amunition and petrol, sailed for Port Moresby in an ancient Dutch vessel, the *Swardenvoert*. Meat and rations generally were in short supply, and despite an aborted raid on the hold where the rations were stored, this unhappy state of affairs continued until they reached Port Moresby.

It is appropriate to digress briefly at this point, in order to comment on the activities of the other future candidates for the 'Services Team'. These were mainly members of the RAAF serving in the European theatres and mainly based in the United Kingdom. In 1942, letters went out from RAAF headquarters to all bases in Britain, seeking cricketers of senior-grade standard (i.e. club or district level in Australia). Two officers, Flight Lieutenants P. N. Cochrane and B. C. Andrew, played a leading part in this exercise, which received an astonishing response. Letters came from all sorts of cricketers of every state, notable among them being Keith Miller, Keith Carmody and Stan Sismey. A match was arranged by Sir Pelham ('Plum') Warner against an England side which included Bob Wyatt, Gubby Allen, the Bedser twins, Alec and Eric, Leslie Compton (Denis's elder brother), Trevor Bailey and former Surrey captain, Errol Holmes. Despite the presence of Miller, Carmody and Sismey, the Australians went down, but it was a start, and in 1943 eight games were played, four won, four lost. They finished with a good win over the RAF, which had a handy side — Bob Wyatt, Cyril Washbrook, Alec Bedser, Paul Gibb and Jack Crapp, among others. The Australians had hoped to be strengthened by Bill Brown, who was expected but was posted elsewhere.

Six members of the RAAF team were chosen in the Dominions' side to play England at Lord's in August 1943 — Carmody, McDonald, Miller, Roper, Sismey and Workman. The fine New Zealand batsman Dempster, Morkel from South Africa and three West Indians, Constantine, Clarke and Martindale, made up the Eleven. The England side bristled with stars — Robins, Ames, Bedser, Bailey, Compton, Evans, Gimblett, Holmes and Robertson. England won by 8 runs and the match was notable for the first real emergence of Keith Miller as a fast bowler. Denis Compton was the unlucky batsman at the receiving end and he told Stan Sismey the first delivery he faced was the fastest since Ernie McCormick graced the scene in 1938.

In 1944, the RAAF received a further boost in its members and talent when Bob Cristofani, Reg Ellis, Ross Stanford and Clive Calvert arrived from Australia. Bob Cristofani had been the terror of the Sydney high schools' circuit around 1936 and 1937, bowling his leg breaks and wrong'uns from a longish run and picking up a few runs as well. Clive Calvert was rather special. A slightly built, gifted all-round cricketer, he adorned the Sydney club scene for far too short a time. He was a graceful batsman, a medium-paced bowler and a charming young man. He lost his life in a mine-laying operation over the Baltic Sea in December 1944. Despite difficulties, the players managed to fit in eleven main fixtures, playing either as the 'RAAF' or 'Australia'. The hard core of an integrated services team was available in England by the time Hassett arrived in the United Kingdom to get things moving in 1945, although Keith Carmody was shot down and imprisoned, only to return shortly after VE Day in May of that year.

It's now time to return to Lindsay Hassett, whom we left hungry, hot and tired aboard a venerable old tub en route to Port Moresby. While there, Lindsay was subjected to the heat and humidity of that coastal town, which is not a suitable place in which to be introduced to the splendour of New Guinea. I speak from postwar experience and concede that the 'splendour' mentioned may not have been especially noticeable to those who dragged guns and fought in the heat during the war. But war or peace, Moresby has little to recommend it.

Lindsay's gun crew was commanded by bombardier Peter Danby, who states that the period in Port Moresby was a 'very stressful time' with 30 to 40 air raids per day. He says that Lindsay gave him wonderful support. Although 'a bit of a rebel', says Danby, 'his marvellous sense of humour was just the sort of antidote required for stressed soldiers'. He adds that Lindsay was 'loyal to the core' and the friendship between the two men extended for many years after the war ended.

For some obscure reason, Lindsay was transferred from the Heavy Anti-aircraft Regiment to a Light Anti-aircraft Regiment, a transfer that resulted in his being separated from George Schofield. While acts of military valour are not available, no doubt Lindsay would have been more than equal to any situation that confronted him. His innovative mind is best illustrated by this account of revised, remedial dressing for sweating soldiers plagued by insects, dermatitis, tinea and the many hazards of tropical service. I'm indebted to Dick Hassett, who provided the article, and the Legacy Club of Melbourne, who included it in their bulletin of 28 May 1987 and kindly agreed to my using it in this book.

## ♦ PRELUDE TO THE VICTORY TESTS ♦

Entitled *The Original Entrepreneur*, the account reads:

> *The recent invitation for items of interest for the Bulletin was not intended to call up your personal experiences, but an item received this week was so priceless, it would be a sin to omit it, so it is presented just as it was received.*
>
> *It concerned a sergeant (probably the Legatee submitting the story, but not known for certain). who on return from a spell with measles in the A.G.H. at Koitaki (NG), was surprised to find the way his blokes were attired. When he left, they all wore standard rig — 'nothing' except shorts and boots. Also all suffered from tinea, for which the only palliative was bright purple 'war paint' liberally daubed over all infected areas.*
>
> *But Lindsay Hassett, of cricket renown, was a member of the detachment, a gunner, an entertainer, and a terrific bloke to have around. He had invented a garment which had changed the life of his mates and, of course, his own. Take one Chesty Bond singlet, standard issue, and hold the singlet upside down, step into the garment with each foot passing through the arm holes. Pull the singlet up until the shoulder straps rest lightly in the groin, tie a bit of string around the waist and let the singlet fall negligently over the hips and thighs. This created a superb style of lap-lap, and solved the perspiration problem, which was causing the worst of the tinea.*
>
> *Finally, Lindsay instructed all of the fellows in the proper way to sit, with a degree of modesty even their mothers would have been proud to see. It is not known whether Hassett registered his design or made money out of royalties.*

Tess Hassett reveals another side to this multi-talented man. Tess says that while in Port Moresby, Lindsay prepared, planted and cultivated a vegetable patch adjacent to his canvas residence. From my knowledge of vegetable growing in most coastal areas of Papua New Guinea, the main crops would have been of the yam and tapioca variety. In the fruit department, bananas would be plentiful, but time may have limited Lindsay's efforts in this area. Tess also said that by some mysterious means, Lindsay acquired a baby's highchair from the table portion of which he'd eat his meals, presumably seated on a stool or some sort of box. A 'one-of-a-kind' example again!

About mid-1944, Lindsay's name was included among those chosen to join the Second AIF Reception Group under Brigadier Eugene Gorman. The group, comprising 150 members of the AIF, was to be located at Eastbourne in Sussex, England, and its duties were to prepare for the return and repatriation of 6,000 plus Australians who were held prisoner in Germany, Poland and Italy. Lindsay Hassett, Albert Cheetham, Dick Whitington and Cecil Pepper were among those chosen for these duties. It's pertinent to point out that in late 1944, after the successful June landings in Normandy, hopes for a speedy end to hostilities were high but sadly a little optimistic.

Gorman's group was to sail to the United Kingdom via the United States, where they had been invited (at Prime Minister Curtin's urging) to take part in a parade down New York's Broadway to demonstrate Australia's gratitude for the contribution made by the armed forces of the United States in thwarting Japan's plans to invade Australia. The length of the march was over 3 miles (5 kilometres) and, as many of the unit were doctors, dentists, lawyers, clerks — even three padres — the standard of marching did not quite attain that reached by the Grenadier Guards, but was probably adequate and little worse than that frequently seen from their own troops by the good citizens of New York.

Ceremonial duties completed, the unit boarded the *Queen Mary* and disembarked at Greenock, Scotland, on 28 August and then entrained for High Wycombe in Buckinghamshire and later to the lovely Saffrons ground at Eastbourne. At this stage of the war, Lindsay Hassett was sporting the three stripes of a sergeant, so too were Cecil Pepper and Charlie Price. Albert Cheetham was a captain as was Dick Whitington.

In the early stages, the newly arrived AIF cricketers, and those from the RAAF who'd been active for some time, preferred to maintain separate identities. There was no real basis of comparison with the first AIF side because air-force personnel were few and far between at that time and the problem of integration did not arise. However, by the time Germany surrendered, it was readily appreciated that something special was required. Accordingly, while retaining both the AIF and RAAF sides as separate entities, a new Australian Services Eleven was formed, thanks mainly to the efforts of Albert Cheetham (Army), Mick Roper (RAAF), John Mallyon (Amenities Officer) and Senior Officer Stan Sismey (RAAF). In due course, the principal members of the squad would be: W/O Hassett (31 Vic. Captain), F/O Bremner (26 Vic.), F/Lt Carmody (26 NSW), Capt. Cheetham (29 NSW), F/O Cristofani (24 NSW), F/O Ellis (27 SA), F/O Miller (25 Vic.), Sgt Pepper (26 NSW), F/O Pettiford (25 NSW), Sgt Price (27 NSW), F/Lt Roper (28 NSW), Sq/Ldr Sismey (29 NSW), F/O Stanford (27 SA), Capt Whitington (32 SA), W/O Williams (29 Vic.), F/O Williams (34 SA) and F/Sgt Workman (26 SA). F/Lt Keith Johnson NSW was manager, Capt. Mallyon (SA) treasurer, Sgt

Maddison (Vic) masseur and F/Sgt Moran (SA) scorer/baggageman.

The team remained officially a service unit and members received nothing more than their service pay. In Lindsay Hassett's case this amounted to 12 shillings per day. Hassett, as a warrant officer, Class II (W/O II), was outranked by most of the other members. He might have had a commission, but turned it down because he did not consider it appropriate to his military duties. Despite some initial querying from RAAF members at his appointment for the whole series, and a feeling that Keith Carmody, when available, had claims to the job, Hassett's position was never questioned. It was widely known that Lindsay had not sought the captaincy. His standing as an international cricketer of some note, plus his personality and obvious leadership qualities, gave him undeniable claims to the post. It was also mandatory that only people who had completed a tour of duty, either in the United Kingdom, the Middle East or New Guinea, would be eligible for inclusion in the squad. This requirement, despite press speculation, ruled out some handy players — Bill Brown, Ian Johnson, Ray Lindwall, Colin McCool and Arthur Morris to name several.

It was the wish of the Australian Prime Minister John Curtin, and, reportedly, days after the German surrender, of Winston Churchill, that some major fixtures be quickly arranged to entertain the British people who hadn't had much entertainment over the past six years of war. And so, some first-class fixtures between England and the Australian Services team were arranged — these eventually came to be known as the 'Victory Tests'.

# CHAPTER 6
# THE AUSTRALIAN SERVICES TEAM

The five games of the Victory series were, and still are by those who took part, regarded as among the happiest matches in which the Australians have ever played. The mood of the English cricket enthusiasts who flocked in droves to the games was one of the most important elements in making the series so successful. Apart from that, the keenness of the contests, always at a high and competitive pitch, never deteriorated into acrimony, far less to the deplorable level of some recent contests. Originally, it was thought that two days would be adequate for the matches, but this was quickly revised to three and all but one of the five contests ended in a result. Keith Miller subsequently wrote that all players 'were happy just to be alive and fit and well', a sentiment that would have been echoed by both players and spectators.

Thousands of Londoners queued overnight at Lord's in wet weather to see the first match which was to begin next day, 19 May, just eleven days after VE (Victory in Europe) Day. England announced a strong side under the formidable leadership of Walter Hammond. With him, Test-players Ames, Edrich, Gover, Hutton, Robins, Washbrook and Wright were the hard core. The Eleven was made up by Griffith, Surrey's wicket-keeper/batsman, Robertson, opening batsman for Middlesex, and Stephenson, an all-rounder from Essex. This side looked strong and, with the preponderance of established international players, the Australian Board of Control's reluctance to give the series official Test match status, appeared more than justified. The sole international in the Australian side was Lindsay Hassett. Cheetham, Pepper, Miller, Sismey and Whitington had all had first-class experience and the others, Ellis, Price, Stanford, Williams and Workman, were all creditable club or district players who, in a sense, had had greatness thrust upon them.

There was an encouraging cable from Prime Minister Curtin on the eve of the match, gracefully acknowledged by the people at Lord's. On the morning of the match, the *Times* came out with a lengthy piece that achieved a nice balance in its review of both teams' capabilities. Entry would be a flat 1/- and spectators were advised 'to bring their own refreshments'.

♦ THE AUSTRALIAN SERVICES TEAM ♦

The Australians, according to Whitington, were subject to serious doubts as to their ability to make a game of it against the star-studded opposition and would be content if they survived without making fools of themselves. Events were to show that on that score their fears were groundless. Stanley Bruce, Australian High Commissioner in London at the time, sat down beside 'Plum' Warner and saw Hassett lose the toss. Cheetham delivered the first ball bowled at Lord's for six years, to Leonard Hutton, who put the first run, a single, on the scoreboard off the fifth ball. It must have been a moment to savour.

Hassett and Miller, who were to play many Tests in the coming years, found that this match had something that no subsequent Test match provided. Australian soldiers were there in good numbers and the English spectators were as pro-Australia as pro-England. John Arlott, prince of commentators, wrote of 'general euphoria borne of relief and nostalgia'.

Cricket is a great leveller. Leonard Hutton, who in 1938 had batted for thirteen hours and fifteen minutes to score 364, was out on this famous day at Lord's, caught by wicket-keeper Stan Sismey off an obscure recently released prisoner of war, Graham Williams, for 1. Williams was a fastish bowler who'd played a few games for South Australia before the war. There were good contributions from Hammond (29), Washbrook (28), Edrich (45), Robertson (53) and Ames (57), and an aggressive 31 from Stephenson. England finished with a respectable but far-from-discouraging (from the Australian viewpoint) total of 267. Keith Miller bowled nine very fast overs for eleven runs for the wicket of his good friend and RAF bomber pilot, Bill Edrich. In the time remaining, the Services lost the wickets of Workman and Whitington and were 2–82 at stumps. Next day, Hassett made a confident 77 before Stephenson bowled him. Hassett played a wild shot at this delivery and paid the penalty. Miller was the rock on which the Services' innings was built. With good support from Stanford (49), Pepper (40) and Williams (53), Miller played a solid rather than aggressive innings of 105 made in three and a half hours. They lifted the score to the undreamed-of total of 455, a lead of 188. This was, by any reckoning, a remarkable effort by a team of spirited spare parts against virtually an English Test side.

Cecil Pepper got among the Englishmen in their second innings with 4–80 off 32 overs. Pepper was a big man who was probably the inventor of the 'flipper'. He was a great spinner of the ball and a punishing middle-order batsman. He hailed from Parkes in the mid-West of New South Wales. Robertson (84) and Edrich (50), again performed well, but Hutton fell to Pepper's top spinner for 21 and Hammond lbw to Ellis for 33. Surely someone, before the series ended, would pay for these comparative failures by two of the best batsmen in the world.

Stan Sismey had dismissed six Englishmen behind the wicket in the match when England's innings ended. The Services needed 107 to win, which they did in an exciting run chase against the clock, with seven men fielding on the boundary at times. Hassett made a brisk 37 after opening with Whitington and was caught at deep mid-off by Hammond from the bowling of Gover. After a couple of run-outs, Pepper (54) and Price (10) saw the Aussies home by 6 wickets. In all, 67,660 people saw the match and net proceeds went to various charities in England and Australia.

The pleasure the Australians understandably took in their victory might perhaps have been tempered a little had they considered the age of three of the England bowlers. Alf Gover, a great toiler under the sun on the Oval graveyard wicket, was 38, Stephenson was 39 and Robins almost 40. However, these thoughts were transient in the euphoria of the moment.

Bramall Lane, Sheffield, was the site of the second match. This ground, scene of many Roses battles and the setting for much Cardus gifted tale-telling, had been badly damaged during the war. Sheffield, an industrial city, was an important target for the Luftwaffe. The England side saw Ames (who played as a batsman in the first match), Robins and Gover replaced by the stylish but short of match practice Holmes, Pope and Pollard. Pope, of Derbyshire, and Pollard, of Lancashire, were similar types of fast-medium bowlers. Both were in their mid-thirties and Pollard, particularly, was very highly regarded by the Australian team of 1948.

The Australians, at Ross Stanford's insistence, brought in Keith Carmody. Stanford had flown with the famous Dam Busters squadron and won a Distinguished Flying Cross. Carmody had just been repatriated from a German prisoner-of-war camp. Carmody's inclusion was fortunate as he was a competent wicket-keeper in a crisis. And there was a crisis in Cheetham's sixth over after Hassett won the toss and sent England in on a damp pitch. A sharp rising ball from Cheetham struck Sismey in the face. The injury required stitching and limited Stan's participation in the game.

Walter Hammond made a masterly century and Washbrook made 63, the latter having been dropped at cover when 2. Pepper tested Hammond to the full and finished with 3–86 off 31 overs bowled in one spell over a period of three hours. Sismey, who saw a lot of Hammond from his vantage point behind the stumps, thought that Hammond hit the ball harder than anyone else he saw. Hammond's majestic off-side play between point and the bowler made his better than average on-side play appear ordinary by comparison. Bowlers generally sought to contain him with a leg-stump attack. Pepper, like Dooland, was unfortunately lost to Australian cricket. Both were leg-spin bowlers of the highest class. In this innings, Hammond paid a noteworthy compliment to the Australian, remarking his bowling as among the best he'd faced — and Hammond batted many times against Grimmett.

The Australians played out time after the England innings closed at a virtually two-man total of 286. However, the next day, in overcast conditions, George Pope moved the ball about in the air to take 5–58 out of a total of 147. Hassett was bowled by a beautiful delivery from Pollard for 5 and Carmody's 42 and Pepper's 21 were the only scores of note.

Saving the follow-on by 10 runs, the Australians did well, Miller was heckled by the Yorkshire crowd for nearly decapitating Hutton with a lively bouncer, then had Washbrook caught at the wicket and baffled Robertson by pace to have him leg before. Hutton made a good 46 and Hammond followed his first innings century with 38. England's 190 left Australia 330 to win in six hours. Workman and Whitington gave their colleagues a great start with a partnership of 108. Workman stuck around for three hours and forty-five minutes and helped Hassett, who made a lively 32. He was then deceived by Pope's outswinger and clean bowled for the second time in the match. Stan Sismey felt that throughout the Victory Tests and those that followed, Lindsay did not bat as well as he could. Perhaps his war service and responsibilities affected him despite many useful and sometimes match-saving innings. Carmody was run out for 14, an event that virtually ended Australia's efforts despite stout contributions by Pepper (27) and Sismey (18). Pollard bowled beautifully to take 5–76 and England won an interesting contest by 41 runs. Both sides earned accolades in the Yorkshire press. It had indeed been a good match — fine batting by Hammond, Washbrook, Workman and Whitington, the knowledgeable medium-paced swingers and cutters from Pope and Pollard, Miller's electrifying spell of express bowling and Pepper's mastery of the magic of spin, all combined to make it a contest to be long remembered by those who played in it. Sadly, 52 years on, there aren't many left.

The splendid crowd support given to the first two games prompted Lancashire to agitate for a piece of the action, and it was soon announced that a fifth match would be played at Old Trafford, Manchester, in mid-August. But it was back to Lord's for the third game. The England selectors responded to some pointed criticism regarding the make-up of their side and, in a rare display of risk-taking, replaced Holmes, Pope and Robertson with three young men whose total ages reached only the middle 50s. These were Donald Carr, John Dewes and Luke White. Robertson could count himself unlucky to be dropped, despite averaging 41 in the games just concluded. Pope had an engagement with his Lancashire league club and Holmes was plainly short of a gallop after six years of war.

Rain delayed proceedings by 40 minutes, but Hammond chose to bat on a slightly sporting wicket. Hutton was in his best 1938 form, a model of sound technique, occasionally interrupted by strokes of the utmost grace and power. Bill Woodfull, Australian skipper of the 1930s, once wrote of Hutton's batting that 'it had a touch of magic'. For my part, I was always surprised when he got out, so complete was his control of all but the quickest of bowling. He was, Cardus said, jointly with Hobbs, exemplar of the classical style.

Bob Cristofani joined the Australian side, which otherwise remained unaltered. Cristofani, late of Sydney High School and the Sydney St George Club, came in for the injured Charlie Price. Cristofani possessed formidable skills with both bat and ball, but unaccountably his cricket fell away on returning to Australia. He pushed his leg spinners through quite briskly and was a more than useful addition to the Services' attack.

Dewes played bravely for 27 until beaten and bowled by a scorching delivery from Miller. Hammond was left stranded by Pepper and was stumped by Sismey. Stan Sismey, Squadron Leader and gentleman in the highest category, had been shot down by the Vichy French while doing escort duty in a Catalina flying boat between Gibraltar and Malta. He was picked up by a British destroyer and spent several months in hospital, where surgeons did their best to remove numerous pieces of shrapnel from his body. Fifty-five years on, pieces of shrapnel are still giving him trouble. As a wicket-keeper, he was of the highest class, and it is unfortunate that, in the early postwar years, Tallon and Saggers were fractionally better with the gloves and a little more impressive as batsmen.

Batting on a drying pitch on the Monday, Hassett saved his side from a total collapse with a good although lucky 68, helped later by Carmody and Cristofani, both of whom made 32. Pollard had the excellent figures of 6–75. At 194, Australia trailed by 60 runs and the prospects looked a trifle dodgy. At the urging of one-time South African fast bowler, Bob Crisp, Hassett tossed the new ball to Miller to open the bowling in England's second innings. Miller's pace was too much for John Dewes, who had been promoted to open following his sturdy first innings 27 and saw his middle stump flattened with indecent haste. Hutton was again sound and thoughtful, and Edrich tough and aggressive. Between them they made all but 37 of England's second innings. Some thought Miller bowled as fast as anyone since Larwood had retired. Hammond had lumbago and did not bat in this innings. Cristofani tidied up the lesser lights, plus Hutton, and the innings closed for 164. This left Australia 225 to win. Hassett was out to Wright for 24, again to a slip catch. Miller made a pleasant unbeaten 71, aided by Sismey with 51, and the runs were scored with the loss of 6 wickets to give the underdogs a 2-1 lead in the series.

At this stage, some of the old spirit had revived in the crowds. Their generous feelings towards the Australians had dissipated somewhat and they dearly wanted an England victory. However, they were generous in defeat and appreciative of the all-round skills of Miller with 7 and 71 and 6–86 in the match and Cristofani with 32 and 9–92, overall both distinguished performances. England had been unlucky in Hammond's inability to bat in the second innings and the three youngsters included in their side had contributed little. Cristofani had demonstrated his claims as a top-class all-rounder and Hassett had made more than a fair contribution both with the bat and as captain. Strangely, as noted earlier, Cristofani was unable to reproduce this form or anything like it when he returned home. However, he more than compensated for this in the success he made of his career outside cricket.

The Australians were sorry to lose Albert Cheetham in mid-series. He was brought back to Australia for discharge. He moved to Melbourne shortly after the war and played no more first-class cricket. Keith Carmody was spelled for the next game, no doubt still a little below par after his sojourn as guest of the Germans. Ross Stanford, who'd generously made way for him in the third game, came back and Jack

Pettiford came in for Cheetham. Jack Pettiford and I played together at school and later for the Gordon Club in Sydney. He died at the early age of 45 after a life dogged by more than a fair share of difficulties and tragedies. Jack was a very useful all-round cricketer, bowling good leg spin and scoring runs briskly in the middle order. A happy man, a good companion and team-mate, he was one who seemed destined to draw the short straw in life.

For England, Carr, Dewes and White, the three youngsters, were unceremoniously dumped and the old guard, Pope and Robertson, recalled, plus Fishlock, a former international. Fishlock, despite a good record with Surrey, was an indifferent performer at Test-match level and his tour of Australia in 1936–37 had been rather undistinguished.

The match was the third to be played at Lord's and was to begin on the August Bank Holiday Monday but weather shortened the playing time, resulting in the only draw of the series. The Australians were given some unwarranted and, at times, venomous 'stick' from the press, which accused the Australians, Sismey in particular, of deliberately slow play, the object being to avoid defeat. According to Whitington, the Australian pre-match plan was not to play for a draw but to achieve a position that would force England to take risks to attempt a win and level the series.

Hassett won the toss and sent Workman in to open with Whitington. Workman got an edge to a Doug Wright leg break and was caught at slip. Sismey was promoted to number three to anchor one end while Whitington got on with it. Sismey stayed around for four hours with his partners Whitington and Miller. With Miller, he added 121 in two hours and later Pepper (57) and Pettiford (32) batted aggressively to see the total reach 388 in 420 minutes. Hassett had failed to pick George Pope's unpredictable outswinger and was taken in the gully for 20. Miller's 118 occupied 200 minutes and the overall scoring rate gave little reason for criticism. Compared with present-day rates, it would border on indecent haste. To make matters worse, Sismey badly bruised his thumb and could not keep wickets, a situation complicated by Keith Carmody having been rested.

Rain and bad light delayed the start on Tuesday until after lunch. Hutton (35), Fishlock (69) and Robertson (25) pushed on at a good rate to be three for 249 at stumps. Poor Jim Workman, standing in behind the stumps, contributed 51 in extras to the England tally for the day. After play finished, Hammond generously and voluntarily told Hassett to use Keith Carmody as wicket-keeper if he wished. That offer was gratefully accepted. On the Wednesday, Hammond drove as only he could in a magnificent innings, curtailed at 83 by a great catch at backward point by, of all people, the relieved Jim Workman. Washbrook 112 and Edrich 73 kept the scorers busy and England passed the Services' 388 in less than six hours, for the loss of 4 wickets. Hassett had many problems containing the batsmen on this day, most of his bowlers taking a fair amount of cane. Next day, England batted on almost to the tea adjournment before Hammond closed the innings. Clearly, Hammond had abandoned any hope of forcing a win some time before. Analysis of run rates, balls and overs bowled, time taken and extras allowed, showed that the scoring rate of both sides was extremely close.

Australia's second innings started badly, Whitington, Workman and Hassett being out with the score only 54. Pettiford made 39 in his first match for the Services; he'd had a good triple — 32 and 39 and 3–62. After his dismissal, Miller (33) and Stanford (39) steered the side home. Lindsay had a bad match, Pollard beating him off the pitch and bowling him for 7. However, his admiration and respect for Walter Hammond had increased and it was a pity that the spirit so evident in the Victory series did not carry over into the Australian summer of 1946–47 when relations between the captains were less cordial.

The fifth and final match of the series was to be played at Old Trafford, where Neville Cardus used to go as a child to watch Test matches, after praying that Victor Trumper might score a century out of Australia 150 all out. If Hassett had a bad match at Lord's a couple of weeks earlier, this was to be a shocker — caught Pollard bowled Pope 6 and caught Griffith bowled Pollard 1. On the other hand, a player of far less batting gifts than Lindsay, Bob Cristofani, was to score a century of which Stan McCabe would have been proud and, as a bonus, captured 5 wickets including those of Hammond and Washbrook for 55 runs.

Japan's surrender after the destruction of Hiroshima and Nagasaki had been accepted and World War II was over when 'hostilities' began at Old Trafford on a typical, cloudy Manchester day which blanketed a greentop Manchester wicket, quite different from that of 1956 when Jim Laker bowled himself into the history books. Hassett must have had serious doubt about batting, but probably guessed that things might get worse if he didn't, Manchester weather being what it is. It was not a highly successful decision because medium-paced seamers, Pope and Pollard, reinforced by the Lancashire member of the club, W. E.

Phillipson, carried too many guns and required no assistance from anyone else in despatching the Services for 173. Miller was 77 not out in one of the finest innings he ever played. Pettiford (28) and Whitington (19) were the only others to post double figures.

Hutton played a patient innings for 64 and, with Hammond in his most authoritative mood, added 97 for the third wicket when Hutton fell once again to Williams, caught at the wicket. Miller had bowled very fast again, Hassett using him in short spells. Apart from Washbrook (38), none of the later England batsmen caused much trouble in the overcast conditions and the innings totalled 243. The deficit of 70 was not unmanageable or critical, with England to bat last, if Cristofani had received even moderate support in his remarkable onslaught on the England bowlers. Bad light, indifferent batting and some questionable umpiring saw the Services at 3–37 by stumps on the second day.

By the lunch break on the last day, the Services had lost 8–105 and were in the unhappy position of having a lead of 39 with 2 'tail-end' wickets standing. It was after lunch that Cristofani launched his murderous assault on the England bowlers. Batting well in front of his crease, he forced the three fast bowlers to shorten their length to avoid having their best deliveries treated like half volleys. Cristofani replied by stepping back and hooking and cutting. His 110 runs came in even time out of 126 recorded while he was at the wicket. Williams had hung on bravely while his partner destroyed the bowling. But it couldn't go on and he was finally out caught at the wicket off Phillipson. Ellis quickly followed and the innings ended at an unlikely 210. Phillipson, still swinging the old ball prodigiously, finished with 6–58 to give him 9 for the match. Needing 141 to win, Hutton, Robertson and Edrich managed the task without much difficulty and England won by 6 wickets, thus squaring the series. Hassett's double failure in this game was unfortunate, but no recognised batsman, apart from Miller, contributed much overall.

In a newspaper article, Lindsay wrote that in all five games both sides had striven to win, despite the ill-informed criticism voiced at the third Lord's match. Lindsay added: 'This is cricket as it should be. These games have shown that international cricket can be played as between friends — let's have no more talk of "war" in cricket.'

Miller had led the batting averages with 443 runs at 63.28, Hassett fourth below Cristofani and Pepper with 277 runs at 27.7. His scores were 77, 37, 5, 32, 68, 24, 20, 7, 6, 1. Cristofani took 14 wickets at 15.21

to be second in the bowling to Charlie Price with 7 wickets at 14 from 35 overs. Ellis, Pepper and Miller had been the chief 'work horses', bowling 189, 180 and 121 overs respectively. Ellis was a very accurate orthodox left-hand slow-medium bowler who could be relied on to keep scoring rates at a reasonable level and was of particular value when Miller and Williams were being spelled. There was little between the English established Test players, Edrich, Washbrook, Hammond and Hutton all scoring over 300 runs with averages over 40 apiece. Pollard took 25 wickets at 23.64. More than 367,000 people attended the five 'Victory Tests', which appeared to justify the concept.

As a wind-up to the serious part of the season, a game was arranged between a Dominions Eleven and England at Lord's. Lindsay Hassett was asked to lead the Dominions side but declined because of ill health. In Lindsay's absence, Learie Constantine was a unanimous choice to do the job. Eight Australians played plus Constantine (West Indies), Donnelly (New Zealand) and Fell (South Africa). Constantine, the son of a slave and a dynamic all-rounder in his younger days, was deeply moved at his election as captain by ten white-skinned players. In this match, Miller played his great innings of 185, described by Warner as the greatest exhibition of hitting he'd ever seen. Hammond scored centuries in both innings and Donnelly a classy 133. In the early postwar years, Donnelly was regarded as the best left-hander in the world. The Dominions won an exciting match by 45 runs.

Hassett's run of 'outs' continued in the "Festival" match at Scarborough when he was caught and bowled by Robins for 19, one of the lowest scores in a total of 506. Cecil Pepper went berserk with 6 sixes and 18 fours in making 168 in 140 minutes. The Leveson Gower X1, understandably demoralised by this, were bowled out twice for 258 and 140, left-hand spinner Reg Ellis taking 5 wickets in each innings. This innings win was seen as a happy conclusion to the tour and the Australians were looking forward to going home, being demobilised and putting the war behind them. But Dr Herbert Evatt had other ideas. He was Minister for External Affairs and Deputy Prime Minister and added a six-week tour of India to the itinerary. As serving soldiers and airmen, the players had no option other than to obey and it was with mixed feelings that they arrived in Bombay on 22 October 1945.

There had been no official Australian tour of the subcontinent, which still included what is now Pakistan. A decade earlier, the Maharajah of Patiala sponsored an unofficial tour under the guidance of one-time gifted Victorian all-rounder, Frank Tarrant, and skippered by Jack Ryder.

On arrival, Lindsay told the local press that his team had come to play cricket, emphasising that they'd do their best to win and expressing the hope that both they and their opponents might 'pick up a few points' from each other. The war had not affected cricket greatly in India and there was a potent assortment of cricketers, particularly batsmen, on hand. Australians who saw the Indian side here in 1947–48 will remember the quality of Hazare, Amarnath, Mushtaq Ali and Mankad. Add to these the talents of Merchant and Modi, who did not come to Australia, and you have a formidable batting line-up. Vijay Merchant could fairly be likened to the Australian Bill Ponsford — a sound player never tiring of scoring runs.

Kumar Shri Duleepsinjhi greeted the Australians and acted as guide and host throughout the nine-match tour which entailed endless miles of rail and bus transport. 'Duleep' was the nephew of the immortal 'Ranji' or, to give him his full title, Kumar Shri Ranjitsinjhi, Sahib of Nawanager, who gave English spectators delight similar to that with which Victor Trumper blessed Australians about the same time. 'Duleep', a charming man, did everything possible to make the Australians comfortable.

The locations were colourful and, at times, frightening. In the north at Lahore, the British garrison was prominent with Punjabi regimental pipe bands playing nostalgic Western music. Red tabs and Sam Browne belts were numerous. By contrast, overhead the skies were at times thick with vultures and on the ground, insects plagued fieldsmen.

Against Northern Zone in Lahore in very hot conditions, Bob Cristofani found it all too much and, after a few overs, disappeared into the cooler shade of the pavilion. As the day wore on and, with some assistance from the umpires, the locals pushed on close to 400 for the loss of 4 wickets as a measure of evening coolness relieved the day's heat. Cristofani felt better and returned to the field hoping to improve his already impressive figures. Hassett made no move to dismiss the twelfth man and watched Cristofani while making a few hand signals to move him here and there, until finally he was still on the field but just in front of the pavilion gate. Hassett finally raised his hand and gave a final unmistakeable signal. Cristofani turned, opened the gate and went through. The whole process took a couple of minutes and intrigued the spectators. The Australians drew the match after much travail and discomfort.

## ◆ THE AUSTRALIAN SERVICES TEAM ◆

Vic Richardson, former Australian captain, was now at New Delhi serving as a welfare officer in the RAAF. The local Maharajah of Patiala was 193 cm (6'6") tall and it was a sight to see him and Hassett go out to toss. This was another heavy-scoring match with Lindsay making 187 and 124 not out, Eddie Williams 100, Amarnath 163 and Mushtaq 108. The Viceroy, Viscount Wavell, entertained the Australians in the evening of the final day. This match and the next at Bombay against West Zone were drawn. The first representative game was played at Bombay. The Australians batting first amassed 531, Carmody and Pettiford making centuries, Hassett 53 and Pepper 95. To this, India replied with 339 and 304, all the stars making reasonable contributions in either or both innings. Needing 113 to win, the Services were 1–31 when time ran out. Duleep was disgusted with what he saw as time-wasting by Merchant. More than 40,000 watched the match on the first day and interest remained high throughout.

After a two-day match in Poona, the travellers flew to Calcutta and it was here in the game against Eastern Zone that Hassett's diplomatic skills in quelling riots were demonstrated as previously mentioned in Chapter 1 (see page 9).

India batted first in the Test match making 386, Mankad (78), Hazare (65) and Modi (75) being the main contributors. The Services replied with 472, thanks mainly to centuries by Whitington (155) and Pettiford (101). Miller made 82 in a hurry, hitting Mankad for four sixes in one over. In doing so, he strained his back and was unable to bowl in India's second innings. Hassett made 18, falling victim to Mankad, who bowled 45 overs in the Australian innings to finish with 4–147. In India's second innings, Merchant was 155 not out when he closed the innings at 4–350. It was a great pity that Australian crowds did not have the pleasure of seeing Merchant bat. There was a ruckus when Roper accused the umpire of cheating after the last of several lbw appeals was turned down. The umpire was upset, 'more than somewhat' as Damon Runyan would say, at this slight to his integrity and demanded that Hassett send Roper from the field. Hassett placated the umpire and said he'd remove Roper from the attack, which he'd intended to do anyway. The match was drawn. What with weariness, doubtful food and water, with dysentery a common side effect, and injuries, the Australians had just about had enough. However, two matches remained to be played in Madras, one against South Zone, which they won by 6 wickets, and the third 'Test' against India, which they lost.

Batting first, the Services made 339. Hassett made a fine 143 and Pepper helped with a punishing 87. However, the Australian bowling was well and truly collared by India, all but the wicket-keeper having a bowl to try to stem the tide. Pepper was best with four for 118 from 41 overs. Amarnath made 113 in his typical flowing style, but Modi was the main stumbling block with a mixture of solid defence and wristy attack compiling 203. The innings of 525 found India 186 ahead. Carmody and Whitington made a fine opening stand of 133, but those who followed failed to build on the satisfactory start and the side was all out for 275. India knocked off the 92 runs without difficulty. The main matter of note was Hassett's clean bowling of Armanath for 9 to give Hassett, temporarily at least, 1–0, the best figures for the match. Whitington also took the valuable wicket of Hazare, caught and bowled, and, with the four best batsman out for 82, there were distinct signs of discomfort among the spectators. However, Kardar and Modi were equal to the task. The Governor of Madras entertained both teams at dinner, and the next day the Australians flew out, playing a three-day match in Colombo en route for home. They won this game by an innings and 44 runs, Miller 132, Hassett 57.

Stan Sismey says that the accommodation provided throughout the tour was generally good. Long train journeys were the greatest hardship — carriage and sleeping accommodation were basic. Some of the grounds, for example Brabourne Stadium in Bombay and Eden Gardens in Calcutta, were extremely well appointed. Victor Richardson eased the transport problem by persuading the AOC Transport Command RAF to provide air transport for the team. This was put in place and thereafter air travel was the order of the day until the team was landed at Fremantle.

The trip home via Cocos Island was not notable for its comfort owing to some crowding, but any inconvenience was minimal compared with the dismay felt by all on arriving at Fremantle. Instead of being allowed to return to their families, the men were told that a six-week tour of Australia had been arranged 'to help put Australian cricket back on its feet'. It would have been understandable for the players, long away from home, to tell the Board or the Army or both, to back off. Like good soldiers and airmen, they did not. Neither Lindsay nor Keith Johnson could persuade the Board even to shorten the proposed itinerary, although, in a laudable act of generosity and altruism, the games were reduced to three days from the original four proposed.

At Christmas 1945, the Services team played Western Australia and salvaged a draw. In Adelaide, much interest centred on the comeback of Don Bradman, who had agreed to play as proceeds of the match were to go to charity. Bradman scored 112 after a somewhat uncertain start on the second day after Services had batted first and totalled 314. Hassett scored 92 in the second innings of 255 and time ran out before any decision could be reached.

In Melbourne, Services were without their captain, Hassett, and Pepper, Sismey and Cristofani, and lost heavily. Cricket and travelling over a long period following years of war service had clearly affected players' health and spirits. In addition, much of their gear was in poor repair. Ian Johnson starred for Victoria in this match with 6–27 and 4–17.

In Sydney, New South Wales totalled 7–551, Alley, Grieves and Barnes scoring centuries. Keith Miller made a fine century against Bill O'Reilly, who was greatly impressed by the young man. Miller, much later, charitably said O'Reilly, at age 41, was far below his prewar best. Services totalled 204 and in the second innings were 9–339 when time ran out. In Brisbane, another draw resulted in Hassett making 67 and Colin McCool taking 11–176 in the match. In Tasmania, there was another draw with some heavy scoring, Hassett again contributing 59, Miller 80 and Cristofani 59. Pepper took 9 wickets in the match.

All in all, over nine months in England, India, Ceylon and Australia, members of the RAAF, AIF or Services teams had played 64 games for 27 wins and 12 losses. The best of them was not seen in Australia at the end of such a long tour, but several players had been brought to notice. Miller was, of course, the outstanding 'find' of the series. Hassett had shown good, if rather variable, form with the bat and had demonstrated skills in leadership and diplomacy that would stand him in good stead in the years ahead. Pepper, an all-rounder of varied talents, was lost to Australian cricket after an ill-judged remark to umpire Jack Scott when the latter turned down his appeal for lbw against Bradman. Pettiford went off to the Lancashire League and Cristofani faded from the scene after failing to reproduce his Services form. Stan Sismey was kept out of the Australian side by the perceived, if not actual, superiority of Saggers and the great Tallon, but played some cricket for New South Wales. Cheetham, Roper, Whitington and Williams retired, and one or two were just unlucky to be overlooked by their home States or stymied by the wealth of talent returning home from the Pacific War and others who'd not been involved in the war. But Hassett, late in his life, could still recall those games as the happiest cricket he'd played.

# CHAPTER 7
# A FEW SHORT ONES FROM LINDSAY

With his friend Ian Johnson, Lindsay wrote a book entitled *Better Cricket*. Shortly after the book was published, a story circulated that a spectator who'd just read the book and had taken his young hopeful to see Lindsay bat, was telling the boy in a loud voice to keep his eye on Hassett: 'Now you watch Hassett — see how he does it. You've read his and Johnson's book. Watch how he stands, look at the way he holds his bat. He's your example. Now watch Bedser — he's going to bowl. Watch how Hassett plays him.'

'Oh, Dad, he's bowled!' As noted before, cricket is a great leveller. Last game's century-maker is quite often this match's 'duck'.

The South Melbourne Club tells the following story about Lindsay and the reflected glory in which one of his admirers bathed. Two cricket enthusiasts in the 'outer' at the MCG were arguing over some technical point in the game they were watching. Opinions became heated and personalities intruded:

'I tell you, I know cricket upside down and inside out,' said one.

'You don't know half as much as I do,' came the reply.

'Don't I? I know more about the game than you ever will.'

'Prove it!'

''Course I can. Have you ever shook hands with Lindsay Hassett?'

'No.'

'Well I have, so shut up.'

The off-field friendship and on-field rivalry between Bill O'Reilly and Lindsay Hassett has intrigued followers of the game for years. The contrast in sizes of the two is one element — Hassett 167 cm (5'6"), O'Reilly about 193 cm (6'3"), Hassett weighing in at around 64 kg (10 stone), O'Reilly at close to 95 kg (15 stone). O'Reilly, with that gingery colouring which suggests (correctly in Bill's case) a short fuse; Hassett calm and unflappable. And yet Bill, who regarded the mild-mannered Stan McCabe as 'the best mate I ever had', put Hassett almost in the same category. It's undeniable that Lindsay Hassett played O'Reilly better than anyone else. I saw Bill bowl in cricket from club to international level. Don Bradman gave Bill a hiding once in Sydney in a testimonial match when he was removed from the attack after dismissing the first three of Bradman's side in the first hour. Bradman, held back in case a rampant Tiger made it four and ruined the Saturday afternoon crowd, was not called upon to face O'Reilly until he was in the 90s. He then delighted the crowd as only he could, calling it a day at 212. Once also during the war, Saggers gave O'Reilly a hiding in a club final. But these were one-off occasions. Hassett did it several times, although losing his wicket more than once.

It's a matter of record that on the memorable Sydney occasion in February 1940, halfway through Hassett's second innings assault, a frustrated O'Reilly stood flabbergasted in the middle of the pitch and yelled: 'And you're not even good-looking, you little bastard'. On another occasion when he'd started scratchily, Hassett finally got down to the bowler's end to be greeted by a frustrated O'Reilly: 'Hasn't that [so and so] bat of yours got any middle?'. Hassett blandly replied, 'Don't need any when I'm batting against you, Tige'. In December 1938, on their return from England, O'Reilly got Hassett twice in the Melbourne Shield match, for 56 in the first innings (caught at the wicket) and 0 in the second innings when Lindsay was given out leg before but believed he'd got a faint edge to the ball before it hit the pads. At the tea adjournment, he came over and sat with Bill. 'You must be getting past it, mate,' he said, 'to have to get a man out like that!' 'Whadya mean?' growled O'Reilly. Sid Barnes, young and brash and nearby, piped up, 'He hit it, he hit it!'. 'You shut up too, you little [so and so],' said Bill and carried on drinking his tea.

Lindsay was one of those rare people whose personality enabled him to get away with pranks and misdemeanours that would find most perpetrators out on their ear. Among these is the story of the hapless waiter who accidentally spilt some dessert down the front of Lindsay's dinner suit, the stain spreading to his trousers. This occurred at a fairly formal dinner at the very upmarket Dorchester Hotel. With the waiter standing horrified nearby, Lindsay removed his coat, lowered his pants, gave the lot to the waiter with the request that he sponge or somehow repair the damage, after which he casually sat down and finished the meal in his underpants, adequately concealed by the tablecloth. To go with this story is Ray Robinson's (the writer, not the batsman) account of Lindsay's arriving late at a party in Durban and signalling his arrival by slipping an ice cube down the back of his hostess's dress. This caused her to jump but Lindsay squared off with an apology and the hostess counted the action a great joke and became one of his fans.

At Suez, returning from their wartime stint in Palestine, the Australians were told that an oil-rich sheikh had 198 wives. In those days, the rules of cricket provided for a new ball after 200 runs had been taken from the old one. Lindsay seized on this to remark that the sheikh 'only needed two more (wives) to get a new ball!'.

Hassett was very fond of Freddy Brown, who led the 1950–51 MCC side to Australia — a side initially given little chance by the scribes of even making a game of the Tests, but a side that surprised everyone, including themselves, by being more than competitive. The start of the first Test in Brisbane was threatened by heavy overnight rain. Brown was understandably unenthusiastic at the prospect of batting on a Brisbane 'sticky' in his first match as captain. At 3 p.m., Lindsay and Brown inspected the wicket. Walking back together, Hassett, poker-faced as ever, Brown anxious as to his reaction, they reached the pavilion gate before Hassett turned to Brown and grinned. 'Let's go and have a drink,' he said. Brown agreed with alacrity and relief.

Inspecting a pitch on another occasion with an opposing skipper, Lindsay walked up and down along the strip, pressed the ground with his thumb, stroked his chin and did all the things captains do on these occasions. As they returned to the pavilion, a spectator enquired: 'What's it like, Lindsay?'. 'Haven't got a clue,' replied Hassett, 'I was just trying to look intelligent.'

Driving with Bill O'Reilly to the SCG, Bill was becoming testy at being held up by cars and people crossing Driver Avenue near the ground. 'Calm down,' said Lindsay. 'They're all going to your testimonial match.' This resulted in a quick change of mood on the Tiger's part.

Sir Donald Bradman in *Farewell to Cricket*, adds a little to the well-known story of Lindsay dropping Cyril Washbrook twice at deep fine leg and then borrowing a policeman's helmet, to the crowd's delight. Don goes on to say, 'A prominent Lancastrian refused to attend the rest of the match because he believed Lindsay had dropped the catches on purpose, claiming that they were too easy to miss and Australia was playing "dead" for the sake of the gate'.

Bill Johnston, a much-loved character and comparable to Gary Sobers in his many-sided bowling gifts but not at all like Gary as a batsman, headed the first-class batting averages in 1953 with the Bradman-like figure of 102 from 17 innings with 16 not outs, a highest score of 28 not out and an aggregate of 102. This was a whimsical arrangement plotted by Lindsay Hassett with the wholehearted cooperation of his team. Some juggling had to be done to shield Johnston from the best bowlers to achieve the not-out innings he played. After his dismissal in the thirteenth game of the tour, against Hampshire, excitement rose as he survived innings after innings in the later games. When the tension was over after the last first-class match, Johnston relaxed against Scotland at Paisley and scorched the field with a rousing 35. This sort of 'nonsense' on Hassett's part was typical of his style and the tactics he would use to unite his colleagues. All were delighted at Bill Johnston's elevation above some of the world's best players and it has been a talking point among cricketers ever since.

Fishing excursions with Bill O'Reilly among the anglers were always interesting, if sometimes argumentative occasions. Bill would start off being cranky, criticising weather, scarcity of fish because of netting or recent rain or being in the wrong spot. This would continue with Lindsay fuelling the O'Reilly anger with niggling remarks until Bill caught a fish. All would instantly change. All would become sweetness and light, at least for awhile until another fish drought set in.

The players returned from New Zealand in a Catalina flying boat which boasted only two bunks. These were commandeered by Hassett and O'Reilly. Presumably Bill Brown either deferred to, or was leaned upon, by the other two.

Returning from England by boat at the conclusion of the 1956 tour, Hassett and O'Reilly disagreed on the method that should be used for community singing. They formed two groups and initially O'Reilly's group proved too strong for Hassett's. But the little man cannily got his lot started on a tear-jerking rendition of 'Danny Boy'. This melancholy ballad proved too much for Bill O'Reilly, an armistice was declared and he quickly had his choir joining in. Peace reigned for the remainder of the voyage.

The O'Reilly temper was embarrassingly evident during a social call on Denis Compton in 1956. Bill, Arthur Morris and Lindsay had been invited down by Denis to meet his new wife. The trio turned up on time and were warmly greeted by Denis and his wife. The latter had, in her arms, two Maltese terriers, obviously spoilt and revelling in their present accommodation. Bill, on his best behaviour, after greeting his host and hostess extended a tentative hand to pat one of the dogs. It bit him. There was consternation. Denis darted off to get some antiseptic and his wife, after putting the dogs on the floor, departed in search of bandaids or something similar. While they were away, Bill, his good intentions and humour shot to pieces, to the mixed concern and amusement of his two pals, picked up the guilty dog and, applying his size eleven boot to its undercarriage, sent it hurtling across the room until stopped by the wall. Unused to this sort of treatment, the dog looked both puzzled and shocked. Slowly and carefully it made its way back to Bill and, on reaching him, sat at his feet looking up at him with respect and some anxiety. There it stayed until Mrs Compton returned with a bandaid and, seeing the dog in this highly apologetic posture said, 'There, he's just showing you how sorry he is'. Lindsay and Arthur were grappling with coughing bouts, having observed the whole incident, and Bill resumed his pose of general benevolence.

A similar incident to that experienced at the Comptons occurred during the same tour at the home of a Leicestershire player who invited Lindsay and Bill to his home on the Sunday of the county's match against the Australians. Their host had a precocious four-year-old son who tested the Tiger's patience severely, first by tipping cigarette ash and butts into his lap, and, following a mild parental rebuke, proceeding to do it a second time. Lindsay watched in horror as the colour started to rise slowly in Bill's neck in a manner familiar to countless batsmen. But, to Lindsay's surprise, his friend exercised great control and laughed the incident off. It earned a sterner rebuke from Dad, but worse was to follow. While Dad was in the kitchen organising drinks, the little horror advanced within a couple of feet of Bill and spat at him. This was more than enough. Bill O'Reilly's feet, along with his general physique, were of substantial dimensions. Quickly raising one foot, he applied it with some force to the lad's midriff, sending him hurtling across the room into the wall, where he collapsed, protesting loudly and indignantly.

The rumpus brought father back hotfoot from the kitchen to ascertain the cause of the disturbance. 'What's the matter?' he asked. Bill and Lindsay, both of whom had drawn satisfaction from the incident, replied blandly, 'He fell over'. To corroborate this answer, which was factually true but perhaps required some amplification, Bill helpfully added: 'The floor's a bit slippery'. The victim did not query this explanation, perhaps sensing that the situation was one where silence is golden.

Lindsay said that Bill regarded 'forward prodders' as 'money from home' and quickly assessed a batsman's length of stay by his ability to get on to the back foot. Bradman advised his colleagues to get as far back as possible when facing O'Reilly and delay their stroke until the very last instant. Lindsay was of the same opinion, altering his method only for the bosie, which he picked from Bill's hand and dropped shoulder, and advanced to hit it high and hard to leg.

A rare pair, Hassett and O'Reilly, now in the next place, picking up where they left off.

## CHAPTER 8
# THE TESTS OF 1946–47

In early 1946, the Australian Board of Control finally yielded to pressure and duty and agreed to start postwar international cricket with a match (later classed as a Test) against our nearest neighbours and comrades-in-arms in two world wars, New Zealand. Only one Test was to be played and that was to be at the Kiwi's capital city, Wellington. Only thirteen players were sent and these received the princely sum of £1 per day, the same largesse as that distributed in Sheffield Shield matches. All were out of pocket, the only bonus being an 'Australian' blazer without the Australian coat of arms. Bradman was unavailable, wisely guarding his health, hopefully for the later contests against England. The thirteen who went were: Brown (captain), O'Reilly (vice-captain), Barnes, Hassett, Meuleman, Miller, McCool, Johnson, Tallon, Lindwall, Toshack, Dooland and Hamence.

There was some criticism that Lindsay Hassett's meritorious service in the Services team had not been recognised by the captaincy or, at least, the vice-captaincy, but little objection could be raised against the two appointed. Bill Brown had long and honourable service in Australian cricket at all levels and was, arguably if Bradman were disregarded, the best batsman in Australia at the time. As for Bill O'Reilly, it was known that the 'tour' was likely to be his last international appearance.

The match itself was badly affected by rain and was all over in two days, Australia winning by an innings and 103 runs. New Zealand found Toshack (6 wickets) and O'Reilly (8 wickets) beyond them in the damp conditions and could manage only 42 and 54. Australia replied with 8–199, Brown top scoring with 67, Barnes 54. Cowie, the great-hearted New Zealand fast bowler, took 6–40. Thankfully, the football season now intervened, and the war-weary and cricket-weary Services team members, and others who'd had less than a picnic in Papua New Guinea, Borneo and other tropical war areas, were able to put their feet up and contemplate what the 1946–47 season might bring forth.

Contrary to their willingness to regard the Victory Tests as 'official', the MCC showed some reluctance in agreeing to a full-scale Ashes tour

♦ THE TESTS OF 1946–47 ♦

of Australia about fourteen months after the cessation on all fronts of World War II activities. The Australian authorities, on the other hand, wanted to get started as soon as possible. Rationing was still in strict force in England and would remain so for some time, and there was a fair measure of understanding of the MCC's position on a long and probably arduous tour in which they no doubt saw themselves at a considerable disadvantage. After all, in the Victory Tests, Australia, with only Hassett of international stature, broke even in the series against England sides fairly well stacked with players of international experience. One can easily imagine the moguls at Lord's asking themselves the question: 'If we could only halve a five-Test series against against a team of enthusiastic amateurs when pitted against half a dozen or more of our best, what hope would we have against the well-fed Aussies at home, with all their players on hand, plus possibly Bradman?'. And their fears were to prove well founded. However, they succumbed to Australian pressure and agreed to send a team.

Those chosen to tour for England were Hammond (captain), Yardley (vice-captain), Gibb, Bedser, Compton, Edrich, Evans, Fishlock, Hardstaff, Hutton, Ikin, Langridge, Pollard, Smith, Voce, Washbrook and Wright. Major Howard was manager of this team and only Hammond, Hardstaff, Fishlock and Voce had toured Australia previously. Hammond, now on his fourth tour, had been and, on recent form probably still was, in the top class of batsmen. Hardstaff had toured in 1936–37 with moderate success, Fishlock was also a 1936 tourist with indifferent credentials and Voce, fine bowler as he'd been, would, at age 37, hardly have improved. Compton, Edrich and Hutton on their first visit promised well and did indeed fulfil that promise. Washbrook, a good player at county level, had some good performances in the Victory games and proved a capable partner for Hutton. Washbrook was an attractive player and splendid coverpoint fieldsman. The two wicket-keepers, Gibb and Evans, were virtually unknown. The number one keeper, Gibb, proved a disappointment and was replaced after the first Test by Godfrey Evans, a mercurial character with both gloves and bat, and possibly the finest wicket-keeper to come from England. Of the bowlers, the Australians (particularly Hassett) had a healthy respect for Wright and Pollard, and Bedser came after a successful home season against India. He was to prove the finest medium pacer since Maurice Tate, which is saying something. Peter Smith was a leg spinner of some skill on English pitches, but played only two Tests in Australia despite capturing 9 wickets in the tour match against New South Wales. Langridge, a great all-rounder at county level, did not succeed in gaining a Test place, but Ikin was to prove useful in the middle order despite collecting a 'pair' in the last Test and was an excellent gully fieldsman. He was to prove pivotal in the series after the controversial incident at Brisbane when a disputed 'catch' went Bradman's way on appeal to the umpire.

Of the Australian players, Bill Brown missed the series because of injury, but the return to cricket of several players after war duty in the Pacific, plus the availability of proven internationals — Hassett and Barnes — and the lustre surrounding Miller after his Victory Test triumphs, suggested the emergence of a strong Eleven. The youthful Arthur Morris, who'd scored centuries in each innings of his initial first-class match before war service claimed him, appeared to be certain of selection, Lindwall was a fast bowler and at age 25, near his peak, and Tallon was widely seen as the best wicket-keeper in the world. Colin McCool and Ian Johnson were both all-rounders of some ability, home from the war, and Toshack and Tribe were left-hand spinners, Toshack leg-spin and Tribe a purveyor of 'chinamen' à la Fleetwood-Smith, but more accurate although less deadly. And then there was Bradman. Following a tentative return to cricket after being sidelined for four years, the Don was slowly gaining strength and recovering the remarkable touch which had haunted bowlers in the years leading up to the war. On the debit side, O'Reilly, Ward and Fleetwood-Smith had, for various reasons, hung up their boots, Stan McCabe's feet had failed to answer the call and Jack Fingleton was busy with his duties as a journalist. Jack Badcock had returned to the family farm in Tasmania, and Ross Gregory and Charlie Walker were victims of Hitler's war.

Lindsay Hassett, in Brown's absence logically appointed vice-captain, had an early look at the MCC bowling playing for Victoria in the game against the tourists. He scored 57 in each innings, had a good look at Bedser and fell victim to his bête noire, Douglas Wright, in the second innings. There was nothing in either innings to suggest a radical change of attitude by Lindsay towards his batting. Perhaps he was enjoying the feel of Victorian turf under his feet and the friendly advice of the spectators. England won this match, their only first-class victory of the tour. A week later, playing for the Australian Eleven again in Melbourne, Lindsay made 28; the following week, a characteristic 114 against South Australia in his prewar style.

♦ THE TESTS OF 1946–47 ♦

Hammond had started the tour well with a double century in Perth, and the massive and serene authority he'd always displayed appeared to have survived the war intact. Sadly, this was later dispelled for a variety of reasons, domestic and cricket, and the last tour of the greatest English batsman of his time was not a happy one. The other known good players, Hutton, Edrich, Compton and Washbrook, all had encouraging starts and the Englishmen came to Brisbane, if not buoyant, certainly not depressed. That changed suddenly and cruelly in the first Test match at the end of November 1946, at the Woolloongabba Ground.

After Barnes and Morris left with only 46 on the scoreboard, smiles and backslapping and general euphoria prevailed on the field. Bedser quickly demonstrated to Morris that he was a cut above the average medium pacer encountered here, and the big man's late outswinger to the left-hander found the edge to fly to Hammond at slip. Barnes soon followed and Hassett joined Bradman who had, to this point, despite some un-Bradmanlike gropings and edgings, displayed an ominous intention to be around for a while. At 28 an event occurred which could well have radically altered not only the match but the series. Bradman chopped down on a full, almost yorker-length delivery from Voce. The ball flew straight to Ikin in the gully, who accepted what he evidently thought was a straightforward catch. The Englishmen applauded and gathered to congratulate Ikin and themselves on the capture of cricket's most valued wicket. They obviously thought Bradman would not hesitate to leave the wicket. When it became apparent that he was still at the crease, an appeal was made to umpire Borwick who had no hesitation in answering 'not out'. Eleven Englishmen were outraged, but the two batsmen, Bradman and Hassett, agreed with the umpire and Hammond and his men simply had to 'wear' it. At any time this sort of verdict presents umpires with a very difficult on-the-spot decision to be given. Bat, ball and ground all converged at the same split second and the umpire has the final word and has to speak it quickly. Bradman was never one to dawdle if he was out and I think he'd have walked had he been sure. He wasn't sure and left it to the umpire. Borwick, possibly in some doubt, gave the benefit of such doubt to the batsman, as he should. Hammond was livid and made some remark to Bradman as he passed him at the end of the over, to the effect that this wasn't a good way to start a series. The relationship between the two men, satisfactory but never particularly warm, caught pneumonia and the chill generated cast a blight over the tour.

It is purely speculative, but not entirely over the top, to consider what might have happened had Bradman been given out. In frail health, might not the Don have said to himself, 'That's it! I've had enough'. He might have been philosophical at the decision, but a scratchy 28 in his return Test match could possibly have brought down the curtain on his amazing career. What had he to prove? The only possible loose end was the small matter of the Oval disaster of 1938, which Bradman would have dearly loved to avenge just to show one and all that his side had drawn the short straw in that engagement. Had he called it a day after Brisbane, the result of the series would almost certainly have been closer, as would the 1948 series eighteen months later. Speculative? Certainly. Likely? Probably not, but interesting.

After this piece of drama, Bradman and Hassett, captain and vice-captain, ground away until the luncheon adjournment, after which Bradman was more like himself. Hassett shut up shop in supporting his captain in a stand of 276 when Bradman, one suspects from sheer exhaustion, hit over a ball from Edrich, a tearaway, quickish bowler who made up in enthusiasm what he lacked in skill, and was bowled. He'd made 187 out of the 276 partnership, not one of his greatest innings but one sufficiently fluent as it proceeded to cause serious heartaches and despondency among the opposition. Lindsay Hassett battled slowly in what was soon to be his usual postwar Test style. His century took almost six hours and made sections of the crowd restless and unconvinced that this was the same player who'd made mincemeat of all bowlers back in the 1930s. Shortly after reaching his century, Hammond, of all people, dropped Lindsay at slip and he advanced to 128 in six and a half hours before Bedser claimed him. He'd gone from 89 when Bradman left, to 128 in company with an aggressive Keith Miller in a partnership of 106. Wright shortly afterwards had Miller leg before for 79, but England's troubles were far from over. McCool (95) and Ian Johnson (47) pressed home the advantage and Lindwall, at number nine, hit a lively 31. The innings closed at 645. Doug Wright had 5–167, including three lbws, in what was a creditable performance in a batting tornado.

Rain in copious volumes left England with the unhappy prospect of batting on a Brisbane wicket, wet to start with and 'sticky' as it dried out. Hammond's 32 and 23 were classic examples of how to cope with wet wickets. Miller was dangerous in the conditions, Toshack at times unplayable after a hint from his captain as to where on the pitch best results could be obtained. Scores of 141 and 172 and a victory by an innings and 332 runs went some way to squaring the Oval account. It was clear that England's batting could not be written off on the strength of the double failure on wet wickets. It was also plain that, despite the obvious class of Bedser and Wright, the visitors would suffer severely from the absence of a fast bowler. Voce, overweight, was a shadow of the fine bowler who'd taken 26 wickets in the 1936–37 series.

The Sydney Test, which I watched in full, saw a marked improvement in the visitors' performance despite another innings loss. The Australian team was unchanged except for the absence of Ray Lindwall, who had chickenpox. He was replaced by Fred Freer, a tall medium pacer from Victoria who bowled Cyril Washbrook for 1 with a sharp off cutter in his first over. Freer played no more Tests and took off soon after the season ended to play in the Lancashire League. Hutton made 39 in his sound, unhurried fashion and surprised everyone with the difficulty he experienced with Ian Johnson, who eventually had him caught at the wicket by Tallon, now at the peak of his form. Johnson, both in this match and later, produced uncertainty for Hutton who, one would have thought, was not lacking in experience in facing off spinners.

Edrich, sound, brave and pugnacious, watched in disbelief as Hammond and Compton both fell to poor shots from McCool's bowling. Having batted against Colin McCool, I was surprised to see Hammond, who was the master of a far greater leg spinner, Clarrie Grimmett (at least in Australia), pinned to the crease by a lesser exponent of the art like McCool. Ikin and Yardley both played well, but 255 was a far from adequate showing on a first day Sydney pitch. Ian Johnson flighted his off breaks well, but 6–42 was a flattering analysis, as I'm sure he'd agree.

Bradman held himself back when Australia batted. He had a damaged hamstring and, after Morris and Johnson went cheaply, Hassett joined Barnes on the third day. Lindsay had been acting-captain during the closing stages of England's innings. Barnes had been getting on everybody's nerves with repeated light appeals on the second day when only 93 minutes play were possible.

Over 51,000 people saw the third day's play on Monday. Barnes had forsaken his stroke-making style, which had distinguished his batting before the war, and with Hassett in fairly low gear, there was not a great deal to excite the multitude. Lindsay was cautious but elegant, and may have been on the threshold of better things when he attempted to hook a bouncer from Edrich, top-edged it and watched as it flew almost in preordained fashion straight to Compton fielding about two-thirds of the way to the fence. Denis did not need to move and took the catch baseball-fashion, just above his head. Hassett had made 34 and departed crestfallen. Miller put some life into the somnolent afternoon session while Barnes grafted away, all pads and backside like Ponsford and, also like that great Victorian, using a bat that seemed to have no edge.

When Miller went just before tea for 40, Bradman came through the pavilion gate to a deafening roar from the patient spectators, many of whom had looked forward to this day and this moment for seven long years. As Barnes walked towards Bradman to brief him on the state of play, a gentleman just in front of me in the old Sheridan Stand, who'd been complaining bitterly about Barnes all day, was moved to give voice to his anger and outrage. 'Ah, Sid!' he bellowed. 'Don't worry about 'im. 'E don't need no drum! 'E knows all about it!'

The Don started quietly, but, after tea, began to overhaul Barnes who'd been in about five hours for 70. The two went on and on to register a record partnership of 405 for the fifth wicket, a record which still stands. After Bradman went for 234 leg before to Yardley, Barnes, with great chivalry and self-sacrifice, got himself out at the same score stating that he did not feel it would be appropriate to outscore his captain. Years later, Arthur Morris had grave doubts about this, stating that he was not convinced and that he'd never known Barnes to give his wicket away in any sort of cricket.

After this, the innings meandered on to 659 when Bradman mercifully closed. Bedser and Wright had toiled manfully, both bowling 46 overs, but the others were clearly below Test class. In England's second innings, Hutton played his miniature masterpiece with eight boundaries in 37 to every corner of the field, an innings cut off in its prime when he trod on his wicket in the last over before lunch. Years later I met Colin McCool by chance and we spoke of that innings. McCool was critical of Hutton who, he thought, should have put his head down and batted through the England innings. I suppose there is some validity to the argument, but nothing can dim the grace and beauty of Leonard Hutton's Sydney innings in 1946. Most who saw it would agree, I think.

Edrich played very well, sound and aggressive when appropriate, and Compton, until caught at mid-off by Bradman off Freer at 54, had looked a certain centurion. Hammond was a little more like Hammond, advancing down the pitch to the spinners. He hit McCool back over his head, but neither hard nor high enough to avoid Toshack fielding at straight hit about two-thirds of the way to the Randwick-end boundary. It was 5–309 when Hammond left, and the side was out for 371. McCool took 5–109 and one wondered what Grimmett and O'Reilly would do with this line-up. Australia won by an innings and 33 runs.

England salvaged a draw in Melbourne in the New Year Test. Arthur Morris justified the selector's faith in him by scoring 155 in about seven hours in the second innings. This was the start of the great left-hander's golden period. Hassett fell twice to Wright, caught at slip by Hammond for 12 and bowled for 9 in the second innings, trying to cut the same bowler. His slow batting in the first innings — 12 in 53 minutes was not appreciated by the big crowd. McCool cracked a lively unbeaten 104 and Bradman did not score a century in either innings. Yardley, an up-and-down medium pacer, got him twice for 79 and 49. Edrich was again in the runs, robbed of another century in the first innings by a bad lbw decision when he was 89. Washbrook had a good double with 62 and 112, but Compton and Hammond were disappointing. England avoided defeat and the crowd appreciated Yardley and Evans' battling on in poor light when an appeal might easily have been upheld. The match was drawn.

England came to Adelaide and strengthened its batting by dropping Voce and replacing him with Hardstaff. Voce's bowling share had to be taken up by second-string operators Edrich, Yardley, Ikin and Compton. Winning the toss, England did well, Hutton in vintage form for 94, Washbrook 65. But it was Compton who caught the eye. He laid to rest some expressed doubts as to his Test-match temperament with centuries in both innings — 147 and 103 not out. Hardstaff justified his selection with an elegant 67 and the side reached a respectable 460. Bedser bowled Bradman for 0 with a delivery Don described as 'the finest he had faced' — a leg cutter it seemed. Morris, now seeing the ball like a pumpkin, made 122, and Miller made, for him, a careful unbeaten 141.

Lindsay Hassett returned to form with 78 in 220 minutes in an innings described as 'cagey'. The adjective would have been greeted with derision in 1938, but was close to the mark in 1947. This was the occasion referred to when he informed Neville Cardus that he was 'wore out'. It wasn't that Hassett was ever uninteresting, at least not to the more knowledgeable, simply because his methods were a sort of compendium of batsmanship — feet correctly placed, bat perpendicular, head over the ball and so on. He could be legitimately compared with Bill Brown, who'd eliminated human error from his game quite early in the piece. It was always a surprise when Brown and Hassett, along with the immaculate Hutton, got out. It seemed almost as though some divine power had decided that the curtain should be lowered. In this Adelaide innings, divine power in the persons, yet again, of Doug Wright and Walter Hammond, suggested that Lindsay go as he'd stayed long enough for any good that he'd done. The Wright/Hassett axis was giving the scribes almost as much food for copy as the Morris/Bedser encounters that were gathering momentum.

With four Tests now played, in two of which England was able to hang on bravely enough to achieve draws, the shortcomings of the England attack were plain to see. The ridiculous rule providing for a new ball to be available to the fielding captain after 55 overs severely disadvantaged the visitors. For the Australians, the rule was made to order. In Lindwall and Miller they had a pair of fast bowlers who rated with Gregory and McDonald of the 1920s. The accuracy of Toshack, combined with the spin of any two of McCool, Johnson, Dooland and Tribe, adequately took care of the 30-odd overs between Lindwall and Miller, finishing with the old ball and restarting with the new. It was a bad rule, still in force in England in 1948. It acted severely to the detriment of England in the immediate postwar years and was a big plus for an Australian team armed with all the heavy artillery. In addition, it was largely responsible for the temporary dearth of spin bowlers. The other minus for England was the comparatively poor form of Hammond, because Hammond, in anything like his best form, would equate to any of the Australians with the usual exception of 'the little bloke', Bradman.

The last match was again played in Sydney, with Hammond a casualty following a match at Ballarat against a Victorian country side. He did not play in the Test, nor did he grace an Australian cricket field again. Apparently a man of moods, Hammond had his share of problems on this tour, as mentioned earlier, and any adverse criticism of him should be tempered by understanding this.

During the break between the third and fourth Tests, Lindsay had appeared in two Sheffield Shield matches, batting in his old form and delighting the cash customers. Against Queensland in Brisbane he made 200, then travelled south to Sydney and almost repeated the dose with 190 against New South Wales. So, with his 126 in the Brisbane Test and 114 against South Australia earlier in the season, plus a century for Victoria against the MCC in the run-up to the final Test, it looked like a good season for Lindsay.

Intermittent rain helped the bowlers in the fifth Test, but the match provided some exciting cricket. Despite a surfeit of bouncers, Hutton added lustre to an already enviable reputation with a fine century before illness overtook him and he sought treatment for tonsilitis, taking no further part in the match. More bouncers scarred the game with the second new ball towards the late afternoon in failing light. Compton trod on his wicket while avoiding a bouncer and two further batsmen lost their wickets despite repeated light appeals.

The distasteful thing about this plethora of short-pitched bowling was that the Englishmen in reply could offer only Bill Edrich, a popgun fast bowler compared with the Australians. Bouncers are best brought to manageable numbers when both sides possess the means to deliver them. It is worth noting, too, that in 1946–47, and later, there were no helmets and other protective equipment, without which no player today would walk through the pavilion gate with bat in hand. Lindwall, great bowler and fine man that he was, reaped a harvest in this innings — 7–63 from 22 overs. England resumed two days later after the second day was lost to rain, and finished at 280. After Barnes and Morris gave Australia a start of 126, Wright bowled Bradman for 12. He'd played a wild stroke at a well pitched-up delivery. Hassett then joined Barnes. Lindsay was again cautious and was given a hard time by the crowd until he was mercifully and brilliantly caught by Ikin in the gully off Wright for 24. It was one of the few attacking strokes he had attempted. Bedser had Barnes caught for 71 by Evans standing up at the stumps to Bedser, as he invariably did. Hamence, in his first Test, remained 30 not out, while the hitherto prolific 'tail enders' all failed and the side was out for 253. This was the only time in the series when England enjoyed a first innings lead. Wright was rewarded for a fine sustained exhibition of leg-spin bowling with 7–105 from 29 overs. He was, like Fleetwood-Smith a few years earlier, a genius flawed by inability to maintain persistent and unrelenting control of length.

Without Hutton, the England second innings was a dismal affair, despite a vintage 76 from Compton. McCool took 5–44, including 4 good wickets of accredited batsmen who connived at their own destruction. McCool was a talented all-rounder, though not a great one, and as a bowler was frequently given some stick in the Sydney District competition before the war. The total of 186 left Australia with 214 required to win.

Morris was run out for 17 and if a Bradman snick had been held by

Edrich at slip, Australia may have been struggling. It was never good policy to drop Bradman. He continued to 63 and, with Lindsay, the pair were fully extended against some excellent bowling by Bedser and Wright. Lindsay Hassett again proved his worth in testing situations and he and Bradman added 98 to put Australia, at 149, within reach of the target. Wright again had Hassett caught brilliantly by Ikin in the gully as he had been in the first innings. He had made a valuable 47 and Miller and McCool sealed the victory with 5 wickets still in hand. Hassett's seven innings in the series had been terminated no less than five times by Wright. In all, Lindsay had scored 332 runs at 47.5, which was more than satisfactory if only occasionally providing the spectators with exciting entertainment.

The England side had won only one first-class match on the tour and that was against Victoria, way back before the first Test. Wright took 23 wickets at 43.04 and Bedser 16 at 54.75. The latter's great days lay a little in the future. Both were admired for the stamina they showed in virtually carrying their side's attack. Hutton made 417 runs at 52, but Hammond's failure, although perhaps not decisive, affected the others.

No England fast bowler was to surface until Fred Trueman appeared in the fifth Test of 1953 at the Oval more than six years later. Shortly after, Statham and Tyson arrived, by which time the fire and fury of Miller and Lindwall had faded and England gained some revenge.

From Australia's point of view, the re-entry of Bradman on the scene was one of the significant events. He was not the Bradman even of ten years before, but still a potent force both as batsman and captain and the years had not diminished his hunger for runs. Whether this was good or bad depended on whether you were an Australian supporter or not.

Comparative figures for the leading batsmen show:

|         | INNINGS | NO | HS  | RUNS | CENTURIES | AVERAGE |
|---------|---------|----|----|------|-----------|---------|
| Bradman | 14      | 1  | 234 | 1032 | 4         | 79.38   |
| Morris  | 20      | 2  | 155 | 1234 | 5         | 68.55   |
| Hassett | 18      | 1  | 200 | 1213 | 5         | 71.35   |

Their ages at the time were: Bradman, 38, Morris, 25, and Hassett, 33. It had been a good season for Lindsay and, at the advanced age (for cricketers) of 33, he could look forward to a few more productive years.

## CHAPTER 9
# AUSTRALIAN SUMMER WITH THE INDIANS — 1947–48

There was considerable interest in the proposed visit by a team from India in the 1947–48 season. At the time of the tour, Lord Louis Mountbatten was in the throes of negotiating a partition of the subcontinent acceptable to both Hindus and Muslims. With this historic and difficult event pending, the Muslim component of the side sent here was bound to have a somewhat touchy relationship with the predominant Hindu group. However, this potential difficulty was largely negated by the keenness with which all had been infused by the Australian Services side's efforts in India in 1945. Indeed, it was widely reported that the Indians of both religious persuasions were looking forward to the tour with great enthusiasm, some going so far as to say how pleased they'd be to meet Bradman in the Tests and how disappointed they'd be if he were unable to play. Their feelings about this may have changed by tour's close, for the Don enjoyed a merry time against a less than penetrative bowling attack and had rather outstayed his welcome.

Australia's interest in Indian cricket up until this time had been marked by a disregard similar to that shown to New Zealand. In the *Oxford Companion to Australian Cricket*, it is described as 'high-handed and unsympathetic'. By contrast, a team from England had toured India in 1932–33, playing three Tests, and Indian sides had visited England three times. The names of Merchant, Mankad, Hazare, Amarnath and Modi were fairly well known to Australians following Hassett's Services side's recent tour. By any standards, the five named would be top-class players in any company, so it was disappointing when Merchant and Modi were unable to join the party.

Seventeen players were chosen to play for India, which seemed too many for a tour of fourteen first-class matches and gave the captain, Amarnath, problems in ensuring that all members had a chance to display their wares. Those chosen were: Amarnath (captain), Hazare, Phadkar, Mankad, Kischenchand, Adhikari, Sarwate, Gul Mahomed, Nayudu, Ranversinghi, Sohoni, Irani, Amir Elahi, Rangnekar, Sen, Rai

Singh and Rangachari. Apart from Mankad, the side lacked top-quality bowlers and looked to all-rounders Phadkar and Nayudu with the captain, Amarnath, and some batsmen who could bowl a bit as back-up. Consequently, there was some heavy scoring on Australia's part.

The Australian side was substantially the same as that chosen to play against England, except that Barnes and Brown shared the second opening spot with Morris while a lanky, fast-medium left-hand bowler of many parts, Bill Johnston, made his debut. Hassett was again vice-captain and seemed to have the captain's job in the bag when the present incumbent hung up his boots. He started the season well playing for Victoria, being 67 not out in the second innings against India after being skittled for one by a tearaway fast bowler named Rangachari in the first innings. In Adelaide against South Australia, he was in his Dr Jekyll role again with a vintage 118, balanced by a duck in the second innings. Len Johnson, a capable medium pacer, toiled long and hard to capture Lindsay's wicket in Brisbane, but only after the perspiring Queenslanders had seen 204 runs stream from his bat. In the second innings, he failed, but got some good batting practice against New South Wales in Sydney with 48. A capable leg spinner, Fred Johnston bowled him.

The Indians, meanwhile, were hampered by rain in their first tour match, although Mankad gave early indications of his quality with 5–68 in Western Australia's innings, followed by 57 in his own side's total of 127. The match was drawn. There was heavy scoring in the match against South Australia, Bradman contributing 156 and two comparative newcomers, Dick Niehuus and Bob Craig, both scoring centuries. Amarnath replied with 144 and Hazare 95 out of a total of 451 in response to South Australia's five for 518 declared. Mankad and Amarnath batted brilliantly in the second innings in a gallant but unsuccessful run chase. Another draw was the result.

Amarnath was still on fire when his side moved on to Victoria. His 228 not out featured every known cricket stroke, all of them executed with a touch of the Eastern magic of his noted predecessors Ranji and Duleep. With his accurate medium-paced swing bowling and brilliant close-in fielding and emergency deputising behind the stumps, he was close to the complete all-rounder. Sid Barnes had similar gifts, but his batting fell short of Amarnath's grace and charm. It was unfortunate that, on this tour, Amarnath's prolific scoring did not extend to the Tests. Lindsay played in this game, being bowled for 1 by medium-fast

Rangachari in the first innings in which only a stand by Harvey and Loxton saved Victoria the embarrassment of following on. Mankad and Hazare were both in the runs in the second innings, despite some excellent bowling by Johnston. Set 333 for victory, the home side had time only for 138, which they reached with the loss of 2 wickets. Lindsay made use of the time to familiarise himself with the Indians' limited bowling wares and was 67 not out at the close.

The visitors suffered their first defeat against the powerful New South Wales side led by Arthur Morris, whose batting at this time was sheer delight. He made 162 in a total of 8–561 declared. Hazare, another whose class was obvious the moment he lifted a bat, as proved beyond doubt by his first-class average of 57.23 and 47.65 in 30 Tests, had a splendid match with 142 against Lindwall, Miller and Co. This was insufficient to save the game, which was lost by an innings and 48. However, the uncertainty of cricket was once more demonstrated when, a week later, the Indians defeated a strong Australian Eleven by 47 runs in an exciting game notable for two rather unusual events. Facing 329, the Australians, before a huge crowd bent on seeing Bradman score his one hundredth hundred, crumbled after this preordained event made its way into the record books. The century of centuries was achieved at the remarkable rate of one in slightly less than every third innings.

The Indians attacked in the hope of a victory and set the Australian Eleven 251 to win in 150 minutes. Early in the run chase, Mankad ran Brown out at the bowler's end. He'd warned Bill about 'backing up' too far, too fast, and when the Australian did it again, Mankad ran him out. This was well within the rules and was accepted by Brown, who acknowledged his error. The Australians, perhaps shocked by this and Bradman's dismissal for 26, were all out for 203 half an hour before the close. I saw this match and the two notable events are etched on my memory as clearly as though they'd happened last week. Lindsay did not play on this occasion.

The Sydney victory was encouraging to the visitors and they built on it with a convincing display in the match against Queensland leading up to the Test. Amarnath again delighted with 172 not out in the first innings, which was the main factor in his side's reaching a respectable 369 in reply to Queensland's 341. Closing at 7–269 in their second innings, Queensland set the visitors 242 to win in 90 minutes, 'a big ask' as the current vernacular has it. The Indians responded boldly, but were dismissed for 217. McCool had a good match with an unconquered 101 and 5–68.

The unlucky Indians drew the short straw in the Test match which followed their brave efforts in the two preceding games. The Australians in good weather on a firm pitch made 8–382. The incredible Bradman made 185 before hitting his wicket with Amarnath bowling, a well-deserved stroke of luck for the Indian captain. With Hassett (48), Bradman added 101 for the third wicket and 120 with Miller for the fourth. There was no play on the third day, a rest day anyway, and the rain drenched the uncovered pitch.

By starting time on Monday, a good old Brisbane 'sticky' was well on the way with a very warm sun working its villainy on the bemused Indians. To face Lindwall, Miller, Toshack and Johnston on such a pitch would have been beyond most of the world's batsmen, past and present. Hobbs and Sutcliffe might have defied the conditions as they did in Melbourne in 1929, but then one pulls up short. The Indians could reach only 58 with Toshack finishing off the innings with 5–2 off 2.3 overs, an analysis which is rather flattering whatever the state of the pitch. Following on, the Indians did a little better with 98, largely owing to a stubborn and brave innings by Sarwate, a slightly built young man who stuck around for three hours for his 26. Toshack took a comparative caning in this innings and conceded 29 runs from 17 overs for his 6 wickets. The loss by an innings and 226 runs was no worse, indeed rather better, than Australia's defeat by England under similar conditions in Brisbane in late 1928 — England 521, Australia 122 and 66.

There was a small measure of revenge for the Indians in the Sydney Test a couple of weeks later, but they weren't to know that, and a significant degree of alarm and despondency was understandably evident as they bade farewell to Brisbane.

While Lindsay was savouring the Test victory, he was surprised and disappointed to learn that his beloved Victorian side had been defeated on the first innings by the Sheffield Shield newcomers, Western Australia, in Perth. Despite the absence of Lindsay Hassett, Ian Johnson and Bill Johnston in Brisbane, Victoria, Shield winners the previous year, had a fairly strong side with the Harvey brothers, Mervyn and Neil, plus Ken Meuleman. As was frequently to happen, Western Australia at home on the WACA Ground proved difficult to beat. Given another half hour the victory would have been more than a first innings' drubbing.

Rain again disrupted the Sydney Test, only ten hours out of 36 scheduled playing hours being completed. The incidence of rain-affected matches in Sydney over the years gives one food for thought

*Above: Lindsay and Tess boating on Corio Bay, 1938*

# LINDSAY HASSETT ◆ ONE OF A KIND

*Left: Lindsay outside his tent in Port Moresby, wearing his patented anti-tinea lap-lap, 1943.*

*Below: Lindsay with Chappy Dwyer and friends, South Africa, 1936.*

# LINDSAY HASSETT ♦ ONE OF A KIND

*Above: Lindsay with Bill Brown en route to England, 1938*

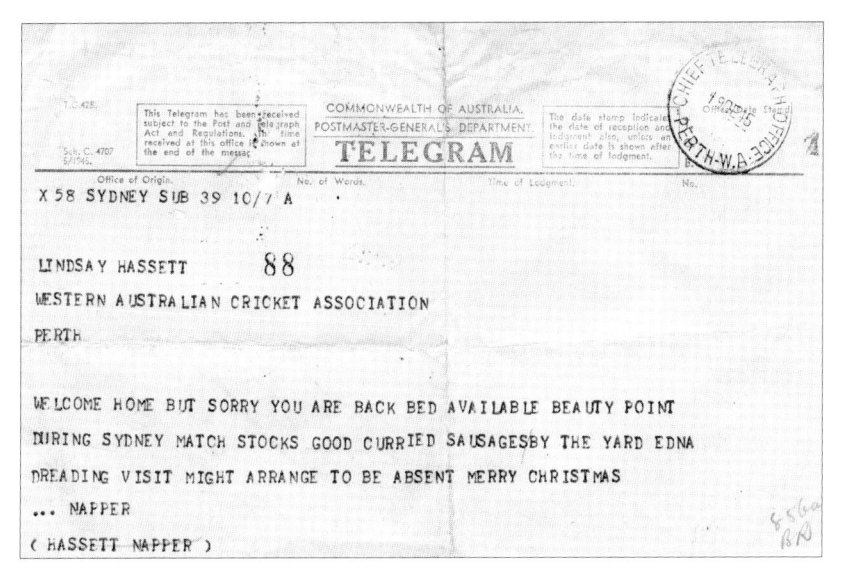

*Above: Telegram sent by Stan McCabe (nicknamed 'Napper' because of his resemblance to Napoleon) to Lindsay in December 1945 upon Lindsay's arrival in Perth after service overseas in AIF and Services cricket team.*

Above: The first postwar Australian side, Brisbane, 1946.
   Back row, left to right: Miller, Toshack, Tallon
   Centre row, left to right: I. Johnson, Morris, Lindwall, McCool,
   Front row, left to right: Hamence, Hassett (vice-captain), Bradman (captain), Barnes, Tribe

*Above: Hassett bats against Surrey at the Oval, May 1948*

*Above: Lindsay and Don Bradman keep an eye on the toss, M.C.G., 1948*

*Above: Lindsay pulls West Indian bowler Ramadhin, 1951*

LINDSAY HASSETT ♦ ONE OF A KIND

*Above: Lindsay bowled around his legs attempting to sweep left hander John Manning, Victoria vs Sth Australia, February 1952.*

*Above: The Australian team at 'The Glorious Days', the Anna Neagle show at the Palace Theatre, London 1953. From left to right: Davidson, Craig, de Courcey, Hill, Benaud (immediately behind Miss Neagle), Langley, Hassett, Hole, Morris.*

*Above: The crowd at the Oval after England regained the Ashes, 1953.*

**LINDSAY HASSETT** ◆ ONE OF A KIND

*Above: Lindsay with Hutton at the Oval after England regained the Ashes, 1953*

# LINDSAY HASSETT ◆ ONE OF A KIND

*Above: Lindsay packs for a trip to England, helped by his daughters Margaret (left) and Anna (right), 1953*

*Above: Lindsay, Robert Menzies and Freddy Brown, Lord's, 1956.*

*Left: Rugged up against the cold with Ian Johnson, London 1956.*

*Above: Lindsay and Ian Johnson at Group Captain Cheshire's 'Kangaroo Hop' function at the Savoy Hotel, London, July 1956.*

*Above: Golfing buddies Brown, Hassett, Lindwall, Fingleton, O'Reilly, in Brisbane in the early 1960s.*

*Left: Lindsay holding a snapper he caught in Port Phillip Bay, 1962.*

*Above: Veterans from the WWII Services team at Lord's, July 1985. From left to right: Colin Bremner, Frank Moran, Larry Maddison, Keith Miller, Reg Ellis, Lindsay Hassett, Ross Stanford, Stan Sismey, Charlie Price (seated).*

*Above: Lindsay, Arthur Morris, Geff Noblet and Freddy Brown at a State Bank reception, Adelaide 1988.*

*Above: Lindsay, Ted and Dick Hassett at Ted's ninetieth birthday, 1989.*

when snide remarks are made about climate in other Australian capital cities, notably Melbourne. The match had its moments. An indifferent batting display by the Indians could return them only 188, Kischenchand top-scoring with 44. With Toshack absent the wickets were shared. When Australia batted, Mankad again ran Brown out for backing up too far before the ball had left the bowler's hand. No Australian player was convincing in the damp conditions. Hassett made 6, Bradman 13, Hazare getting the best bowling figures of 4–29. Hazare was a useful medium pacer with 565 first-class career wickets. On this day, he kept the ball up and let the wicket help the batsmen cooperate in their own downfall. The Indians' second innings was a melancholy affair until time ran out with the visitors 7–61. Had the weather dried out, one more day would almost surely have seen an Australian victory.

After defeating NSW Western Districts at Bathurst and playing a draw against another country side in Canberra, the Indians moved south to Melbourne for the New Year Test match. There they encountered a Bradman who added yet another rare achievement to his record. Although he'd previously scored centuries in each innings of some matches, he hadn't managed to do it in a Test match and against India's threadbare attack, he'd never have a better opportunity than in the current season. In each innings he was almost the Bradman of old. Bill O'Reilly, in writing of his hundredth century innings, had said: 'There's no answer when Bradman is Bradman'.

In the first innings after Barnes left, Bradman and Morris carried on to 99 when Morris was bowled by the deceptively guileful Amarnath. Bradman and Hassett then added 169 before Hassett was leg before to the persistent Mankad for 80. He'd gone run for run with his captain in a satisfying innings on his own ground. This partnership was the cornerstone of the innings, which ended at 394. Amarnath and Mankad both had 4 wickets.

The Indians got off to a good start with Mankad and Sarwate having an opening partnership of 124, no mean feat against an attack comprising Lindwall, Miller, Johnston, Johnson and Dooland. However, the innings fell away, the most disappointing feature being Amarnath's continued failure in the Tests after his dazzling early form. His Test match innings to date were 22, 5, 25, 14, and in the present match he added 0 and 8. Overnight rain, with some promise of sun, persuaded the Indian captain to close 103 runs behind at 291 in the hope of trapping the Australians on a drying pitch. Bradman foiled this by sending tail-enders in first but, after four had fallen for 32, he and Morris, in an unbroken stand of 223, took the score to 4–255. Rain again wrong-footed the unhappy Indians and they were quickly shot out for 125, Australia winning by 233 runs. By this time, one could reasonably surmise that our visitors had had a surfeit of two things on this tour — Australian weather and D. G. Bradman. They would gladly have waived any further contact with either.

As it turned out, the Adelaide weather was guiltless in the batting orgy that overwhelmed them on the Anniversary Day weekend — guiltless for both sides, but more guiltless for the team that won the toss. And that team was Australia. The home batsmen would have found the prospect of facing a run-of-the-mill Indian attack on a perfect Adelaide pitch on days one and two, nothing short of mouth-watering. The Indians were in good heart when they arrived in Adelaide after defeating Tasmania by an innings in Hobart, Amarnath and Hazare making centuries and the captain taking 5 wickets cheaply in the match. A cloudless sky, a lost toss and a 'couch stuffed with runs' to bowl on quickly dampened their enthusiasm.

Australia made 674, Barnes 112, Bradman 201 and Hassett 198 not out. Hassett and Bradman had a partnership of 125 and when Miller joined Hassett, a further 142 runs were added before Miller left. Lindsay and the lesser lights ripped into the tired bowlers adding a further 151 before the last wicket fell late on the second day. If it wasn't quite the prewar Hassett, it was something like it often enough to whet the appetite for more. None of the bowling figures would be treasured by their owners, part-timers Sarwate and Hazare being the most expensive. Lindsay's innings would remain his highest in Tests. It lasted 342 minutes and included 16 fours.

The Indians did well after two early losses and Amarnath looked set for a big score until, at 46, he mishit Ian Johnson to be caught by Bradman. Hazare was his usual versatile self, equally at home defending or attacking, and his 116 was boosted by a punishing century from pace bowler Phadkar, who demonstrated his all-round ability by scoring 123 and outpacing his more illustrious partner in a partnership of 188 which lifted his side's total to a respectable 381, albeit still 293 behind their opponents. For Australia, Ian Johnson had the best figures of 4–64. Following on, Mankad, Amarnath, Kischenchand and Rangachari all failed to bother the scorers, but the great Hazare left his stamp on the game with his second century, an heroic 145 when all around him wickets were tumbling like ducks in a shooting gallery. After six poor scores in previous innings, he was due for a change of luck and he seized the opportunity to join a rather elite group of Test-match centurions in both innings. When the last wicket fell at 277, India still trailed by 16 and lost the match by an innings and that deficit. Lindwall had the remarkable second innings figures of 7–38.

By this time, the visitors would gladly have called it a day but the drama had to be played out and Melbourne offered no relief unless it was that Bradman had to retire with a torn rib muscle when 57. Lindsay's absence from this match left the door ajar for yet another batting champion in the slight figure of nineteen-year-old Robert Neil Harvey. His 153 gave promise of a brilliant career, a promise amply fulfilled. Brown made 99 and Loxton 80 in another mammoth total of 8–575. In reply, India managed 331, with Mankad 111, Hazare 74 and Phadkar again with 56 not out. Following on, they had little heart for the chase and the side collapsed for 67, Australia recording its fourth win by an innings and 177 runs.

The 'not out' in Adelaide helped Lindsay's Test figures:

| INNINGS | NO | HS | RUNS | AVERAGE |
| --- | --- | --- | --- | --- |
| 4 | 1 | 198 no | 332 | 110.7 |

Australia won the series 4–0 with one Test drawn. There was general disappointment at Amarnath's poor Test performances and this, coupled with the absence of star players Merchant and Modi, contributed to the scale of the defeats. On the bright side, in Hazare and Mankad there were players of world class and Amarnath's comparative failures were repeated by another great player, Denis Compton, in Australia three years later. Amarnath's 1,162 tour runs at 58.10 included five century innings. Hazare made 1,056 runs at 48 with four centuries while Mankad was the outstanding bowler with 61 wickets at 28.43. Lack of class bowlers, particularly of pace, gave the Australians a comfortable ride, except when some pitch abnormalities disturbed their equilibrium, as at Sydney. Bradman's dream lead-up to another England tour would produce resigned sighs at Lord's and throughout the kingdom.

Lindsay finished the season with a Shield match against South Australia where he made 0 and 22 and a century in a Testimonial match at Melbourne.

The next engagements would be in England.

## CHAPTER 10
# BRADMAN'S UNDERSTUDY — 1948

On the home front, the Hassett family, which at this stage comprised Lindsay, Tess and Margaret (born in 1943 while Lindsay was still serving in the Army at Port Moresby) were living in a rented house in Toorak, a rather upmarket Melbourne suburb. There was no prospect of moving at present and plans to do so were placed on hold.

When Lindsay was discharged from the Army, he returned to his old accounting firm for a time until his friend, George Schofield, arranged a job for him with a firm known as 'Swiss Dye', Lindsay's position being in public relations. This did not last more than about six months, as his employers were not much in favour of granting Lindsay time off for his cricketing activities and, with a tour of England looming, this was scarcely satisfactory. So he left. This occurred in late 1947 and it was then that Stan McCabe made the loan available to him to get him started in a sports store (see p.13). Initially, the operation was conducted on modest lines in one room on the first floor of a building in Elizabeth Street, Melbourne, and it was here that Lindsay suffered the embarrassment of having to send out to the Melbourne Sports Club for a pair of boots of the size requested by the governor, Sir Dallas Brooks.

Lindsay's accountancy training stood him in good stead in formulating cash-flows, controlling expenditure and costing, and the business flourished quickly. He moved from there to more commodious premises in Swanston Street, then to Little Collins Street. From that time, the business expanded to Geelong, Ballarat and some of Melbourne's new shopping centres. By 1959, Lindsay sold the businesses, retaining an interest in them but not a controlling one. Soon afterwards, management problems forced the businesses into receivership.

Opinions vary as to whether Bradman's 1948 Australian team was the greatest to leave our shores with England in its sights. There are many who support either the 1921 or the 1902 team, and these were certainly great combinations. But Bradman's team went through undefeated, something the other two mentioned did not succeed in doing. The Test matches of 1921 went Australia's way by three Tests to nil with two

## BRADMAN'S UNDERSTUDY — 1948

matches drawn. In 1948, the result was an Australian victory by four games to nil. A point that seems to have been ignored, however, is that England's greatest batsman, Jack Hobbs, did not play in any 1921 Test matches, comparative unknowns such as Dipper, Brown, Russell, Hardinge and Holmes all filling the important opening spots against McDonald and Gregory, roughly the equivalent of Lindwall and Miller. Suffice to say that the 1948 squad was a very good one which would have been hard to beat at any time by any combination. Those chosen were Bradman (captain), Hassett (vice-captain), Morris, Brown, Barnes, Loxton, Harvey, Miller, Johnson, Hamence, McCool, Lindwall, Tallon, Saggers, Ring, Johnston and Toshack.

Ten players were 30 years old or older and the youngest was Neil Harvey 19. Lindsay Hassett enjoyed a good relationship with Bradman and there was no apparent anti-Bradman cave as arguably had been the case ten years before.

The team travelled aboard the *Strathaird*, breaking the journey at Colombo where Bill O'Reilly, covering the tour for the Sydney *Sun* newspaper, was appalled by the price of beer. Lindsay received a warm welcome from the Singalese (now Sri Lankans) who remembered him from the Australian Services team visit about two and a half years before. The match was unusual in that it was found the pitch measured only 20 yards (18.8 m). This problem was overcome by delivering the ball from a point about 2 yards (1.8 m) behind the crease.

In Aden, Lindsay was also given a warm reception. Many uniformed English gentlemen came aboard the ship to renew acquaintanceship, having played cricket against Lindsay when he was serving in the Middle East and enjoying cricket against British Services teams.

The Australians were fêted in the days leading up to the opening tour match at Worcester. There was practice at Lord's on most days and social gatherings in the evening. Bradman did not suffer as a speaker by comparison with some of the noted orators on hand at these gatherings — Norman Birkett, Oliver Littleton and Canon Gillingham, among others.

The opening matches of the tour meandered along in time-honoured fashion. Hassett's 35 was followed by 0 and 12 in the Yorkshire match in which he led the Australians, who gave their absent captain, Bradman, some anxious moments before scraping home in the end. At the Oval, Hassett reached his best form with 110 against Surrey before Bedser bowled him. On the hallowed turf at Fenners, he was 61 not out before Bradman closed the innings at 4–414, but followed this with his second 'duck' at Oxford. Hassett was captain in the Oxford game and at one of the pitch-rolling exercises, the Oxford captain, Pawson, an engineer, asked Hassett what roller he'd like.

'What have you got?' asked Hassett, poker-faced.

'Heavy, medium and light,' answered Pawson.

'Have you got a spiked one?' asked Hassett, still straight-faced.

'I don't think so,' answered Pawson seriously, 'but I'll make sure.'

And he went away to enquire. This episode earned Pawson the soubriquet of 'Spike' thereafter.

The match against MCC took place at Lord's, where spectators witnessed the unusual spectacle of Bradman being out at 98, caught by Edrich at slip off an Army bowler named Deighton. For Bradman, dismissals in the 90s were rare through his career.

Hassett played a half-century innings here that delighted the eye — 'the prettiest half-century of the whole summer,' said Fingleton. In an effortless display, he despatched the ball to all corners of the field before being leg before to left-hand bowler Jack Young. Later, sixes galore sped from the bats of Miller and Johnson. Laker was the main victim of these attacks yielding no less than 9 sixes, most of which landed in the vicinity of the Tavern. Barnes was fielding very close to the batsman at short leg (bat pad now) and came in for some criticism, but Barnes took all the risk (without a helmet) and was to get his comeuppence later in the tour. At Lord's he missed a couple of possible catches, probably due to being too close. He pretended to ask Hassett to come and change position with him, but when Hassett approached as though to comply, Barnes quickly motioned him away. Hassett skippered the side at Southampton against Hampshire and, after trailing the county by 117 to 195, managed to salvage an 8-wicket victory. This was the second match in which Hassett, as captain, had given himself a fright before scrambling out of it to snatch victory. His own contributions were modest — 26 and 27.

At Trent Bridge, Nottingham, for the first Test, England recalled Hardstaff on his own turf and included Barnett, a fine player before the war but, at 38, pushing on a bit; Laker, the off spinner; and Jack Young, the Middlesex orthodox left-hand finger spinner. All the others had toured Australia in 1946–47. Yardley was captain and struck the first blow for England on an overcast day. As things turned out, it may have been a good toss to lose. Hutton and Washbrook were soon in trouble, Miller and Lindwall being difficult to handle in the conditions.

Compton and Edrich stayed for a time, but when they departed and Hardstaff followed for 0 and Barnett for 8, England at 5–48, were in a parlous position. Yardley and Evans were quickly out and, at 8–74, the innings showed every sign of a debacle. Then came Laker, not especially noted for his batting, but by no means a rabbit. He played the Australian attack as though they were a pretty average lot and made 63 in just over even time. With Bedser, the pair added 89, a partnership that should have exposed the recognised batsmen to something akin to the wrath of God. The innings ended at 165 which, even at this early stage, was clearly going to prove insufficient. Johnston had the best bowling figures with 5–36 from 25 overs.

Barnes and Morris gave the side a good start with 73 on the board before Morris was bowled by Laker for 31. Arthur Morris considers Laker the best off spinner he faced, edging out the South African, Tayfield, by a small margin.

The Englishmen pulled out all the stops in trying to remove Bradman early. Bedser attacked his leg stump with close-in fieldsmen on the leg side and the lad from Bowral took some time to settle down. He saw Barnes brilliantly caught by Evans for 62 and Miller caught at slip, both off Laker who had three pretty good wickets for 22 from 12 overs. Australia was 3–121 when Brown joined Bradman. Bill Brown was not himself at number five and he departed for 17 leg before to Yardley, a better bowler than he looked from the pavilion. Hassett was next and he and his captain set about consolidating a position which, at 4–185, although far from dangerous, was rather less than the strong batting line-up had anticipated. Both batsmen were slow, but free-scoring was difficult with Charlie Barnett commissioned to bowl a foot outside leg stump with a leg-side field. Bradman was less than impressed by these tactics and allowed one over to pass without attempting any stroke. Yardley had seen and heard enough of Bradman to appreciate that this was the point in many of his innings that the Don, through his early uncertainties, was eager and able to take any attack apart, and Yardley was determined to slow things up. Bradman still went to his century in just over three and a half hours, a scoring rate that would border on the indecent in recent Tests. Lindsay was also 'doing a Micawber' and waiting patiently, oblivious to organised, sardonic clapping from some spectators. Bradman was 130 at stumps.

After some meaningful overnight discussions between Bedser and O'Reilly, the Surrey man moved Hutton from leg slip a little towards the square-leg umpire, whereupon Bradman flicked the Bedser inswinger on his pads straight to Hutton, who didn't have to move. Bill O'Reilly belonged to the Mailey school of advocates of the 'freemasonry of bowlers' or, as Mailey had put it some years previously, 'Cricket is like art; it is international'. Hassett was still progressing steadily, his caution tempered by a six off Laker but pinned down by left-hand finger spinner Jack Young, who bowled 11 successive maidens. Despite this, Lindsay had made 53 in the two-hour morning session. Just after lunch, he reached his first Test century in England in just over five hours. He then displayed many of his vintage strokes before Bedser bowled him at 137, made in just under six hours from 385 balls. The Australian tail wagged vigorously, thanks mainly to Ray Lindwall, a pretty good performer at number nine, who played freely for 42. The innings closed at 509, Bedser and Laker gaining most of the wickets. Yardley had kept the run-scoring at a subdued level and, with a deficit of 344 and two days plus one session left for play, a draw was his only option.

In England's second innings, after Washbrook and Edrich completed miserable doubles, Hutton was at his most gracious and elegant best and Compton, after some hair-raising antics, was with him at the close, the score 2–121. These two carried on next day until Hutton was bowled by a ball from Miller that skidded past Hutton's 'half-cock' forward prod. There was an interruption of play at 12.35 p.m. owing to rain after Hardstaff had had everyone on the edge of their seats with airy flicks and snicks, one of which was dropped 'emphatically', as Cardus might say. Before play resumed close to 1 p.m., Hassett hid the ball in the heap of sawdust at one end of the pitch and scooted to the boundary. It took Miller a few moments to locate the missile and excavate it. At lunch, England was 3–191, Compton 63, Hardstaff 31.

After lunch, Hardstaff almost decapitated Barnes at 'bat pad' or 'silly leg' as it was termed in those less enlightened days. Compton reached his century in 227 minutes with 12 fours and was promptly dropped by Ian Johnson in the slips. At stumps, England, at 6–345, had wiped off the deficit. Yardley had made a fighting 22. Compton (154) and Evans (10) were the not-out batsmen.

Next day, Compton overbalanced dodging a Miller bouncer and fell on his wicket for 184, one of the great innings in Test-match history. Evans laid about him for 50, but ran out of partners and the innings ended at 441.

Australia needed 98 in three hours for victory in poor light and uncertain weather conditions. Bedser bowled Morris and had Bradman again caught by Hutton at backward square leg for nil. This occurrence in successive innings pushed a couple of small wars and a murder or two off the front pages of the newspapers. Lindsay Hassett came in ahead of Brown and Miller, the latter having bowled 44 overs in England's innings. With dark clouds threatening, Lindsay was not inclined to dawdle, and he and Sid Barnes wiped off the deficit without further trouble. Barnes was 62 and Hassett 21 at the close, Australia winning by eight wickets. Bradman's duck was his first in a Test in England and his slowest anywhere.

Against Northamptonshire, Hassett led the Australians to an innings victory and himself top-scored with 127. At Bramall Lane, Sheffield, Yorkshire again pressed the visitors hard, but Bill Brown, with 113, and Ernie Toshack with 7–81, secured a draw.

The Test match at Lord's in June is one of the highlights of the English season, both cricket and social. On a sunny day, the old ground — by no means the most commodious in the world for spectators or players with a playing surface that falls short of some others — still has an ambience so unique that to watch a Test match there is one of life's great experiences for cricket lovers. To play in a Test match at Lord's must surely be the pinnacle of a cricketer's career.

So the Australians, particularly those who had not played in a Lord's Test (and only Bradman, Brown and Hassett had had the honour), were looking forward to the second Test match with keen anticipation. There were no changes in the Australian side, but England welcomed the return of Wright, replaced Barnett with Dollery and Young with Coxon. Dollery was a marginally better choice than Barnett, and Coxon, a fast-medium bowler from Yorkshire, added some strength to the bowling. None of the replacements performed sensationally.

Bradman won the toss and Australia batted. Barnes was out for 0 and Bradman once again fell to the Bedser–Hutton trap devised by Bill O'Reilly, and left for 38 compiled in less than his best style. Morris, playing beautifully, was joined by Hassett. Morris went on to 105 and Hassett had his fair share of luck, being dropped when 37 and again at 42, only to be yorked by Yardley at 47. Miller and Brown both went cheaply but the tail wagged, Tallon making a splendid 53 and Bill Johnston and Toshack applying the long handle for 29 and 20 not out respectively the next morning. The tail had added 92 runs in just over an hour.

England started badly with Hutton, Washbrook, Edrich and Dollery all out with just 46 runs on the board. Lindwall had three of these and Ian Johnson accounted for Hutton. Yardley and Compton put some stiffening into the batting and carried on until just after tea, when both fell for the addition of only one run and England finished the day in dire straits at 9–207. Lindwall, after softening Bedser up with a few bumpers, bowled him for 9 and the innings closed for a quite inadequate 215, just 135 runs behind Australia.

Barnes made the Lord's century he'd promised himself and Morris played well in an opening stand of 122. Bradman proceeded on his way, inevitably it seemed, to a century at Lord's when he was brilliantly caught by Edrich at slip for 89. During this innings, Bradman frustrated the Bedser–Hutton plan by pushing his leg at the ball, a riposte he'd have scorned in his younger days. Barnes was caught at deep fine leg, hooking Yardley after he and Bradman had added 174 runs. Next man in was South Melbourne's pride and joy, Arthur Lindsay Hassett. His stay was as brief as it could be. He snicked Yardley into the stumps and departed looking mystified. In typical Hassett fashion though, he was pleased to resume his seat in the dressing room watching John Bromwich playing tennis at Wimbledon on television. He derived some comfort from the fact that he'd missed only a couple of points of the tennis. Miller then enlivened things with some soaring sixes that put in jeopardy the less agile in the stand. Bradman ended the slaughter at 7–460. This left England with the small matter of 596 runs to score for victory in 600 minutes, a period reduced by rain.

In appalling light, Hutton and Washbrook opened against Lindwall and Johnston. Neither batsman was convincing and Hutton, in particular, played poorly and his departure was greeted in chilly silence by the spectators. Compton, Dollery and Evans tried hard against a determined and accurate attack in miserable conditions and the curtain fell at 186, a loss by 409 runs. Toshack had 5–40 but he profited from the softening up provided earlier by Lindwall and Bill Johnston.

In the ten days between the Lord's Test and the third Test at Old Trafford, the Australians dealt out severe punishment to Gloucestershire and Surrey, with victories by an innings, and 10 wickets, respectively. Lindsay was in the runs against Surrey recording his second century (139). There was shock and disbelief, however, when the England side for the Test was announced. England's world-record holder and arguably her finest batsman, Len Hutton, was dropped. The only people who were pleased were the Australians — they had a healthy regard for Hutton and, of all English batsmen, he was the one they best liked to see disappearing through the pavilion gate. His replacement was George Emmett of Gloucestershire, a capable player at county level but out of his class as a Test batsman. Wright, too, was dropped for the more accurate but pedestrian Jack Young. Pollard came in for Coxon, a good selection, and Jack Crapp, a sound left-hander, for Laker. The England selectors appeared in the early stages of panic, casting about for a team that might prove competitive. This side looked a little light on bowlers, with only Bedser, Pollard and Young available.

For Australia, Bill Brown made way for Loxton. Brown, a fine player over many years, had batted out of position at number six with only moderate success, but his omission in this match may have been regretted in the light of events.

England won the toss and there was some fiery bowling from Lindwall and Bill Johnston. Compton sustained a nasty blow, attempting to hook a Lindwall bumper and dragging the ball on to his face. After repair work, he returned to play a brave and match-saving innings of 145. There was some good low-key support from two or three others and the innings closed at 363. Barnes collected a rib-cracking blow as Pollard laid into a short ball late in the innings, and took no further part in the match. Old Trafford, never Bradman's favourite ground, bade him farewell after he'd scored 7, and Hassett, after moving along well, was out driving Young, whom he'd tried to force out of the attack, to be caught at cover by Washbrook for 38.

In the England innings, bumpers were frequent, Lindwall exchanged words with umpire Davies for 'dragging', and Lindsay Hassett twice dropped Washbrook. This was the occasion when he amused the crowd by borrowing a policeman's helmet and holding it in front of him. England was pleased to secure a first-innings lead for a change, but rain spoilt their pleasure and the whole of Monday was washed out. There were 21,000 people who had paid their money to see this day of no play, but there were no refunds. Play finally got under way at 2.15 p.m. on Tuesday with little hope of a decision being reached, Australia needing 316 to win in about three hours. Showers interrupted this brief period and Morris and Bradman took no risks until the game fizzled out just before 6 p.m., with Morris on 54 and Bradman on 30. The weather possibly robbed England of a win in this game and it was noticeable that Pollard gave the attack a far more formidable look. He and Bedser between them took 7 wickets for the match.

The Test match at Headingley, Leeds, like its counterpart ten years before, was one of the greatest matches ever played. Lindsay's part in it was undistinguished, but he demonstrated his team spirit as well as his versatility by opening the batting with Morris in both innings. This was due to Barnes's absence, still recovering from the blow he'd received from Pollard's bat at Old Trafford, a blow which Barnes modestly claimed 'would kill any ordinary man'.

For England, Emmett had played his one and only Test and departed for the southern beauty of Gloucestershire. One would imagine that the absence of Hutton on his own Yorkshire patch at Leeds would not have been well received and might well have caused the second English civil war or some similar unpleasantness. Cranston, a Lancashire dentist, came in for Dollery, and Laker was restored in place of Young.

After Yardley had won the toss, Hutton and Washbrook came out to a great ovation, one imagines directed towards Hutton whose omission from the Old Trafford Test rankled bitterly in Yorkshire hearts. The 'Old Firm' brought up the first opening partnership of 50 for the series amid general euphoria, and the two went on steadily with a little help from Lady Luck when Hassett dropped Hutton on 25 at square leg. Lindsay's thoughts probably took wings back to 1938 at the Oval when Ben Barnett missed an easy stumping chance off the same batsman who showed his appreciation by proceeding to 364. Counting the two misses from Washbrook's bat at Old Trafford, Lindsay had now grassed three in a row.

At lunch, England was 0–88, Hutton 46 and Washbrook 41, which gave Bradman food for thought as he ate his chicken salad or Yorkshire pudding. The two continued in fine style after the interval against some fairly indifferent bowling. With the score reaching 150, Bradman conferred with Hassett and brought on Ian Johnson to bowl to a run-saving field, pending the new ball's becoming available. This occurred at 165 and Lindwall bowled Hutton in his first over with the new ball. Hutton was out playing the bane of English batsmanship — the half-cock forward prod. Edrich saw Washbrook to his century at 5 p.m.. It was a chanceless innings made in 230 minutes with 16 fours. Alec Bedser came in as night watchman and England saw the day end at 2–268, with Edrich 41 and out of the batting horrors.

Bedser hung on next day and dealt severely with both Toshack and Johnson and, with Edrich, added 155 runs. Morris was introduced to bowl his left-hand 'chinamen' and was promptly hit into the crowd at square leg by his friendly enemy. Bedser went at 423 and Edrich soon followed him. The batting fell apart after this, the need for quicker runs taking its toll in wickets. The side was all out for 496 after being 2–423.

Bedser got Morris cheaply, but Hassett, who opened with Morris in the absence of Barnes, was there at stumps with Bradman and 63 runs on the board. Next morning, Pollard had Hassett caught for 13 at slip by Crapp off his second ball. Next over, Pollard clean bowled Bradman for 33 and immediately became a candidate for a knighthood at the very least. Miller and Harvey then put a stop to this nonsense, Harvey in his first Test, Australia in trouble at 3–68. The two batted with great resolution and aggression, both batsmen being especially severe on Laker. Miller was out at 189 and Loxton continued the good work with a punishing 93. Harvey was out at 294, but Loxton went on, well assisted by Lindwall, who nursed the tail through to the respectable total of 458 — a good recovery.

Next morning, after a second century opening partnership, England pushed the score along and was 2–209 at tea. Evans savaged the bowling late in the day, which finished with England at 8–365. This was a lead of 400, an unheard-of task for a side in the fourth innings. However, with Bradman in the opposition and out cheaply in the first innings, Yardley was taking no chances. He batted on for two overs, closing at 8–362. This tactic enabled him to have the heavy roller on the pitch before play started, the idea hopefully being to crumble it a little for Australia.

The outcome of this run chase was a triumph for Australia and a bitter disappointment for England. The pitch played well, such final-day spin as it held being beyond the ability of England bowlers to exploit. The batting of Don Bradman on his last appearance at a ground and before a crowd, both of which he'd made his own, and his young partner, a left-handed batsman fit to rate with any left-hander of any time, were beyond praise.

Denis Compton, a part-time spinner, had Hassett early to a brilliant catch from his own bowling for 17, but after that England had to drain the bitter cup offered to them as a result of poor team selection. Laker was dealt with harshly, but what was required was a spinner like Doug Wright. Grimmett and O'Reilly would have given a written guarantee to remove any opposition for under 250. What we sadly saw (or heard) was the introduction of Hutton into the attack. Hutton bowled a leg break occasionally in the nets or in a county game when the result was immaterial. His four overs cost 30. Morris went along to 182, playing every stroke in the book, and was out at 358 in an innings he understandably sees as a high point in his career. After Miller was out for 12, the Don, tired but triumphant, was still there at the end. He fled the ground as his thousands of Yorkshire admirers converged on him. As batsman and captain, he had been the architect of a famous victory.

The fifth Test at the Oval had little to recommend it or remember it by, except that Morris scored 196 and had to be run out. England batted poorly in both innings; Don Bradman got a 'duck' in his last Test innings to a leg spinner named Hollies, who would have been most welcome at Leeds; and Ray Lindwall took 6–20 in the England first-innings debacle, his best Test-match figures.

Australia won a disappointing contest after the excitement of Leeds, by an innings and 149 runs. This gave them the series 4–0, a reasonable assessment of the two teams' respective merits. Lindsay Hassett, at 44.3, was seventh in the batting averages, with 310 runs from 8 innings with 1 not out. Morris led the table with the remarkable total of 696 runs at 87, Toshack was fifth with an average of 51 having been only once out. Both Miller and Brown of the recognised batsmen finished below Hassett, Miller on 26, Brown on 24.

Bradman took the remaining games seriously, being anxious to complete the tour undefeated. Lindsay made the most of the games in which he played, being not out 200 in the game against the Gentlemen of England at Lord's in a total of 5–610. He followed this with a modest 103 at Taunton against Somerset and 151 against South of England at Hastings. Lindsay's double century at Lord's showed a measure of determination with aggression in his last tour appearance at the 'Cathedral of Cricket'. His centuries at Taunton and Hastings were in lighter vein and showed him in his best prewar style.

The long tour was over. Lindsay had done his best to relieve Don Bradman of routine duties and enable him to cope with the adulation accorded him throughout England, whether on cricket fields, at functions or via the mail. Bradman was, it seems, grateful for this and spoke highly of Lindsay, both as vice-captain and batsman.

Lindsay's complete tour figures are impressive. In 27 innings, he had 6 not outs, 1,563 runs at 74.43, with 7 centuries and 4 half-centuries. These figures showed a significant improvement on those achieved ten years before. He'd been praised by his captain and was well regarded by his team-mates, for whom he provided a vital bridge to the more reserved captain, and confirmed his high place among Australian batsmen, past and present.

Although Wisden's choice of its 'Five Cricketers of the Year' for 1948 did not appear until the 1949 issue of the 'Cricket Bible', it is appropriate to end this chapter by mentioning the selection of Lindsay Hassett. The year was probably unique in that all five chosen were Australians — Hassett, Lindwall, Johnston, Tallon and Morris. Of Lindsay Hassett, the responsible scribe wrote, inter alia:

> Hassett was the ideal vice-captain to Bradman, combining cheerfulness with leadership. He was coached at the South Melbourne Club and, apart from Bradman, few cricketers have started so well on tour as he did in 1938. His innings at Leeds that year sealed Australia's victory in that match. He is entitled to much of the credit for the success of the Victory Tests by providing relaxation from war worries and making cricket attractive and ensuring that it was played in the happiest possible spirit.
>
> In the 1948 season, after a moderate start, he put together 6 hundreds in his last 17 innings, winding up with scores of 200 not out, 103 and 151. Despite postwar slowness, he was still master of almost every stroke due to superb timing, nimble footwork and strong wrists. He played hooks, pulls, cuts and glances with casual ease and was a master of back play. Not many Australian batsmen have fared better on a wet pitch and few handled O'Reilly in such summary fashion. He was one of the best outfielders in the world.

With regard to Linsday's outfielding, Ray Lindwall might have reservations!

# CHAPTER 11
# A DRUBBING FOR THE SPRINGBOKS — SOUTH AFRICA 1949–50

The Australian tourists arrived home from England, soon to be plunged into a domestic season followed by a tour of South Africa with five Tests scheduled. A Testimonial match for Bradman in Melbourne started the season between an Eleven led by the Don himself and one by Lindsay Hassett. There was some crowd-pleasing cricket and some clowning by Sid Barnes, which did little to mend his fences with the Board of Control. It was arranged that Bradman would bat on the Saturday afternoon, which he did, scoring 123 after obligingly being dropped at 97 by Colin McCool at slip. Hassett batted twice in the match, making 35 in the first innings and a brisk 102 in the second. Lindwall, Morris and Meuleman also scored centuries in a run feast in which both sides totalled 836, the match ending in a tie.

After scoring 104 against Queensland in Melbourne, Lindsay failed twice against New South Wales, also at home, followed by 56 and 24 against South Australia, once again in Melbourne. Journeying north for a return match against Queensland, Lindsay put the locals to the sword with 205, gathered in a fashion that suggested batting was one of the simplest arts. Keith Miller had him cheaply in the return match against New South Wales in Sydney to wrap up the Sheffield Shield. The Victorians journeyed to Perth for their final game against Western Australia who, owing to distance, did not play the six mandatory games like the other States but had their season's results assessed on a proportional basis. Lindsay scored 40 and 1 in the west.

Two of the 'mother' states' brightest and best, Alan Kippax and Bert Oldfield, were honoured in a Testimonial match at the SCG in early February. Don Bradman turned out to honour his old team-mates and the match would have been a happy finale to the season, with Don appearing for the last time on the ground, always dear to him, where he'd started more than 20 years before. As usual, the Board did not let its critics down, casting a pall over the proceedings by omitting Barnes, a favourite in his own state despite his antics, none of which was of the nasty variety but leant rather towards mischievousness. There was again some heavy scoring, Bradman making a lively 53 until, to the horror of all present, he was caught by Ken Meuleman running with a lofted legside shot that he could legitimately have dropped but chose to catch sensationally one-handed. Being a Victorian, Meuleman was not spared by the crowd on the Randwick-end 'Hill'. Jack Moroney scored 217 and Lindsay, with 159, rolled back the years with a scintillating array of dazzling strokes. The beneficiaries of this game received just over £3,015 each and it had served a dual purpose, being used as a trial match for the tour of South Aftica.

The selectors, Dwyer, Ryder and Bradman, chose a strong side, but were roundly condemned for their omission of Keith Miller, widely regarded as the world's leading all-rounder. This was indeed a curious omission, but the selectors had the embarrassment early in the tour of having to ask Miller to join the team after Bill Johnston was injured in a motor accident. Brown and Barnes were not available and Toshack, though apparently available, was not considered. Those chosen were Hassett (captain), Neil Harvey, Ian Johnson, Bill Johnston, Loxton, Lindwall, Moroney, Morris, Saggers, Walker, Archer, Tallon, McCool and Noblet. 'Chappie' Dwyer was manager. It was said that the Board had named Hassett, a Catholic, captain only after a ballot of all Board members, Lindsay getting the nod by the odd vote in thirteen received. Sectarianism may not have yet died in the postwar era, although there were signs throughout the community that it was mortally ill.

An event of some importance in the lives of Lindsay and Tess Hassett, as well as daughter Margaret, was the birth of Anna shortly before Lindsay took off for South Africa. Anna was born six years after Margaret and Lindsay would have had mixed feelings at having to leave his expanded family so soon after Anna's arrival. During the tour, his great friends Stan and Edna McCabe had a welcome addition to their family in the birth of a daughter, Christine, and the tourists hoisted one or two in her honour.

Before arriving in Durban in October 1949, Lindsay Hassett, during a shipboard interview, made the prudent but interesting comment that while he had 'some very fine cricketers under me, as an international combination, they are entirely unproven'. This was true enough for, of the victorious 1948 Ashes party, some notable figures were now missing — Bradman, Brown, Tallon, Barnes, Toshack, Miller and Ring. Tallon had withdrawn from the original party selected and was replaced by Gil

Langley of South Australia. Hassett's caution was soundly based as it took some time for the team to be welded into the formidable combination it finally became. The rise of Neil Harvey to top quality among world batsmen was the main bonus to Australia from the tour, which also rounded off the captaincy of Lindsay Hassett. With the best will in the world, being second-in-command to a figure like D. G. Bradman would tend to modify any originality or radicalism in tactics in case they met with disaster. Now he ran his own outfit and it was soon apparent that a leader of quality and initiative had emerged. The promise he'd shown while leading his school team was now bearing fruit.

As noted in Chapter 2, Lindsay had some fairly unsuccessful tonsil surgery early in the tour of South Africa and he was not free of its impact at any stage. However, it failed to stop him from playing a full part in the tour, both as captain and batsman throughout.

The hard core of South African batting, as judged by performances against England, still comprised the 'old guard' of Dudley Nourse, Eric Rowan, Bruce Mitchell and Walter Wade. There appeared to be a scarcity of young players. Dudley Nourse was 39 years old but still a formidable attacking player. Fourteen years before, Clarrie Grimmett, who took 44 wickets in five Tests on the 1935–36 tour, considered Nourse not far short of Bradman as a batsman. Nourse greeted Hassett in Durban and the tone for the tour was set immediately. Lindsay replied to Nourse's greeting with, 'How are you Dudley? I hope you aren't feeling too well'. Rapport was quickly established and maintained throughout the tour.

After a trial run against Zululand, the Australians met Natal, where Lindsay scored 44 before falling to 'Fish' Markham, who'd achieved instant fame the previous year by skittling Denis Compton. Dudley Nourse lost no time acquainting the visitors with the fact that age had indeed not wearied him as he went on to an unbeaten 104 in the second innings of the Natal game, holding the Australians to a draw. It was about this time when Bill Johnston had his accident and his return to duty appeared likely to be delayed. Miller was despatched at once, answering the summons quickly and without rancour.

At Benoni against Northern Transvaal, Lindsay made his first century of the tour, an even ton out of a total of 4–331 declared. Hassett and Harvey both displayed their class in a 10-wicket victory. Another easy victory followed at Bulawayo against Southern Rhodesia, Hassett being 66 not out when the innings ended at 398. Lindsay did not play against

♦ A DRUBBING FOR THE SPRINGBOKS — SOUTH AFRICA 1949-50 ♦

the Transvaal at Johannesburg where the Australians had considerable difficulty against off spinner Athol Rowan, who had 15 wickets for 68 in the match. Rowan was a slow off spinner who, when the wicket gave assistance, could be a problem to all batsmen. Ian Johnson saved this game for Australia taking 6-22 in the last innings with the Transvaal failing by 15 runs to achieve the 69 runs required for victory.

Lindsay had some needed batting practice against the Orange Free State with a sound 96 out of a total of 3-405 declared and the tourists went into their first Test at Johannesburg with 5 wins and 3 draws under their belt.

After Moroney and Morris both departed with only 2 runs on the board — Moroney run out, Morris caught at backward square leg off McCarthy — Miller left at 71, but Hassett and Loxton with 101 restored the position. Lindsay's innings was described as of 'considerable quality' in the press and 'featuring classical unhurried strokes'. His century came up in 190 minutes and when rain caused play to finish early, he was 109 not out from a total of 4-190. The tonsillitis was taking its toll and Lindsay was exhausted. He was out early next morning for 112, which included 7 fours from 283 balls faced, a sound and well-constructed innings, appropriate to the situation when he came to the wicket at 2-2. Loxton's 101 was made in 150 minutes and Ian Johnson, that underrated cricketer, contributed 66 in the total of 413.

Christmas festivities were beyond Lindsay Hassett on this occasion. He had turned in at 8 p.m. on Christmas Eve and took things very quietly on the day itself. After the rest, he'd been able to complete his innings and carry out his duties when South Africa batted. Eric Rowan made a brave 60 when all around were crumbling before the early tour absentee, Keith Miller, who had some of his best figures — 5-40 from 15 overs. Following on after their last wicket fell at 137, the South Africans did a little better. Nourse, who'd fallen to Ian Johnson for 0 in the first innings (it's surprising how often the frequently criticised Ian claimed the wickets of the best batsmen — Len Hutton always had difficulty with him), made a good 36 and there were moderate contributions from one or two others, but Bill Johnston, back from injury, carried too much of the heavy artillery and took 6-44. Ray Lindwall went wicketless in the match.

Cape Town was the site for the second Test, played on the New Year weekend. The Australians kept their winning combination intact, as did their poorly performing opponents, possibly because, apart from Bruce

Mitchell (whom the Australians were happy to see omitted), there were not any better players about. It must be said that the side restored their country's dignity to some extent although beaten by 8 wickets. Batting first, the first five Australian batsmen's scores were Morris 42, Moroney 87, Miller 58, Hassett 57 (caught and bowled Mann), and Harvey 178. At 7–526, Lindsay brought the massacre to an end by closing the innings. None of the bowling figures impressed but Tayfield showed signs of future danger with a tidy display, although 2–141 from 37 overs wouldn't warrant any trophy.

For the Springboks, Nourse (65) and Rowan (67) fared well in the first innings and, following on, Nourse, in a punishing display, saw his side to a total sufficient to force his opponents to bat again. After a lethargic exhibition in South Africa's first innings, Ray Lindwall fired in the second with 5–32. For South Africa, 'Tufty' Mann, an economical left-hand orthodox spinner, took 6 wickets for the match and was treated with respect.

Lindsay's captaincy was now gaining plaudits as he grew in confidence and the team relationships were excellent, despite the captain's penchant for late nights (or early mornings!) and revelry in which he expected to be joined by other team members. Luckily, there was a preponderance of players who'd had experience of their captain's late-night capers and suitable steps were taken both to isolate themselves (behind locked doors) and warn the newer chums what to expect.

At Port Elizabeth against Eastern Province, Lindsay scored a tidy 50 and followed with 106 not out against Border at East London. The opposition here was not overstrong, and Australia's 4–425 closed inspired such awe in them that Eastern Province could manage only 72 and 60. Talent was thin in parts of the 'Union' at this time, but the reckoning, when it came 20-odd years later, was devastating.

Despite calls in the press for the recall of Bruce Mitchell, the selectors stuck to the Eleven that had lost the first two Tests. The Australians left the winning combination intact, but they were to get a sharp shock in this match before clinching a third victory, albeit by the more modest margin of 5 wickets. Batting first, Eric Rowan, a solid performer, happy to keep anyone that would listen apprised of the game's progress, proceeded to his century, with Dudley Nourse again contributing a well-constructed 66. Together they pushed the side's total to a respectable 311. At this point, rain intervened with its usual unfortunate effect on Australian batsmen, who fell easy prey to the off spinner Tayfield who took 7 wickets for 23 in only 8 overs. Hassett's contribution was on a par with most of the others — lbw Tayfield 2. Arthur Morris thought Laker a better bowler than Tayfield, Ian Craig the reverse.

The South African second innings was a further debacle, Ian Johnson taking 5 wickets and Bill Johnston 4 in a total of 99. This left the Australians 336 to win, which they reached, thanks mainly to a superb not-out innings of 151 by Harvey, an innings he rates the best he ever played. It is interesting to speculate on the outcome of the match had Nourse enforced the follow-on after the Australians' disastrous first innings. As things happened, Hassett asked his bowlers to keep the Springboks at the crease as long as possible to give the pitch time to dry out before the Australians batted again. Nourse came in for some heavy criticism over his tactical 'failure' in the game, all with hindsight of course. Morris and Loxton gave the brilliant Harvey all the support he needed to clinch the victory and the series.

Johannesburg was the venue once again for the fourth Test and the South African selectors took the axe to the Springbok side which, though showing some improvement, was still performing a little below what the populace expected. After all, Springboks had long contested supremacy with New Zealand on the rugby field and it was humiliating for loyal South Africans to see the cream of their cricketers humbled by Australia, a country which, up to that time, occupied the bottom spot in the hierarchy of the chief rugby nations. Wynne, Watkins, Smith, Wade and Cheetham were replaced by Begbie, Draper, Melle, Fullerton and Winslow. All these except Draper, the wicket-keeper, came from the Transvaal. Melle, a fastish bowler, added some life to the attack and Fullerton performed well with the bat. In addition, Fullerton carried out the wicket-keeping duties.

Australia batted first. Morris and Moroney made an opening stand of 214 in a display described as 'drab' in some newspapers. This description may not have been far from the truth because the Australian innings of 465 was not terminated by closure until the fall of the eighth wicket late on the second day. Miller was aggressive in scoring 84 and Hassett, after sending Lindwall in at number four to liven things up but seeing him depart for 5, batted on solidly while Neil Harvey laid about him to some effect being not out 56 when the plug was pulled. Hassett was bowled by McCarthy for 53. Michael Melle was impressive with the ball and made all players wary, finishing with 5–113.

Eric Rowan was again in the runs with 55, but Nourse had one of his rare failures. Fullerton played well for 88 and, helped by Tayfield with 40, pushed his side on to 352. Batting again, and in a hurry, Moroney made his second hundred for the match and Harvey, who had developed a great and enduring rapport with South African bowlers, made an even century when Melle bowled him. Time ran out before a decision could be reached, but it could be claimed that the home side was slowly on the improve. It did not last, and in the final match at Port Elizabeth, the Springboks suffered a crushing defeat and were virtually back to square one.

The Australians, batting first, were 7–549 when Hassett applied the closure. Morris made 157, Harvey 116 and Hassett 167. This welcome century came after two country games following the fourth Test in which he made 2 and 6 against Griqualand West and Natal. The century innings of Hassett's was more in keeping with his prewar style. It was described as 'an innings of considerable quality, featuring classical, unhurried strokes'. It lasted 261 minutes and he faced 283 balls.

The home team's showing must have depressed the spectators. The first innings yielded only 158 and worse came in the follow-on, only 132, of which Nourse made 55. Australia won by an innings and 259 runs.

Before this game started, Hassett nominated his deputy, Arthur Morris, to advise Ray Lindwall that 'he was being rested' in favour of Geff Noblet. Neither Arthur nor Ray was very comfortable with this piece of intelligence. One wonders what the result might have been had Lindwall played.

The tour came to a close with a match at Cape Town against Western Province where they played a draw and a win against a South African Eleven at Johannesburg. Lindsay gave these games a miss. In Tests he'd batted six times to total 402 runs at 67.00, coming second to Harvey with 660 runs at the Bradman-like average of 132. On the tour, despite the captaincy cares and tonsillitis, Lindsay made 855 runs at 61.07 with 4 centuries. The Australians 4-0 victory in the Tests matched the results of Victor Richardson's team in 1935–36 and they were again clearly much the better team. Relations between the captains and players were excellent. Chappie Dwyer's sure but sensitive hand was visible in all they did, both on and off the field.

When Lindsay returned to Melbourne to his wife and two daughters, he described Cape Town and Durban as beautiful cities, more than able to hold their own against the more famous metropolises. He added: 'I shall always look back on my six months in South Africa as among the happiest of my life, despite the fact that I was suffering from tonsillitis most of the time. Life is more leisurely there than in most other places.' Most of the team would have echoed these sentiments.

There followed a winter of family pursuits, fishing, golf and gardening, before the 'Ashes' tour of 1950–51 disturbed once again the even tenor of life for the Hassett family.

There was also the small matter of the family business to oversee.

## CHAPTER 12
# FREDDY BROWN'S ENGLISHMEN — 1950–51

The England side that came to Australia in 1950–51 did not look likely to extend the home team greatly. Nor did it, in the stark terms of success achieved, for Freddy Brown's team was beaten 4 to 1 in the Tests. There was, however, one significant end result for, at Melbourne, in the fifth Test, England won by 8 wickets, its first victory over Australia since the debacle at the Oval in 1938. The selection of F. R. Brown as captain, at first puzzling, proved a singularly happy one. Brown had been here in 1932 with Douglas Jardine's predatory outfit. He did not play in a Test and his performances in other games were few and unimpressive. Brown was an instant success with Australians. One Sydney city fruit barrowman peddling his wares shouted: 'Lettuces with hearts as big as Freddy Brown's'.

He and Lindsay Hassett had met in the Middle East during the war and had played some cricket together before Brown was captured in Tobruk by the Germans and spent three years as a prisoner of war in an Italian camp. This caused Freddy to shed some weight, but was unable to quench his optimism and love of cricket. At 40, however, he seemed an odd choice as the captain to rejuvenate English cricket. But rejuvenate it he did. Australians love a fighter and are generous to underdogs, and they took Brown to their hearts, unreservedly and with appreciation. His by-now solid build and ruddy countenance, and the pleasure and pride he took in his team's performances, reflected a personality acceptable to Australians of all ages. It was common to hear usually intensely one-eyed Australians express the hope that 'the Poms' would win. Perhaps one reason for this turnaround was that an England win appeared highly unlikely.

From Australia's point of view, looking back it is fairly clear that this series marked the start of our decline, confirmed in England in 1953 and brutally demonstrated in Australia in 1954–55. Another factor in the results of the Tests was the sad and inexplicable failure of Denis Compton. Compton batted 7 times for 53 runs, his scores being 3, 0, 0, 23, 5, 0, 11, 11 not out. Had he batted to his capacity and proven ability the series may have gone rather more England's way.

The England team comprised Brown (captain), Compton (vice-captain), Bailey, Dewes, Close, Sheppard, Simpson, Hutton, Parkhouse, Washbrook, Evans, McIntyre, Bedser, Berry, Hollies, Wright and Warr. The tried and true performers were Hutton, Washbrook, Compton, Evans, Bedser and Wright. The all-rounders were Bailey, Brown and Close. There were unrealised hopes and expectations that newcomers Dewes, Close, Berry and Warr, or at least some of them, would come good. In the event, none did. Warr was a happy tourist and a most likeable man, but, as a pace bowler, he was inadequate. Close suffered from a high degree of the misplaced confidence of youth, a malady from which he recovered in later years. Dewes was a solid left-hand opening batsman who never attained Test class. Berry bowled orthodox left-hand spin of the type suitable to English conditions but fairly useless in Australia. Sheppard was a bit ahead of his time. Simpson and Parkhouse were the best of the newcomers and both played some useful innings, while Bailey redeemed some dismal batting performances with several spells of economical fast-medium bowling. His best times were to come and his nuisance value in later series made Australians tear their hair.

Lindsay Hassett's position as captain was unchallengeable and he picked up his friendship with Brown where he'd left it nearly ten years before in Egypt. Brown, who'd shed 22 kg (3 stone) while a prisoner of war, was fast regaining the lost avoirdupois and, with his cheerful ruddy face, was what many Australians saw as 'the typical Englishman', possibly one who'd spent his life cultivating 'England's pleasant pastures'. He'd captained 'the Gentlemen' against 'the Players' and redeemed a dismal situation with a brilliant century and a few wickets. This all-round performance no doubt sealed the job for him, a job he'd probably considered never likely to be his.

Lindsay had started the season well with a century (113) against South Australia, but could muster only 18 in the second innings. At home against New South Wales, he was in his old style and made 179, falling to a very useful leg spinner, Fred Johnston. A youthful Richie Benaud had him lbw for 8 in the second innings.

The Englishmen, meanwhile, had not set many pulses racing in the lead-up games to the Brisbane Test, although Close scored a century in the west and Compton was running into the form which he held throughout the tour except where it counted most, in the Tests. The fielding was indifferent and there was much interest in the 'mystery' bowler, Jack Iverson, of whom the Englishmen had heard some disquieting snippets of information. Bailey and Brown were having some success with the ball and Hutton looked ominously safe — the complete batsman as he moved on to his 92nd first-class century in the tour game against South Australia. Evans was brilliant. The MCC won the match against South Australia after an exciting run chase, scoring 185 in 105 minutes, Evans sealing the victory with 5 fours off 6 balls.

Compton led the side against Victoria after Brown damaged a finger. Iverson worried the life out of Washbrook who should have been caught at slip off the ball 'Big Jake' Iverson made to run on straight instead of his stock off spinner. Later, he nearly turned Compton inside out as Denis tried to unravel him. Bailey bowled beautifully, skittling Meuleman, having Harvey caught at short leg by Sheppard and clean bowling Lindsay Hassett for 19 as an encore.

Morris and Miller gave the Englishmen a leather-hunting at Sydney in a total of 3–509. Bedser was recovering from influenza and the newly laid Sydney pitch was slow and depressing to all bowlers. Hutton made another century and both he and Washbrook dished out some punishment to Lindwall. The match was drawn. Moving on to Queensland, rain curtailed play and there was little joy for England except a sound century to John Dewes, a century that guaranteed him a place in the first Test side.

Australia picked Moroney rather than Burke to open with Morris (Barnes being otherwise employed) and Iverson came in for McCool. England discarded the younger players Close, Warr and Berry, but retained Dewes. Brown had more than his share of worries, not the least of which was his side's slipshod fielding. He gave the team a stern 'pep talk' on the eve of the match and, in the upshot, the visitors performed well above their own or anyone else's expectations.

Hassett won the toss and Moroney registered the first half of his 'pair', being caught by Hutton off Bailey in a position close to that occupied by the four fieldsman when he caught Bradman a few times in England in 1948. Morris, Harvey and Miller brought the score to 3–116 when Miller fell for 15. Hassett was next and had some anxious moments against Doug Wright who, after a settling-in period marred by long hops and no-balls, was now well and truly on the spot. Evans caught Harvey brilliantly and at 4–118, Australia appeared to have lost the plot. Worse was to follow. Bedser found a beauty for Hassett on 8, a leg cutter, pitched on leg stump and taking the off bail, a similar delivery to the one with which he'd bowled Bradman in Adelaide in 1946. Hassett complained later that the Surrey bowler seemed to save this type of delivery for him. With 5 out for 129, England unexpectedly found themselves in a commanding position. Loxton (24), Lindwall (41) and Ian Johnson (23), restored some dignity, but 228 was a total far removed from that expected on the first day of a Test match against the present England side. Bailey took 3–28, Bedser 4–45 and Brown 2–63. Wright had terrible luck once again in a Test match, beating the bat regularly but interspersing his testing deliveries with no-balls and the occasional long hop. Arthur Morris once said that he could not remember any bowler who beat him as often as Wright without getting his wicket. He took 1–81 from 16 overs.

Heavy rain fell overnight and there was no play on the Saturday. Hassett kept Brown in suspense, calling for frequent inspections of the pitch. Brown was understandably reluctant to see his batsmen attempting to cope with a Brisbane 'sticky'. At 3 p.m., the two captains walked back and, at the pavilion gate, Lindsay relieved Brown's anxiety, saying, 'Let's go and have a drink'. The clouds on Freddy's face dispersed instantly. Sunday was a rest day and, on Monday, play began on a drying wicket. Washbrook top-scored with 19 and at 7–68, Brown closed the innings with the intention of knocking over a few Australian batsmen before the pitch dried out. This stratagem proved successful, seven of our best and brightest being out for 32. Moroney, Morris, Loxton and Lindwall registered 0, Hassett was out lbw to Bailey for 3 and Harvey, the only one to get double figures, top-scored with 12. Bedser had 3–9 and Bailey 4–22. Hassett had narrowly averted a hat trick after Morris and Loxton (elevated in the batting order) fell to Bedser. Lindsay did not stay long and was quick to cut his losses, close the innings and get the Englishmen in for a second round on the still mischievous pitch. At 7–32, Australia was not far short of its lowest 'all out' score of 36 against England at Birmingham in 1902. Two closures on the one day set the statisticians searching vainly for a precedent.

England now needed 193 to win. Brown had 97 minutes to negotiate before the close, but, in that time, his team managed to lose 6 wickets for 30. Any hope England had of winning rested on Hutton taking the bowling by the neck next day, this depending, of course, on having partners to stay with him. Iverson put paid to this, capturing 4 wickets in a hurry while Hutton, in lonely defiance, made 62. England could manage only 122 and Australia won by 70 runs. Hutton played with the mixture of defence, aggression and elegance expected of the master batsman. This was an extraordinary match. Australia had the best of the conditions in batting first, but their performance on day one was disappointing. England should have done better in the last innings, but suffered from injudicious shots and a run-out. Hutton lent further weight to the belief of some that he was the best batsman in the world. Lindsay Hassett handled his bowlers shrewdly and, on the score of tactics, there was little between the two captains.

Lindsay was soon back in the state side for the Melbourne game against Queensland where he scored 127 and 28 not out in displays reminiscent of days gone by. The second Test followed hard on the heels of this Shield game. The luckless Moroney, who'd registered a pair in the Brisbane Test, was unceremoniously dropped and despatched to the outer darkness. It seemed a trifle hard on a player who'd done well in South Africa a year before, but Moroney was never much of a favourite, either with the crowds or the hierarchy. Ken Archer from Queensland replaced him, but there was no other change. England replaced an injured Compton with Parkhouse, and Close came in for McIntyre.

Hassett won the toss again and Morris and Archer opened the innings. Morris was quickly out and with Archer and Miller following shortly afterwards, it was up to Hassett to get the innings back on the rails, the more so when Harvey went. There were now 4 out for 93. Loxton and Hassett restored the position to some extent. Lindsay drew on his experience to counter some splendid bowling from Bailey and Bedser, and reached a sound and valuable 50 in 97 minutes before he was yorked by Bailey when 52. The lower half of Australia's batting offered feeble resistance and the side was out for 194.

England did little better, the top half of their batting performing poorly against the fast bowlers. Brown, with a vigorous 62, and Evans, with 49, saved the day and saw the side through to 197 — a meagre enough lead of 3 runs, but an event certainly not in the script at the start of the season. This curious match continued to unfold in unpredictable fashion when Brown and Bedser bowled the home side out for a paltry 181. Hassett fell to his opposite number, Brown, for 19, caught in the gully by Bailey. This left England 179 runs to win, a target one would have imagined well within their capacity. However, some cracks in the pitch were opening up and batting would probably not be easy. Time was not a factor as there remained three days plus an hour of play if needed. Brown had adopted the doubtful tactic of dropping Hutton, his best batsman, opener at that, down the order. It hadn't worked in any of the innings so far and it didn't work on this occasion. Nobody was good enough to stay with Hutton who, in desperation at 40, attempted to force things a little but skied a short ball from Johnston, to be caught near the square-leg umpire by Lindwall. England failed by 28 runs in a disappointing display but, on the other hand, the home team had suffered a severe fright and were probably lucky to get away with a win. In their four innings to date, the Australians by and large had done little to inspire confidence. Harvey's 74 at Brisbane and Hassett's 52 in Melbourne were the only two scores over 50. England was slightly but decisively worse — Brown alone fulfilled the batting role with his 62. In addition, he had 5 wickets to his credit or 7 wickets for the series so far.

Lindsay played in the Shield match against South Australia, also in Melbourne, and made 69 out of a total of 271. It was a relief to be playing in a match where the strain and responsibility were less heavy and he would demonstrate in these innings that he'd not lost all the strokes that made his batting sheer delight to watch. Comparison with Stan McCabe, the other great stroke player between the wars, is inevitable. Both played with an ease and power which had their roots in timing and balance. The difference probably was that Stan was predominantly a back-foot player who could drive 'on the up' while Lindsay was equally at home forward or back. Perhaps a fairer comparison would be with Alan Kippax or Archie Jackson of that golden era of New South Wales cricket.

The Sydney Test saw some resurgence in the home team's batting. Compton returned from injury and replaced Close, but Denis failed again, disastrously for his team. Hutton, restored to the opening spot, made 62 after Brown had won the toss and was well supported by Brown (79) and Simpson (49). In their total of 290, Iverson failed to take a wicket, giving no indication of the wrath to follow a few days later. Lindwall broke Bailey's thumb and Wright strained a groin muscle in England's innings and neither was able to bowl. This left Bedser, Warr and Brown to do virtually all of the bowling. The three toilers understandably were not anxious to get through their overs too quickly. This told against the cricket as a spectacle, particularly as Miller was in his most circumspect mood in batting through most of the innings to be 145 not out when the last wicket fell at 426. Lindsay Hassett had made 70 with a mixture of defence and aggression in 192 minutes, but generally the batting was fairly plebeian, partly due to the slow over rate.

Hassett appeared to give his wicket away after the umpire had refused an appeal for caught behind the previous ball. Bedser bowled 43 overs to take 4–107, Warr 36 overs for 0–142 and Brown 44 overs for 4–153. Brown in most games bowled his medium-paced cutters and swingers rather than the leg breaks of his younger days.

Trailing by 136, England started its second innings with high hopes. All went well until Iverson was brought into the attack. The wicket had abandoned its bland character and was now taking spin and taking it sharply. Hutton quickly fell to a remarkable catch by Tallon. Hutton had snicked one low to Ian Johnson who just got his left hand under it at slip and scooped the ball up for Tallon to take a diving catch. This was a mortal blow and thereafter disaster followed disaster in dismal succession. Washbrook made 34 by guess and by God, Compton 23 in a manner calculated to give the less talented players the horrors, Simpson and Bailey were both scoreless. Iverson did the damage to finish with 6–27 from 19 overs. Flicking the ball with the second finger of a very large hand, his stock ball was the off break. Once or twice in each over, by a slight movement in the direction towards which his thumb was pointing, he'd straighten one or cause it to turn fractionally towards the off, and nobody had as yet fathomed when this delivery was on its way. A couple of New South Wales batsmen worked it out later in a Shield match and gave Iverson some severe punishment.

England was all out for 123, losing by an innings and 13 runs, a defeat which rather negated the excellent fights of the first two Tests. The Iverson factor was probably decisive — his bowling in the second innings when the wicket was taking spin was top class. On the debit side for Australia, the batting against a severely limited England attack was ordinary. Ian Johnson, coming in late in the innings, seemed the only one to appreciate that runs were there for the taking. However, there was no denying that the Ashes had been retained by the better side, albeit not as easily as had been anticipated.

In the three weeks before the Adelaide Test was due to start, Lindsay took part in two away Sheffield Shield games. In Brisbane against Queensland, he made 29 and 30 not out, and at Sydney his 82 was worth watching and he followed it with 27 in the second innings.

For the Adelaide Test, Jim Burke came in for Loxton. England was without Bailey (with a damaged finger) and he was replaced by reinforcement Roy Tattersall. Warr was retained and Sheppard replaced Parkhouse. Hassett won the toss and was quickly at the wicket when

Archer left without scoring. Morris, whose form in the Tests had been poor, was grateful to have his captain as partner and the two proceeded steadily until Hassett, on 43, fell to his old hoodoo man, nicking a Wright leg break to Evans. Morris now got a move on with Harvey and Miller to reach his century in 215 minutes. This was his seventh century against England, the only Australian ahead of him being Bradman with 19. He moved steadily to 200 in 445 minutes with 22 fours, finally being bowled by Tattersall for 206 when attempting a big hit. The innings closed at 371. Bedser, Warr and Wright shared the wickets.

The highlight of England's innings was Hutton's 156 not out in making which he carried his bat. This was widely applauded as a great innings by a great batsman with little support from the other ten players, including Compton. Iverson, on the bland Adelaide pitch, was not the menace he'd been in Sydney, but he bowled accurately, always requiring vigilance, particularly for the ball that went straight on or turned fractionally towards the off. His 3–68 from 26 overs was a fine effort from a bowler who had never seen a Test match until he played in one. Hutton played Iverson with growing confidence and his innings included 11 fours and occupied 370 minutes. England finished with 271, which did little justice to Hutton's heroic display.

Morris was run out that evening, but Hassett and Archer carried on next morning until Lindsay fell again to Wright, lbw for 31, shortly after Archer had mishit Tattersall to be caught by Bedser at mid-wicket. Miller was out for 99 trying a back cut but hitting his stumps instead. He'd protected Burke playing in his first Test and next day the young man went on to a century, being severe on Wright. Hassett delayed the closure until Burke reached his century. The batting, indeed the cricket, was fairly ordinary this day. Brown and the team manager had been in an accident on the previous night and Brown's absence seemed to infect the team with a feeling of lethargy. Hassett closed at 8–403, leaving England the small matter of 503 runs to get in just under eight hours, a task beyond better sides than this one.

Despite some promising starts by Washbrook, Hutton, Simpson and Sheppard, the lower order failed dismally and the side was out for 228. Compton recorded yet another failure on this occasion, failing to trouble the scorers at all. Australia chalked up their fourth victory by 274 runs. The English impetus apparent in the first two Tests had been derailed, thwarted or just plain stopped. Generally, the match, as a spectacle, had little to recommend it.

In the state match against England, Hassett made 232 but came in for criticism for negative cricket. Victoria had batted first and, at close of play, Hassett required 27 runs to reach his double century. It took him 75 minutes to achieve this and the game was put back to some extent. This situation was aggravated by Hutton and Bailey when the MCC batted, the main object appearing to be to allow Bailey to reach his first century in Australia. The game finished in a draw, neither captain appearing anxious to take the necessary steps to achieve a result. There were elements of unwelcome farce towards the end, with Loxton keeping wickets and tail-end England batsmen opening the innings. With the final Test to be played on the same ground the following week, these antics tended to leave an unpleasant taste.

Bailey was back in the Test side for Warr and, for Australia, Graeme Hole replaced Archer. Burke was to be Morris's opening partner.

Hassett won the toss for the fourth time in the series and after Burke left for 11, Hassett and Morris added 88 for the second wicket. Bedser troubled both batsmen and at lunch only 48 runs had been scored, the slowest pre-lunch session in the series. It did not improve much after lunch and there was some jeering directed at the two batsmen. Morris, particularly, was out of touch, taking almost three hours for his half-century. He was out at that score leg before to Brown, who also accounted for Harvey and Miller. Hassett, with wickets tumbling, pushed the score along with some vintage drives and cuts. He was brilliantly caught at slip by Hutton off Brown's bowling for 92 — a mixed innings which had flowered after a slow start. He'd batted 212 minutes and hit 9 fours. The innings closed for 217, Brown having 5–49, figures he could scarcely have visualised in his dreams.

The England innings was marked by some high-class batting by Hutton (79) and Simpson (156 not out). Simpson's knock was marked by some splendid on-side play in the area between square leg and mid-on and he was unconquered at the end. None of the others helped greatly, Compton continuing with his wretched run of outs to be caught at slip off Lindwall for 11. However, England finished at 320, a lead of 103.

The Australian second innings started badly, Morris and Burke both being out with only 6 runs on the board. Hassett and Harvey played soundly against some pretty good bowling from Wright and Bedser. Harvey played brightly for his 52 but Hassett was slow — with wickets falling, it was understandable that he should take a sheet-anchor role. At stumps, Lindsay was 44, made in 173 minutes, and Hole was 18. The total was 4–129, so Australia's lead was only 26 runs with 6 wickets standing.

Early on the Wednesday, Wright bowled Hassett with a leg break that clipped the top of the off stump. Hole played some good strokes but the end was near and Bedser fittingly took the last 2 wickets, Johnston 1, Iverson 0. Australia's total of 197 left England 95 runs to win. Bedser had 10 wickets for the match.

England lost Washbrook and Simpson and rain threatened to thwart an English victory. The batsmen hastened to knock off the runs and, with 8 still wanted, Hassett took the ball and made as if to bowl, amid much cheering. He then changed his mind and gave the ball to Hole. Next over, however, after a conference with Hutton, he did bowl — a slow full toss to Hutton. The theory was that Hutton would hit the delivery for 4 and he and Hassett would share the stumps as souvenirs. Hassett pulled a set of stumps up as he delivered the ball, but Hutton miscued and got only a single, so the stumps had to be put back. On the last ball of Hassett's over, Hutton hit the winning run. Despite Compton's failures on this tour, it was fitting that England's two greatest batsmen should be in at the end, an end that marked England's first victory against Australia since 1938. There was great enthusiasm at England's win, with thousands invading the field and a great crowd around the Members' Stand chanting, 'We want Brown'. Brown appeared and spoke briefly and graciously. Hassett then appeared in an umpire's hat. After congratulating Brown, Lindsay complained that the presence of so many pretty girls in the crowd had distracted his players.

Lindsay Hassett had enjoyed a fairly good season. In the Tests, he made 366 runs at 40 and in first-class matches, 1,423 runs at 64. It should be remembered that he was now 37 years old and it's hard to recall quickly other postwar Australian cricketers, apart from Don Bradman, who were still playing at that age and performing at or even near this level.

Jack Fingleton wrote approvingly of Lindsay's performances as captain, noting that he got about his business quietly and effectively without the necessity for lengthy field conferences. If some of his moves appeared unorthodox and subject to criticism, the critics were usually silenced because almost invariably they proved successful. Hassett assumed the important number-three position in the batting order when this position proved unsuitable for Neil Harvey. With Morris out of form early, the number-three position demanded a degree of solidity that did not suit the aggressive Harvey, so Lindsay assumed the responsibility of getting the innings on course. Bradman could play either the attacking or defensive role as the occasion demanded, but geniuses are as uncommon in cricket as anywhere else.

All in all, in a season of some surprises and in the absence of Bradman, Lindsay Hassett could be quietly satisfied by his performances on and off the field. Off the field, relations between the teams were far more relaxed than in the 1946–47 series when Hammond and Bradman were at their respective helms. E. W. Swanton, in his account of the tour, made special mention of Lindsay Hassett's part in this cheerful rapport:

> *The personality of Lindsay Hassett had a great deal to do with this. He had been a popular member of the 1938 team to England, he had captained the highly successful Services team in 1945 and had come a third time as vice-captain to Bradman in 1948. It would be hard to find a more charming opponent or colleague in any game than this whimsical little man.*

# CHAPTER 13
# JOHN GODDARD'S WEST INDIANS — 1951–52

The West Indies side that toured Australia in the 1951–52 season had enjoyed a successful tour of England in the Northern summer of 1950 and the praises of several of its players were being widely sung in world cricketing circles. The 'three Ws', Weekes, Worrell and Walcott, had laid about them with the bat, and two bowlers, Ramadhin and Valentine, had mesmerised English batsmen. Valentine was a slow orthodox left-hand finger spinner who imparted prodigious turn, while Ramadhin, Indian born, had a bewildering arsenal of deliveries which batsmen were likening to witchcraft or black magic. Bowling with his sleeve rolled down, his hand leading his arm over quickly, it was difficult to detect the direction of spin from the hand and he was quick enough through the air to make detection in transit a matter of intelligent guesswork.

The authorities denied the tourists the usual acclimatisation period in the various states before the Tests started. The schedule provided for a one-day match against the Prime Minister's Eleven in Canberra, two shortened games against country sides from New South Wales and Queensland, and a first-class engagement against the Queensland state side in Brisbane. This truncated program put the tourists up against it when confronted by Australia at full strength in a Test. However, they did surprisingly well in the series, winning the third game by 6 wickets and losing the fourth by 1 wicket. Once again there were signs of a gradual decline in our cricket, first observed in the Ashes series of the previous summer.

The following is the team broken down into its components:

| | |
|---|---|
| Captain/batsman: | Goddard |
| Vice-captain/batsman: | Stollmeyer |
| Batsmen: | Weekes, Worrell, Rae, Christiani, Marshall, Rickards |
| All-rounders: | Atkinson, Gomez |
| Wicket-keepers: | Walcott, Guillen |
| Pace bowlers: | Trim, Jones |
| Slow bowlers: | Ramadhin, Valentine |

As well as being the number-one wicket-keeper, Walcott was one of the 'three Ws'.

Lindsay Hassett was outspoken and critical of the arrangements made for the tour itinerary, accusing the Board of Control of 'sheer stupidity'. Indeed, administrators and players indulged in some testy jibes at each other early in the season. All of this culminated in a celebrated court case involving the Board, the *Daily Mirror* newspaper, a Mr Raith and Sid Barnes. None of the parties emerged with much credit, the Board least of all. What angered Hassett most was that the coming series would, in many minds, determine the best team in the world, and that any such appraisal would be undermined by the unfairness of the tour program.

Lindsay played no Shield cricket in the weeks preceding the Test. The visitors' match in Canberra was shortened by rain, but they defeated New South Wales Country by 8 wickets at Newcastle and drew the Queensland Country game at Townsville.

In the game against Queensland, Ramadhin and Valentine were rested and the paucity of the visitors' attack without them was soon evident. After McCool routed 'the Windies' for 198, taking 6–83, Queensland replied with 455 and dismissed the visitors again for 282, Gomez defiant with a splendid 97 not out. Queensland won by 10 wickets. Gerry Gomez was to prove a more than useful all-rounder on the tour.

Changes to the Australian side for the Brisbane Test were Archer for Burke, Langley for Tallon and Ring, the Victorian leg spinner, for McCool. Sid Barnes was still embroiled in a continuing donnybrook with the Board and was 'persona non grata'. Goddard won the toss and the Windies batted against the formidable Australian attack without even having seen them on the field, let alone having faced them. The scales were heavily weighted against them. The pace of Lindwall, Miller and Johnston was entirely new to them and a score of 216 was, if not adequate, then certainly creditable and, as it proved, competitive. Of the 'three Ws', Weekes and Worrell performed well, but Walcott got a scorcher into the pads from Lindwall first ball and was leg before. Miller was reproved by umpire Barlow for too many bouncers and the fast attack was vigorous and constant, Hassett keeping Lindwall, Miller and Bill Johnston bowling throughout the first session.

When Australia batted, Hassett continued in the number-three batting spot as he'd done the previous season, but played all around a

Ramadhin delivery and was bowled for 6. Miller and Lindwall restored dignity after 5 wickets had fallen for 129, Lindwall's 61 including 9 fours and 1 six. The side was out for 226, so that the visitors' 216 took on an air of respectability. Valentine had 5–99 and Ramadhin's sole wicket, Hassett, left him with the unflattering figures of 1–75 — he had bowled much better than they indicate and he'd undoubtedly helped his 'spin twin' to the choicer result.

In their second innings, after being 5–96, the West Indies, through Weekes (70) and Gomez (55), recovered to total 245, Ring with 6–80 being the destroyer. This left Australia 236 to win. Hassett had a good look at Ramadhin and Valentine, occupying the crease for 94 minutes, scoring 35, receiving some heckling for what was seen as slow play and finally falling lbw to Ramadhin. The crowd's criticism of Hassett took no note of the facts first, that he was the captain, batting at number three after one opener had departed for 4, and second, that it was important for the most experienced player to get the innings on track against some top-class bowling. In the event, Australia won the match by 3 wickets, Ramadhin, on this occasion, grabbing the figures with 5–90. Reviewing the match in the light of the circumstances in which the Windies had been obliged to play, they could take some comfort from the result which was far less than clear-cut and gave promise of better things to come.

Lindsay had fallen twice to Ramadhin and things were not about to improve, for in the state game at Melbourne, Ramadhin had Lindsay leg before, again for 12. The Windies might well have won this match had not rain interfered. This would have been a great morale booster coming up to the Sydney Test, due at the end of November. On the plus side, Walcott and Stollmeyer had returned to form with scores of 75 and 94.

Batting first again in the second Test at the Sydney Cricket Ground, several of the Windies batsmen got runs in a respectable total of 362. However, after having Australia at 2–27, Lindsay Hassett was given a crucial let-off when, only 7, he was dropped behind the stumps by Walcott, who juggled an attempted hook stroke but could not hang on to it. He went on to 132, adding 235 with Miller who finished with 129. Lindsay's innings occupied 381 minutes and on that basis could be described as slow. Reports of the game stated that he was not 'stodgy' but always interesting, his defensive play again an example for young cricketers. Alan 'Johnny' Moyes, while acknowledging this, felt that defence had been 'overemphasised'. There were 11 fours in the innings.

Scoring 517, the Australians had a handy lead of 155 runs and the West Indies, batting again, endured a barrage of bumpers from Miller and Lindwall. Lindwall was reported to have bowled 15 of these deliveries in 40 balls. It is surprising that the umpires did not intervene. Had the bowlers and Hassett been able to cast their minds forward 25 years, it may have given them pause for the Australians were destined to get these back, pressed down and flowing over. Goddard and Gomez contributed well in both innings, but the Australian speed attack was fierce and unrelenting, capturing 14 of the 20 wickets that fell in the match. Of the remaining 5, Ian Johnson got 4, Hole 1 and Ring 1. The Australians scored the 137 runs required with the loss of 3 wickets, Hassett being not out at the death with 46, despite a run-out mix-up. Missed catches probably cost the Windies the match and there was some distaste at the excessive use of short-pitched bowling by the Australians. The visitors had nobody capable of replying in kind.

Between the second Test and the third at Adelaide, two Shield matches took place between Victoria and New South Wales. In the first of these played at Melbourne, Lindsay made 92. Moving on to Sydney, he was less successful with 14 and 7. As well as that, he pulled a muscle which kept him out of the Adelaide Test to be played over Christmas 1951.

There was a bad mix-up in recasting the Australian side as a result of Hassett's absence. As vice-captain, Arthur Morris assumed the captaincy. Sid Barnes had been named as a replacement for Lindsay, but was virtually barred 'for reasons other than cricketing ability'. Hassett, pulled muscle and all, was named twelfth man and local paceman, Geff Noblet, was included in the side. This left Morris with five bowlers and five batsmen if Miller is classed only as a batsman. Morris was, and still is, livid about this fatuity. Worse was to follow for Arthur, as we'll see.

Since the Sydney Test, the West Indies had suffered defeats against South Australia and Western Australia in this crazy tour arrangement, losses which were scarcely propitious omens as lead-ups to an important Test match.

Poor Arthur Morris! Winning the toss at the Adelaide Oval is usually like winning the State Lottery for cricket captains, but on this occasion, Arthur was deceived. Moisture below the surface started to rise, deliveries would skip or kick without rhyme or reason, and Australia was out for 82. Frank Worrell, a medium-paced left-hand bowler with not much claim to Test match success, took 6–38 in this collapse. The West

## JOHN GODDARD'S WEST INDIANS — 1951-52

Indies, with 105, did little better, finding Bill Johnston almost unplayable on the drying pitch. Weekes top-scored with 26. Batting again, Australia struck trouble with Valentine and could muster only 255 — Valentine 6–102. The West Indies knocked off the 233 runs needed, Gomez and Christiani being in at the finish with 46 and 42. The West Indies won by 6 wickets; Lindsay Hassett was delighted at not having participated in the defeat while Arthur Morris felt, with justification, that he'd been conned and left holding the messy baby. The visitors were jubilant.

The fourth Test proved to be an exciting engagement. The Australian selectors were experiencing difficulty in settling on an opening partner for Morris, who was not having a great season. Having tried Burke and Archer, they turned back to Jack Moroney who, at his last appearance, registered a 'pair' in the first Test against England the previous season. Hassett returned to restore the side's balance and Noblet was omitted. The West Indies were also having difficulty in finalising the opening positions, Rae and Marshall having had little success. For this match Rickards was tried.

The West Indies won the toss and, after a bad start, Worrell scored a very fine century — the first scored by the Windies on the tour. He batted for four hours and hit 7 fours. Miller took 5–60 but the Australian fielding was indifferent. The total of 272 proved to be just sufficient.

When Australia batted, both openers fell cheaply and Hassett was run out for 15 when moving along in good style. Harvey's 83 was the only innings of note and the side was all out for 216, the medium pacer, Trim, having the surprising figures of 5–34. Batting again, the Windies performed poorly, four of the last five batsmen registering nil, with two run-outs thrown in. This left the home team 260 to win. Thanks mainly to Hassett they achieved this, but if the two tail-enders, Johnston and Ring, hadn't held out in a stand of 38 for the last wicket, the West Indies would have equalised the series. Lindsay's innings was played out in his 'sheet anchor' role. His batting was described as 'stubborn', relieved occasionally by a boundary when he judged the ball to be loose enough. His 102 took 323 minutes and critics might well have reflected that without the captain's knock, Australia may have suffered a heavy defeat. The spin twins took 8 of the 9 wickets that fell — 5 to Valentine, 3 to Ramadhin.

The West Indies had a successful short tour of Tasmania, winning both matches comfortably. Returning to Melbourne, they played a return match against Victoria. This proved an exciting match, Lindsay

Hassett making a challenging second innings declaration which left the visitors 210 minutes to score 297. Walcott and Christiani both scored centuries in the run chase and the Windies won by 4 wickets. Hassett had a satisfactory double with 56 and 43.

In the final Test, played at Sydney, the Australian selectors discarded both openers, elevating two Victorians, Colin McDonald and George Thoms. The match was marred by persistent bumpers from Miller and Lindwall. Batting first, Australia was dismissed for 116, Hassett falling to Gomez for 2. Gomez was moving the ball about in unpredictable fashion on a very hot and humid late January day, and finished with 7–55. The West Indies could muster only 78 in reply. Nineteen wickets fell on this day. The second innings produced better results for Australia's batsmen, Hassett and Miller laying the foundation for a respectable score. Lindsay was caught at slip off Valentine after a solid 64 and Miller and Hole made good contributions. The total of 377 left the West Indies to score 417 runs to win in the fourth innings. They could muster only 213, which included a fine century by Stollmeyer. Australia won by 202 runs to wrap up the series 4-1.

Hassett's Test-match performance was more than satisfactory. His contributions as captain and batsman were vital to the team's success, while his footwork and concentration were remarkable. Batting eight times with 1 not out, he totalled 402 runs at an average of 57.4. He'd led his side capably and relations between the teams were good, despite the excessive use of the bumper. Hassett probably took the view that a law of cricket was available to deal with intimidatory bowling, but the umpires, in the main, appeared reluctant to use it.

With the departure of the West Indians, the season was now drawing to its close. The visitors had learnt the hard way that Lindwall and Miller were vastly different from Bedser and Bailey and that quick-footed Australian batsmen bore little resemblance to the England crease-huggers whom their spinners had immobilised. The lessons were well learnt and were amply revenged in due course. From Australia's point of view, the downward trend noticeable in 1950–51 was more obvious and the ageing half of the team could scarcely be expected to reverse it. Younger replacements of the top class were not all that obvious.

Lindsay wound up the season in rousing fashion with 229 out of 537 against South Australia in Melbourne. In this innings he was scarcely recognisable as the Test match Hassett. The strokes of yesteryear flowed freely from his bat to the delight of his colleagues and the Melbourne crowds. At the age of 38 he'd totalled 855 runs from 15 innings, once not out, average 61.07 with 3 centuries. Overall, few would argue that there were not a couple more seasons to enjoy before he joined his old mates, Stan and Bill, in retirement. One would involve a series against the South Africans, of whom Lindsay had the happiest memories, and, last of all perhaps, 'the Poms' in England.

# CHAPTER 14
# THE SPRINGBOKS SURPRISE AUSTRALIA — 1952–53

The decision by the South African authorities to seek the Australian Board of Control's agreement to receiving a touring party in the 1952–53 season was greeted with lukewarm enthusiasm on both sides of the Indian Ocean. South African critics, through the media, expressed the opinion that such a tour would be farcical and humiliating for South Africa. They dwelt at length on the heavy defeats suffered in 1949–50 despite the presence of Dudley Nourse, the Rowans and 'Tufty' Mann, all of whom had either hung up their boots or, in Mann's case, shuffled off this mortal coil. The Australian Board, smarting under the financial losses sustained during the West Indies tour the previous year, were unenthusiastic about greeting a team of virtual unknowns with the likelihood of incurring a further loss.

The ageing great South African batsman, Herbert Taylor, took a different view. He believed the young team had good prospects because of its youth and ability to field well. He thought that the absence of any 'star' players might work to the team's advantage, forcing them to pull together and not depend on the performances of one or two individuals. And how correct this proved to be! With Bradman gone, the Australians were still facing a similar problem, admittedly on a larger scale.

There were no enthusiastic newspaper headlines heralding the coming of this South African team. To soothe the financial anxiety of the Australian Board of Control, the South African controllers were prepared to underwrite any monetary loss incurred by the Australian authorities. It was unfortunate, too, that the tour coincided with an all-out set-to between the New South Wales Cricket Association and the Board arising from the retirement of Sir Donald Bradman from the Selection Committee and the election of Phil Ridings instead of Chappie Dwyer in his place. This meant that New South Wales, which provided a large proportion of the representative cricketers, was not represented on the Committee at all. The row blew over, more or less, despite occasional rumblings from the parties concerned. All in all, the

♦ THE SPRINGBOKS SURPRISE AUSTRALIA — 1951–52 ♦

South Africans arrived in Western Australia to find distrust and bitterness, not towards them, but within the 'cricket body politic', to coin a phrase. That they ignored or overcame this was to their great credit and, in the end, the tour was a most enjoyable and satisfactory one.

Those selected were:

| | |
|---|---|
| Cheetham | Captain/batsman |
| McGlew | Vice-captain/opening batsman |
| Funston | Batsman |
| Murray | All-rounder |
| Endean | Batsman and reserve wicket-keeper |
| Norton | Batsman |
| Innes | Batsman |
| McLean | Batsman |
| Waite | Opening batsman and wicket-keeper |
| Mansell | Spin bowler |
| Fuller | Fast-medium bowler |
| Watkins | All-rounder |
| Keith | Left-hand bowler |
| Melle | Fast bowler |
| Tayfield | Off-spinner |

Ken Viljoen, one-time Test batsman, was manager.

Lindsay Hassett, now in his fortieth year, got straight into things and played two Shield games before the first Test match scheduled to start in Brisbane in early December. Against South Australia he scored 1 and 91, and at home against New South Wales, 4 and 31. In the latter game, Sid Barnes registered a powerful 152 in a vain effort to persuade the Board (which had won the court case) to let bygones be bygones and select him for the Brisbane Test. Sid, a bit of a hard case but fairly harmless and, possibly, the best batsman in the country (barring Bradman) in the early postwar years, was destined never to play for Australia again.

The South Africans, probably owing to their country's geographical position, started the tour in the west and were given eight games in which to warm up before the Tests started. The West Indians had not been so lucky.

The visitors played a one-day game at Northam in Western Australia and four of their batsmen had useful practice in a drawn match. Against the West Australian state side in Perth, Jacky McGlew, in a remarkable exhibition of concentration, made 182 in eight hours and had to be run out in the end. Tayfield, with 5–98 off 48 overs, quickly demonstrated that his reputation as perhaps the world's best off spinner was not overstated. This match and the next against South Australia were both drawn. In the latter game, the locals led by 153 on the first innings and might well have won given the necessary time. Most of the South African batsmen were running into form and Tayfield again showed that he'd be quite a handful. Melbourne had had a wet spring and the MCG pitch was rather under-prepared. Lindsay Hassett had been involved in a car accident and was nursing a bad knee, so Doug Ring took over the captaincy in the state game against the Springboks.

The South Africans had elevated Jack Iverson to bogey-man status, but, in a low-scoring game, 'Big Jake' took only 3 wickets. He'd missed a season and did not appear to have the bite which had flummoxed the Englishmen a couple of years previously. What emerged from this low-scoring match was that the visitors were a first-class fielding team and that Tayfield would carry a heavy responsibility. The batting looked as though it might be more than adequate and McLean and Funston had delighted spectators with their, at times, risky stroke play.

In Sydney against a strong New South Wales side, the visitors met their first defeat. Endean showed good form with the bat and Tayfield, with 8 wickets for the match, was beginning to assume larger-than-life proportions. Off spinners generally have not fared exceptionally well in Australia, but Tayfield to date in 4 first-class matches, had captured 25 wickets. The state side won this match by 5 wickets, Barnes underlining his futile claim to a Test spot with 43 and 79 not out.

Moving further north, the Springboks had a 7-wicket win against New South Wales Country in Newcastle and drew a game in Bundaberg against Queensland Country. In the state game against Queensland, there was some heavy scoring, Don Tallon rolling back the years with some spectacular driving in making 133 and Russell Endean having an excellent double with 181 not out and 87. Tayfield bowled 50 overs to take 4–195 against several batsmen in a hurry on their own pitch — apart from Tallon, Colin McCool, the two Archers and 'Slasher' Mackay all got runs, Mackay in his own measured and idiosyncratic style.

For the Brisbane Test, Morris came back, replacing Thoms, and Johnson returned for Benaud, whose time had not yet arrived although he was named twelfth man. There was some resentment that Langley was selected ahead of Tallon, particularly after the local man's impressive century in the state game. But Tallon's wicket-keeping credentials had become a little tarnished although he still made it to England in mid-1953. Don Tallon, widely regarded by his contemporaries as the best of a distinguished lot of Australian wicket-keepers, had been unfortunately omitted from the 1938 side to England when Ben Barnett and Charlie Walker were chosen. Walker lost his life in the war and Barnett spent most of the war in a Japanese prisoner-of-war camp in Malaya and it would be churlish to criticise their 1938 selection. Tallon, however, was the best wicket-keeper in the country at the time. The name of S. G. Barnes in the side was noticeable for its absence in the coming Test match.

Hassett won the toss and batted. Both Morris and McDonald were out after a 55-run opening partnership and Hassett joined Harvey, who'd come in at number three. The two pushed the score along in a partnership of 155 in even time — Harvey was first out for 109 after a dazzling display picking up where he'd left off against the South Africans three years before. Lindsay Hassett, the anchorman in the partnership, was out shortly after, cleverly caught at the wicket by John Waite off the medium pacer Watkins for 55. In view of the collapse that followed, it was as well that Hassett had stuck around with his younger colleague. From 4–216 when Hassett left, the side crumbled to be all out for 280. Michael Melle, quickest of the bowlers, had the good figures of 6–71 from 20 overs, despite almost having been omitted because of indifferent form in the early games. The South African fielding in this innings was first class, quite as good as anything seen since the war. Oddly enough, Tayfield, the star bowler, had 0–59 — a temporary phenomenon.

The visitors failed to capitalise on the poor batting of the opposition and their own excellent out-cricket. Half a dozen of them got a start, but top-scorer was John Waite with 39. Ring took the bowling honours with 6–72 — flattering figures, but then, one can do no more than get the batsmen out and Ring did this admirably. Fielding and returns to the wicket-keeper were lamentable and Langley had a wretched time gathering the ball in wide at his feet or above his head. The partisan Brisbane crowd didn't spare him.

Australia's second innings was a fairly brittle affair, although Morris got some runs in a patchy display. Hassett was out hitting a full toss from Melle straight to McGlew at mid-wicket — he made 17. Neil Harvey rounded off his game with 52 and had to be run out. Hole and Lindwall got a few but the batting was ordinary. Tayfield had 4–116 off 33 overs and the innings closed at 277. This left South Africa with 337 runs to win. Funston and McGlew gave the locals a fright with some stubborn batting, adding 96 for the third wicket. Once they were separated, wickets fell fairly quickly, Lindwall, despite a stomach upset, bowling splendidly to take 5–60. The delivery that ended McLean's threatening innings was a beauty, just taking the bail. The Australian fielding was a marked improvement on the first-innings exhibition. South Africa could manage only 240 and Australia won by 96 runs. However, the South Africans had given a very good account of themselves and, although beaten, had brought their hosts back to the field with something of a shock. In the five years since 1948, there'd been a significant decline in Australian cricket and comparisons between the two sides, most of all their fielding, should have started the alarm bells ringing in the Australian hierarchy.

Lindsay did not play in the Sydney match between 'An Australian Eleven' and South Africa, and Phil Ridings, selector and South Australian captain, led the locals. Quite a number of young players were given a game and it was good to see Benaud, de Courcey and Carroll get some runs. The match was drawn.

The second Test match in Melbourne at Christmas gave the Australians the greatest jolt they'd received since Tests had resumed after the war. For Australia, Richie Benaud came in for Ian Johnson. The visitors left well alone. On this occasion, they got a good start by winning the toss. It availed them little. Miller and Lindwall were deadly in the humid conditions and 3 wickets fell for 27 before McLean and limpet-like McGlew added 36 to bring the score to a still-sad 4–63. Things didn't improve much and wickets fell fairly regularly until Tayfield and Murray added 51 for the ninth wicket. The side was all out for 227. It didn't seem many but eventually proved adequate.

The Australian innings was a triumph for Tayfield. He took 6–84 from 29 overs, including the caught-and-bowled prize wicket of Arthur Morris, with a catch that belongs to the legends of cricket. Morris jumped to drive Tayfield and Cheetham, at silly point, got his fingers to it causing it to fly towards mid-off. Recovering from his follow-through, Tayfield turned quickly, dived, got his right hand under the ball before it hit the grass and held onto it. For a change, Neil Harvey went cheaply and Hassett fell to Mansell bowling his innocent-looking leg breaks. Miller batted aggressively for 52, but the batting was again showing the brittleness that had marked recent innings. The visitors fielded impressively and Australia finished just 16 runs ahead at 243.

In the second innings, Endean, batting at number three, was unconquered at the end with 162 and, with a total of 388, Australia was looking down the barrel, needing 346 to win in a fourth innings against a bowler well able to exploit any advantage resting in the pitch. Lindsay, at number four, made 21 in correct and sedate fashion, adding 42 for the third wicket with Neil Harvey who got partly back into the run-getting groove with a bright 60. Lindsay in this innings was looking set for a good score, but fell leg before to a sharp off break from Tayfield. Benaud (45) and Ring (53) added 61 for the ninth wicket, but Tayfield got them both in the end. Australia was dismissed for 290, Hugh Tayfield's 7–81 from 37 overs giving him a memorable 13 wickets for the match. The only off spinner to challenge Tayfield in Australia would be Jim Laker, who took 11 wickets in three Tests in 1958–59, and opinions vary as to who was the better bowler.

As far as Australia was concerned, this was a loss of some meaning and there were cries all around for some new blood. But who? Hassett, Harvey, Morris and Miller could hardly be relegated, Benaud and Hole were comparative newcomers and scarcely deserved to be dropped. It would have required a brave selection committee to drop Lindwall and Bill Johnston, neither of whom was exactly decrepit. Ring had done well at times with both bat and ball. From being a team of world-beaters, the Australians had to accept that they'd come back to the field and were now just a good team among other good teams who were improving while the Australians had not yet bottomed. In assessing Lindsay Hassett's stewardship, this has to be borne in mind. Two other things stuck out — one, our fielding, once our pride, was now markedly inferior to that of the South Africans, whereas in 1948 it had provoked wonderment among the English; two, we had not adjusted to the absence of Bradman. Indeed how could we? How could anyone? For 20 years he had been the equivalent of two top-class batsmen. The problems, though not insoluble, took Australia until around 1958 to solve.

The South Africans drew the game against New South Wales and had a first-innings win against New South Wales Country before returning to Sydney for the third Test, where the euphoria of the Melbourne victory was rudely shattered. The state game was marked by an extraordinary performance by seventeen-year-old Ian Craig who made 213 not out in the team's total of 416. I saw much of this innings and Craig batted with the aplomb of a veteran, handling all bowlers in a confident fashion. Tayfield was playing in the game and finished with 1–114 from 32 overs. Young Craig's subsequent career did not unfold in the way that many of the scribes predicted. He was dogged by ill health, had a miserable tour of England in 1953 but recovered in part on his second tour in 1956, and was named captain of an untried side that visited South Africa in 1957–58. It was much to his credit that this team of learners completed the South African tour undefeated. It was after that tour that a severe dose of hepatitis, together with work responsibilities, ended his Test career. A charming man, he was well regarded by those who played with him, Lindsay Hassett in particular.

No changes occurred in either team for the Test match. South Africa was pleased to win the toss, but underrated the liveliness of the Sydney pitch, still the fastest in the country. Lindwall and Miller disposed of the Springboks for 173, Funston top-scoring with 56. Australia replied with 443, Lindsay came in at the fall of Morris's wicket and had made 2 in the 46 minutes before lunch. Immediately after lunch, he was out without adding to this, attempting a big hit off medium pacer Murray, miscuing and giving Funston an easy catch at mid-on. Enter the scourge of the Springboks, Neil Harvey. In a faultless and fiery display, he made 190 in six hours with 21 fours. Miller made 55 and Ring 58 in a total of 443. Tayfield had the best figures with 3–94 from 38 overs.

In South Africa's second innings, McLean gave further evidence of his class with a fine 65 and the reliable Endean made 71. Lindwall and Miller were again troublesome on the lively pitch and Lindwall finished with 8 wickets for the match. South Africa made 232, which left the side 38 runs short of Australia's total. The visitors lost by an innings. There was criticism of the number of bumpers bowled by Lindwall and Miller.

The South Africans had a heartening tour of Tasmania, winning both games by an innings. Funston scored an unbeaten 109 in the Hobart game and McGlew made a painstaking 110, also unbeaten, at Launceston.

The South Africans struck a bad patch with injuries at about this time, the most serious being that to Tayfield who'd suffered a broken thumb. This improved sufficiently for the star bowler to play in the Adelaide Test, but he was severely handicapped. Despite this, he captured 4–142 from 44 overs in Australia's first innings, which totalled 530. Colin McDonald, batting in extreme heat, played a fine opening batsman's innings of 153. Morris had gone for 1 and then Hassett and McDonald added 275 for the second wicket. Hassett's innings was a mixture of restraint, later blossoming into the recognisable stroke-playing style of earlier days. To illustrate the Jekyll and Hyde nature of this innings of 163, Hassett had contributed only 73 in 206 minutes before rain washed out play on the first day. The report of the game says that Lindsay 'was painstaking up to his century, which took 270 minutes. After his century, he was the essence of elegance.' In all, he batted 359 minutes for his 163, the last 50 coming up in 87 minutes. He was finally out caught at mid-off from a 'tired man's shot'.

The South Africans had ample time to regret that Hassett had been dropped at second slip by Watkins when 4. Much later, when 132, he should have been caught at deep mid-on by Endean. This was a routine catch and Endean was the last man one would have expected to grass it. The partnership of 275 with McDonald broke the previous record of 274 held by Woodfull and Bradman in the second innings of the third Test against South Africa in Melbourne in January 1932. On that occasion, Woodfull made 161, Bradman 167. Harvey made only 84 in this innings, almost a failure for him against South Africa. He made up for it in the second innings, however. Lindsay incurred some criticism for not closing the innings late in the afternoon to give his bowlers an hour or so against the tired Springboks. However, Lindwall and Miller were unfit, Lindwall bowling only 13 overs and Miller 2 in the match. Perhaps Hassett felt it wise to insure his side against loss by scoring as many runs as possible. So they carried on to 530, Hole making a good 59 and the consistent tail-ender Ring making 28. The South Africans had blotted their fielding reputation by dropping simple catches, but this was a team of high morale and enthusiasm and they made the most of the rest day on Glenelg beach.

The Springboks put in a solid effort on days three and four, totalling 387, Funston, Waite, Endean and Watkins all contributing. Bill Johnston and Richie Benaud took 5 and 4 wickets respectively. With a lead of 143, the Australians pushed ahead, Arthur Morris playing his best innings for 77 while Neil Harvey attacked, displaying a bewildering number of strokes. Both were dismissed to marvellous catches by Endean, Morris at mid-wicket off Melle, Harvey low at cover. Harvey's innings was one of his best, which is saying a lot. The name of Neil Harvey should be engraved on the hearts of South African cricket and cricketers of the period.

Hassett closed at 3–233, not batting himself. This left the visitors 255 minutes to get 377 runs to win. Never did they look like achieving this difficult task and when time ran out they had lost 6–177 and were happy to finish with a draw. This had been a disappointing match for the South Africans, missed chances in the field, particularly that of Hassett, having contributed in large measure in putting them well on the back foot.

Although the match against Victoria, prior to the final Test to be played at the MCG, was drawn, it was noteworthy because of the effort of a young batsman, Headley Keith. He scored centuries in each innings. Another young player, Gerald Innes, also scored a century and he would have appreciated Lindsay Hassett's thoughtful and generous action when he was 99. At this point, the drinks appeared, but Hassett waved the carrier off — he did not want the young man's concentration broken by a drinks break at 99. Innes went on to score a notable century, a memorable event on one of the world's most famous cricket grounds. Hassett, fell for 7 in the match and the visitors ended with a draw much in their favour. The scores were South Africa 401 and 228, Victoria 260 and 0–21. Neil Harvey 'failed' with 69!

For the final Test, Miller and Lindwall, both of whom were carrying injuries, were replaced by Craig and Noblet, and Ron Archer came in for Hole. For the South Africans, Keith replaced McGlew, who was nursing a damaged finger, and Murray came in for Melle. Australia again won the toss and the start was delayed following an overnight downpour, but the pitch was easy and the weather pleasant. Morris and McDonald gave their team a start of 122 before McDonald was out for 41. Morris played well before being unluckily run out for 99, sacrificing his wicket for Harvey. The latter again savaged the Springboks' attack, first with Hassett then with Craig. Hassett was in his cautious mode until run out by a direct hit from Endean in the gully for 40. Harvey and Craig carried on, the former in devastating form, punishing all bowlers. At 205, he mishit a forcing leg-side stroke to extra cover to be caught by Cheetham off Fuller's bowling. He had batted for just under five hours. Craig made a good 53 in his first Test outing and the total climbed to 520 at about 5 p.m. on the second day.

Most of the South Africans made solid contributions in their reply, the reliable Waite making 64, Watkins 92 and McLean 81. Benaud and Ring took some heavy punishment, forcing Hassett to make frequent field changes to contain the flow of runs. McLean, batting at number six, flayed all the bowlers until he was unlucky at 81 to be given out leg

## THE SPRINGBOKS SURPRISE AUSTRALIA — 1951-52

before to a ball to which he appeared to get a faint edge. Cheetham and Mansell were then together in a lively partnership of 111 for the seventh wicket and the score mounted to 435 before the last wicket fell — a deficit of 85.

Not a bit discouraged, the visitors bowled Australia out for 209, Ian Craig top-scoring with 47. Lindsay made 30 in his innings, using his feet well to the spinners but not doing much when he got to the pitch of the ball. He was out pushing forward to Mansell and giving Endean a low catch close in at mid-on. After Benaud left for 30, the innings came to an end fairly quickly for 209. The Australian batting in this innings was, in many instances, very ordinary, with little effort being made to hit over the heads of the predominantly close-set field. However, 295 runs were needed if the visitors were to win, not an easy task on the final day. But the Springboks were more than equal to it and reached the goal with 6 wickets in hand. When the score reached 4–285, Lindsay Hassett took the ball and was smartly hit for 3 fours by McLean to win the match for South Africa.

This was a notable win despite the absence of Lindwall and Miller. The ground fielding and catching were outstanding and they played as a team, all keen, all giving 100 per cent plus and demonstrating how their performance had improved over the course of the tour — they had indeed matured.

As for Lindsay Hassett, he batted eight times for 346 and averaged 43.25. His batting generally gave spectators little to enthuse over despite its value to his team. Perhaps the car accident in which he'd been involved had had a bad effect. His captaincy and field placing were sound and thoughtful, and relations had been maintained at an excellent level, both in the team and with the visitors. This whole season was, in fact, one of Lindsay's less prolific ones — 779 runs at 38.95.

After a drawn game against South Australia and a win against Western Australia, the South Africans left for home, well satisfied with their achievements. Australian cricket lovers had enjoyed the visit very much.

# CHAPTER 15
# CRICKETING SWAN SONG — ENGLAND 1953

No sooner had the final Test match of the South African tour ended in mid-February than the Ashes tour of England in the northern summer of 1953 loomed up. This was to be a memorable summer for the British, apart from the fact that an Australian cricket team was due in April — indeed, it's fair to say that the coronation of Queen Elizabeth II was foremost in British minds. There was talk of a second 'Elizabethan age'. Winston Churchill, in his eightieth year, was Prime Minister and the young Queen, an appealing, decorative and industrious figure, carried the nation's and Commonwealth's hopes and aspirations.

So it was a good year to be in England and Lindsay Hassett, who would turn 40 late in the summer, was looking forward to the tour which would be his cricketing swan song. The family was now living at Hampton, a suburb south-east of the City of Melbourne and close to Port Phillip Bay. It is also adjacent to Sandringham, the site of the Sandringham Club which Lindsay Hassett occasionally visited. The girls were growing up — Margaret 10, Anna 4 — and Tess was as happy as a cricketing wife can be, in charge of two lively children, with the prospect of Lindsay's absence for the coming six months.

It was as certain as most things in life that when the party for England was named, Lindsay Hassett's would head the list. He was the obvious choice on all counts — captaincy record, ability, experience and personality, as popular and respected as any sportsman with both colleagues and opponents. And so it turned out. Those selected were:

| | |
|---|---|
| Hassett | Captain |
| Morris | Vice-captain/batsman |
| Archer R G | All-rounder |
| Benaud | All-rounder |
| Craig | Batsman |
| Davidson | All-rounder |
| de Courcy | Batsman |
| Harvey | Batsman |
| Hole | Batsman |

| | |
|---|---|
| Hill | Bowler |
| Johnston | Bowler |
| Langley | Wicket-keeper |
| Tallon | Wicket-keeper |
| Lindwall | Bowler |
| McDonald | Batsman |
| Miller | All-rounder |
| Ring | Bowler |

There were seven players from New South Wales, five from Victoria, two from South Australia and two from Queensland. Mr George Davies was appointed manager.

The side boasted only two recognised opening batsmen — Morris and McDonald. This suggested that Hassett would be required to fill in from time to time. Hill was really the only surprise selection. He was a right-hand 'quickish' slow bowler, who pushed the ball through and relied on top spin rather than leg spin. He apparently elbowed Ian Johnson out of the side. Johnson was to be recalled for the 1954–55 Tests and led the side to the West Indies in 1955 and England in 1956. Len Hutton would have been pleased at Johnson's omission. Lindwall (31), Miller (33) and Johnston (31) were the pace trio and, from the England point of view, it appeared that these redoubtable bowlers would probably not be the force they'd been in 1948. Australia had resorted to youth in the selection of Ron Archer, aged nineteen, Benaud, 22, Davidson, 23, Craig, seventeen, and de Courcy, 26 years of age. Of these, Benaud, Archer and Craig had been blooded against the Springboks, but de Courcy and Davidson were newcomers. Hole was persevered with because of his obvious potential, a potential never fully realised. It seemed that the captain would need to nurse these young men along. Lindsay certainly did this and all have expressed appreciation of his interest in them. Alan Davidson, in particular, was virtually unknown to Lindsay, but early in the tour, Alan scored 60 at number eight batting against Leicestershire, who boasted two top-class Australian bowling imports in Jack Walsh and Vic Jackson. Lindsay, watching this, complimented Alan, adding that he would give him a chance higher in the batting order. Thereafter, Alan Davidson came in at number six or seven.

The party sailed on the *SS Orcades* on 22 March 1953 and played the usual warm-up games in Tasmania and Western Australia and, en route, stopped briefly in Colombo. Critics and cricketers in England, while freely acknowledging that any Australian side would prove hard to beat, were understandably cheered by the knowledge that, for the first time since 1926, they would not have to contend with Bradman on English soil, for which he'd shown a marked affinity. The absence of Barnes, too, was a plus for the Englishmen, Sidney George having intimated to the Board that they knew what they could do with their 'Ashes' tour. Alec Bedser was especially pleased that 'The Artful Dodger' would be only there as a reporter. Bedser considered Barnes a most difficult batsman to dislodge.

Lindsay Hassett enjoyed the voyage. He had the ability to mix with the younger members of the team, a couple of whom were babies when he made his first trip in 1938. The fancy dress ball provided an ideal opportunity for Hassett's inventiveness. The team trooped into the dining room, all dressed in the flowing robes of 'Sons of the Desert', ignored their normal seats and squatted cross-legged on the floor and served themselves from a communal pot thoughtfully provided by one of the stewards. Calling themselves 'Hassett's Private Army', the routine quickly dispelled any reserve of other passengers and a lively night was had by all. The team became very popular on board as a result of this and other off-the-cuff activities. Lindsay detailed Ray Lindwall to lead the team against the ship's officers, whom they beat at deck cricket.

The team was warmly greeted at Southampton by some MCC notables including H. S. Altham and R. W. V. Robins. At Waterloo Station, former England captains Douglas Jardine (much mellowed by the years), Gubby Allen and Freddy Brown were waiting. There were numerous former Australian cricketing greats in England to cover the tour for various media outlets — Barnes, Fingleton, Mailey and O'Reilly had come with the team. Bertie Oldfield and Don Bradman arrived a little later. The first official lunch of the tour was given by the British Sportsmen's Club at the Savoy, with 450 guests present. Sir Alan Herbert, Member of Parliament, essayist and humorist, had put together some verses which were printed on the menu. The first two verses were:

*Baby Bradman in her pouches,*
*Here's our favourite foe once more,*
*And the wounded lion crouches*
*With a most respectful roar.*

## CRICKETING SWAN SONG — ENGLAND 1953

*Welcome 'home' good Captain Hassett!*
*Rich in runs you'll give us pain:*
*But we have one ancient asset*
*English grass — and English rain!*

The 'Baby Bradman' referred to by Sir Alan was Ian Craig, whom some were anointing as the successor to the mighty Don — this was unfair to the young man as well as unlikely.

The Australians practised at the Lord's nets, where spring rain had rendered the pitches slow beyond the experience of the younger Australians. The social one-day match at East Molesey was won by the Australians, Lindsay loosening up with Arthur Morris in an aggressive partnership for the second wicket. Among the opposition was George Tribe, expatriate Victoria bowler of 'chinamen' who'd played for Australia in the 1946–47 Tests. Tribe took 6 wickets but they cost him 112 runs from 14 overs.

As had been the custom until recently, the tour proper began at Worcester. The weather was cold and the wind bracing, to put it charitably. Hassett made only 2, falling to the seamer Whitehead. Miller (220 not out), Hole (112) and Archer (108), repaired the losses sustained by the failure of early batsmen, taking Australia's total to 7–542 in reply to the county's 333. Australian bowling and fielding were below par, but this would soon be remedied with further acclimatisation and a bit of sunshine.

At Leicester, in fine weather, the Australians lifted a couple of gears, the fielding improved and Neil Harvey shone with the bat, making an unbeaten 202. In this innings, Alan Davidson, batting at number eight, impressed spectators and scribes as well as his captain, with a murderous attack comprising 11 fours and 1 six in compiling 63. Lindsay, batting at number three and looking ominous, was bowled for 18 by a leg cutter from Charlie Palmer, a delivery which delighted the bowler almost as much as it puzzled the batsman. Australia won by an innings and 154 runs, Doug Ring and Jack Hill shining with the ball.

Hassett missed several games due to inflammation of the tendons in his forearm. At Bradford against Yorkshire, the Australians won by an innings and 94. In the county's first innings, Lindwall's fifth delivery crashed through Hutton's bat, which seemed to have been impeded by a new pair of pads. Leonard departed amid a tangible silence from beyond the boundary, but redeemed himself in the follow-on with a solid 65, during which he had a good look at the bowling of Jack Hill. The latter took 4 wickets in the second innings after Benaud sent the County packing with 7–46 in the first innings.

The Australians did well on the green-top at the Oval, bundling Surrey out for 58 and 122, Ron Archer taking 11 wickets for the match. In the tourists' innings, Harvey top-scored with 66. Peter May, in whom many England hopes were placed, failed in both innings — to Lindwall for 0 and Archer for 1. In the first innings, Lindwall lifted himself into top gear in a successful effort to unsettle May before bowling him. May, now seen by good judges as England's finest postwar batsman, was picked for only two Tests in the series and had only moderate success. The best of May was not far distant, however.

Lindsay was still missing when the Australians travelled to lovely Fenners to play Cambridge University. Catching the students on a rain-affected pitch after making 383 themselves, they shot the University out for 130 and 147 for another innings win. Ring took 9 wickets in the match.

At Lord's, the MCC fielded a strong side, but there was little joy for either side in the match. Compton and Bailey got a few runs in the second innings but no Australian shone, although Lindwall again illustrated his underrated ability with the bat, making a lively 33 batting well down the order. Hassett was still resting his arm and was to miss the game following this one, against Oxford University, before returning for a warm-up match against the Minor Counties.

The MCC match was drawn but Oxford was beaten by an innings, Jim de Courcy finding his timing and footwork in an impressive century. For the University, a future notable, Michael Colin Cowdrey, appeared, but showed few signs of his quality with 3 and 5. Hill, Benaud and Ring were all turning in consistent performances with the ball.

At Stoke-on-Trent against the Minor Counties, Hassett played well for 32, despite a still-troublesome arm. Harvey made 109 on a wicket scarcely fit for play and certainly fraught with danger to the county's players short of match play and form, with Lindwall in full cry. He took 7–20 in the first innings but Hassett took pity on the opposition in the second innings, resting him completely.

There was some sterner opposition at Old Trafford, home of the Lancashire County Club, MacLaren and Tyldesley, and also famous for its consistently unpredictable and inclement weather. A violent storm had hit the ground with rain and wind during the Roses match against

♦ CRICKETING SWAN SONG — ENGLAND 1953 ♦

Yorkshire, followed by a fine day but more rain on the night of the Australian's arrival. This washed out the first day's play. Batting first on a suspect pitch, the Australians were less than comfortable, particularly against Brian Statham, a fast bowler of note whose career path over the following years was to be strewn with Australian wickets. Hassett made 34 before slow left-hander Malcolm Hilton made one stand up and fly off his bat to Ken Grieves at slip — Grieves was another promising Australian cricketer seduced by the Lancashire League and County. Hassett had enjoyed some useful practice after his lay-off. The team totalled 298 and dismissed 9 Lancastrians for 232 before time ran out in the shortened game.

Moving on to Nottinghamshire, there was disappointment that here, too, rain curtailed play and prevented a result. Hassett sent the county in and bowled them out for 208, with Hill having 5–62. Hassett played a delightful knock with all his strokes on display before falling to Goonesena, a leg spinner from Ceylon (now Sri Lanka). The team was pleased to see Hassett running into form because, for the success of the tour, it was essential that his contribution be a worthwhile one — particularly as the selected opener, McDonald, was having difficulty in coming to terms with English conditions. Time ran out with the Australians 6–290.

At Hove against Sussex, Hassett partnered McDonald in opening the innings. Ironically, it was Hassett who failed with 8 while McDonald, after a painfully scratchy start, put difficulties behind him and, to everyone's satisfaction, made 106 and had to be run out. Australia made 325 and bowled the county out for 218, Johnston and Hill sharing the wickets with 4 each. Hassett batted beautifully in the second innings, at times putting even Neil Harvey in the shade with his array of strokes. Both scored not-out centuries — Hassett 108, Harvey 137.

For the last match before the Test against Hampshire at Southampton, Lindsay decided to hand the captaincy over to Morris and stayed in London for net practice at Lord's. The reason appeared to be that he was anxious for as much practice as possible because he'd decided it would probably be necessary for him to open the innings in the Test match. One might think match practice would be preferable but, as things turned out, the Southampton wicket did not suit seam bowlers, spinners taking most of the Australian wickets. Harvey made another sparkling century and Morris was now batting in something like his best form. The Australians won by 158 runs.

For the Test at Nottingham, many of the Australians picked themselves — Hassett, Morris, Miller, Lindwall and Johnston. Tallon had shown good form and, of the young men, Benaud and Davidson had all-round qualities that could not be overlooked. The opening spot with Morris was something of a worry. McDonald, despite his recent century, could hardly be chosen. Lindsay was still reluctant to be cast in the opening role except as a last resort and the selectors, with some misgivings, turned to Graeme Hole. With his high back lift, Hole was scarcely the ideal opener, being more suited to conditions when the ball had lost its shine and there were a few runs on the scoreboard. However, Hole got the nod and had an unhappy experience. This left only another bowler, probably spin, to be chosen and the choice was Hill or Ring. The former had bowled consistently well and was selected.

For England the opening spot with Hutton was a concern — Washbrook and Edrich were deemed 'past it', a little prematurely as it later turned out. Don Kenyon of Worcestershire was finally chosen. Trueman, an automatic choice normally, was in the RAF on service and had played no first-class cricket and Lock had a damaged spinning finger. This prompted Wardle's inclusion. Tattersall was preferred to Laker, a curious choice, and Sheppard had no form to recommend him. The final Eleven was Hutton (captain), Compton (vice-captain), Kenyon, Simpson, Graveney, May, Evans, Bailey, Wardle, Tattersall and Bedser. This was a handy side, but, for various reasons, fell short of the optimum. If rain had not frustrated England on the last days, it would probably have been good enough to win.

Australia won the toss on a grey day with rain about, but elected to bat on a firm, dry wicket. Hole, unfortunately, was bowled in Bedser's first over. Enter Hassett who, with Morris, pushed the score along to 124 when Morris, at 67, fell leg before to his old antagonist who was swinging and cutting the ball in bewildering fashion. Lindsay's innings was, in the context of the match, vital. Slow he was, but equally at home forward or back, he cut and drove elegantly, a straight drive off Bedser to the boundary being especially memorable. His century took five hours, forty-five minutes, and was his ninth in Tests. Finally, Alec Bedser removed him with a splendid leg cutter that clipped the off stump. Lindsay made 115, Morris 67 and Miller 55. When Lindsay returned to the dressing room, he was asked what happened. After giving the matter some thought, he replied, 'Well, it looked like Alec's normal inswinger and I shaped to play it as such. Then, late in flight, it swung more and I followed it. After pitching, it changed course like a fast leg break and hit the top of the off stump. But it still shaved the edge of my bat as it passed. I reckon I can't be such a bad player after all.' Hole, Harvey, Tallon, Lindwall, Hill and Johnston all failed to score and all of England rejoiced when the last wicket fell at 249, Bedser having 7–55. The last six Australian wickets had fallen for 5 runs, and this on a good pitch. Don Bradman must have wept.

England's rejoicing was shortlived, Lindwall bowling like an avenging fury in poor light against some pretty ordinary batting. Hutton made 43, Graveney 22 and Wardle was 29 not out in the sad total of 144. Hassett set aggressive fields with four slips, gully and three leg slips, Compton made 0 but Hutton, the maestro, played with easy authority in a batting catastrophe. The innings closed just before lunch on the third day.

Bedser and Tattersall destroyed the Australian second innings, to the discomfiture of the Australian Prime Minister who was a spectator, the only bright spot being the batting of Arthur Morris who made 60 and was not dismissed by Bedser. Tattersall had that honour. Hassett received a spiteful delivery from Surrey's pride, which caught the bat's shoulder and dollied to Hutton at short leg. He'd made 5. Nobody else did anything and the innings closed for a lamentable 123, Bedser 7–44 to finish with 14–99 for the match. During this innings, 'Deafy' Tallon misconstrued a Hassett instruction 'to give the light a go' as 'give it a go', meaning 'attack the bowling'. Tallon passed this message on to Davidson and the pair laid about them briefly for 15 and 12 respectively — probably little harm was done by the error. This left England 228 runs in arrears with one day plus an hour to play. Rain on the Sunday night prevented any play until late in the afternoon on Monday, leaving only about two hours for play. The match sadly petered out, Hutton and Simpson having some useful batting practice against an Australian attack content with containment. Hutton was 60 and Simpson 28 at the close. Arthur Morris had a couple of overs at the finish. The match was drawn, but England may well have won had the weather behaved. Bedser and Hassett were the outstanding performers.

The Australians moved further north to Chesterfield, home of the Derbyshire County Club. The county boasted a top-class seam bowler in Cliff Gladwin, who played in only a handful of Tests but sent 1,653 batsmen packing in his first-class career. He got Lindsay Hassett twice for 5 and 0. The match was again rain affected, but the home team had the distinction of being the first to dismiss the Australians twice. Colin

McDonald had a good double with 28 and 51 and Graeme Hole top-scored for the match with a second innings 73.

The return match against Yorkshire was played at Bramall Lane, Sheffield, where many Roses matches have been graced by the pen of Neville Cardus. When the Yorks and Lancastrians played, Cardus said that after the captains tossed, no word passed on or off the field between the teams, except to appeal, which they did loudly and repeatedly. It was a little more civilised on the occasion of the 'Aussies' match. Hassett and Morris both missed the game and Miller assumed the captaincy. Putting the county in to bat, he suffered the indignity of seeing the locals amass the highest ever total recorded by the county against Australia. Hutton made a studious 67, analysing all bowlers with scholarly care, and Bill Sutcliffe, son of the great Herbert, made 57. For the visitors, Miller made 86, six chances being dropped in an untidy display both by batsman and fieldsmen, and the Australians, with 323, trailed the county by 54. Time prevented a decision and Yorkshire's second innings was of academic interest only. Three wickets fell for 220 with the maestro, Hutton, making a polished 84. If Lindsay Hassett had witnessed any of this match, the reports suggest that he may not have been overly impressed by some of his team's cricket.

For the Lord's Test, Ring replaced Hill and Langley came in for Tallon, who'd been prone to error in the Yorkshire match. England omitted May and brought in the solid Willie Watson from Yorkshire, replacing Simpson. Freddy Brown was again called to the colours and, with three bowlers plus all-rounders Bailey and Brown, the side seemed a little overweight in the bowling department. Brian Statham was to get his chance instead of Tattersall so that Wardle would be in sole command of the spinning side of things unless Brown reverted to his old style of wrist spin.

Although this match was drawn, it had all the excitement needed. There were fine centuries by Hassett and Hutton, and an extraordinary rearguard action by Watson (109) and Bailey (71) that denied Australia a victory.

After winning the toss, Hassett opened the innings with Morris, Hole being dropped to the more suitable number-five spot. The first wicket partnership of 65 got the side off to a good start, which Harvey built on, with what was for him, a moderately struck 59. Lower down, Alan Davidson justified his captain's confidence with a hard-hitting 76 at number seven. Hassett's innings of 104 proved the cornerstone on which the total of 346 was eventually built; despite some luck, he was in control. His innings occupied 291 minutes taken from 251 balls received and he was seventh out at 291. Bedser took 5–105 and runs were hard to come by from any bowler.

England began shortly after lunch on the second day and Hutton (145), Graveney (78) and Compton (57) all scored freely. By lunch on the third day England had lost 2–275, but when Hutton fell to Johnston, wickets tumbled quickly and hopes of a very big lead had to be modified. Only Brown (22) and Wardle (23) resisted the fierce bowling of the Australian speed men. Hutton's fine innings lasted 338 minutes and when he'd reached 123, he'd recorded his 2,000th run against Australia. At 372, England had the modest lead of 26.

Hassett went cheaply in the second innings, but the decision appeared doubtful. Evans, catching the ball from Statham down the leg side was in no doubt as he threw the ball up in triumph and Lindsay accepted the decision without demur. He'd made 5. Morris (89) and Miller (109) delighted the crowd in a stand of 165. Graeme Hole made 47 and Lindwall batted in his usual aggressive style for 50, being especially severe on Wardle. The last wicket fell at 368, which left England 343 to win. The start was disastrous — Hutton 5, Kenyon 2, Graveney 2, the three top-order batsmen out for 12. Watson and Compton stopped the rot briefly, but, at 4–73, and only all-rounders and bowlers to come, all seemed lost from the English point of view. Trevor Bailey had other ideas. This sort of situation was right up Bailey's alley. He and Watson were in stark contrast in their respective demeanours. Watson said nothing, but Bailey chatted brightly to the close-in fieldsmen as he gradually pressed them into the ground. From before lunch, they batted down the long afternoon, gathering confidence as they went and adding 163 for the fifth wicket. Watson went first, Bailey 10 runs later at 246, whereupon Brown (28) and Evans (11) saw their side home to a draw. It was indeed a famous rearguard action with tension on the field and among the spectators and scribes. Don Bradman, whose nerves have always been of the cast-iron variety, commented at the end that he wouldn't be able to stand the strain of any future Test of this type.

Moving on to Bristol, the Australians put the Gloucestershire side through the mincer by 9 wickets. The shade of 'W. G.' hovers over the Gloucester ground and thoughts of the great Walter Hammond frequently find utterance in the voices of cricket enthusiasts, for

Hammond had claims to be 'the perfect cricketer'. He was a man of imposing physique, a majestic batsman in the line of Hobbs and MacLaren, a bowler whom many thought might have rivalled Maurice Tate had he so desired, a slip fieldsman second-to-none among Englishmen and a person respected by his colleagues despite the reserve which some have mentioned. To find an Australian counterpart, one would not go past Stan McCabe, Victor Trumper or Keith Miller.

Lindsay Hassett played but his contribution was limited to his well-honed captaincy skills, for he made only 1, falling to off spinner Mortimore. Harvey adorned the occasion with 24 fours in an innings of lustre such as few past or present have possessed. He and de Courcy, whose on-side play was worth the gate money to see, added 160 for the seventh wicket. For the county, Tom Graveney, who'd have seen something of Hammond in his later years, played stylishly for 52, and in the county's second innings, George Emmett, who'd taken Hutton's place in the 1948 Old Trafford Test, surprised the Australians with a polished century. The Australians won by 9 wickets, Australia 9–402 and 1–33, Gloucester 137 and 297.

Morris led the side against Northamptonshire, who were undefeated to this point in the County Championship. The county boasted a new fast bowler, Frank Tyson, who was to spell much woe for Australia eighteen months later. Running from somewhere close to the sightboard (if there'd been one), he speared two or three lightning-fast deliveries into Morris's thigh, blows which invoked some unavoidable rubbing and stretching by Arthur, much to Freddy Brown's delight — he was fielding close in on the leg side. 'How do you like it, son?' he chortled. Arthur had the last word though. He went on to make 80 after McDonald departed for 4 and Hole for 0 after brief but decisive encounters with Tyson, whose speed was totally unfamiliar to them. Harvey scored another hundred and Tribe took 5–97 for Northants. The county was bowled out for 141 and 120 in reply to Australia's 323, the tourists winning by an innings and 62 runs.

For the Old Trafford Test, England recalled Edrich for Kenyon, Simpson for Brown and Laker for Tattersall. Trueman was chosen in the twelve, but, with rain about, he was relegated to the twelfth-man spot. For Australia, Bill Johnston's knee was again troublesome and he was omitted. De Courcy came in for Benaud and Archer for Ring so that the attack comprised Lindwall, Davidson, Archer, Hill and Miller when required. Rain prevented any play on the fourth day, eliminating any hope of a decision and resulting in some questionable elements of farce in the last day's play.

Hassett won the toss for the third time, a toss that Hutton may well have been happy enough to lose — Lindsay opened with Morris and saw Morris 1 and Miller 17 clean bowled by Bedser. Lindsay was out for 26 with no addition to the score, which stood at an unhealthy 3–48. He'd played well for his 26, with some good strokes against the very testing opening spells of Bedser and Bailey. The latter bowled him with a sharp off cutter against which Lindsay did not offer a shot. With the score at 3–48 and Harvey and Hole in occupation, disaster almost followed when Harvey edged Bailey and Evans, moving across towards slip, dropped a catch that he'd have normally pouched with his eyes shut. The two young men then set about them and, with luck on their side, the score rose to 221. Intermittent showers and a greasy ball did not help the England bowlers, nor did Laker's absence with a pulled thigh muscle. He was able to resume on the second day. De Courcy made a good 41, but the tail failed to wag after Harvey was out at 256 and the innings closed at 318. The mighty Bedser once again took the bowling honours with 5–115 from 42 overs.

When England batted soon after lunch, Hutton saw Edrich and Graveney depart in quick time, but then, with Compton, a good partnership developed. Edrich had fallen to Hill, whom he'd not faced before, following an inspired bowling change by Hassett, bringing on the Victorian spinner very early in the innings. Edrich was out playing the English half-cock shot, the leg spinner finding the edge for a comfortable catch to Hole at slip. Hill tested Hutton to the full early in his innings. Hassett at forward short leg had a bit of fun with the crowd, missing a bumpball from Compton's bat and bringing his cap into play when Miller tossed the ball back to him, much to the crowd's enjoyment — they remembered the policeman's helmet incident five years previously at the same ground. Hutton was leg before to Lindwall for 66 and Compton fell at the same score, so it was 4–126 when rain intervened and continued throughout Monday.

The weather was so wretched that many expressed the hope that it might terminate the dismal proceedings altogether. It didn't and, on the last day, England had to reach 169 to avoid the follow-on. Despite some early loss of wickets, the tenacious Bailey and mercurial Evans put the issue beyond doubt and, with the tail, brought the total to 276. With no likelihood of a decision, Hassett tossed the ball to Morris when Bedser came in and invited Morris to get a little of his own back. The first ball Arthur Morris bowled to his 'enemy' was a 'chinaman' which bowled Alec Bedser and ended the England innings. The Australians allowed Morris, smiling cherubically, to lead them in. 'I never knew it was so easy,' said Arthur.

An hour remained for Australia to bat and lose 8 wickets for 35; Hassett caught Bailey, bowled Bedser for 8. Hutton still appeared to be taking matters seriously but the Australians regarded the whole 'innings' in a lighthearted manner. The bowlers' averages profited by the farce. The match ended in a draw.

Middlesex, the London metropolitan county comprising areas north of the Thames, were at this time pushing towards the County Championship and were Australia's next opponents. The match was, as usual, played at Lord's and the Eleven that took the field appeared strong on paper with names such as John Robertson, Bill Edrich, Denis Compton, Fred Titmus and Jack Young appearing on the score card. As things turned out, rain on the first day restricted play to 85 minutes. Hassett, continuing the Australian innings until all were out when he might have closed and pressed for a win, made the county's second innings of fairly academic interest. Hassett had the excuse that, with two Tests still to be played, it was important that all his players obtain batting practice. This sort of situation usually generates some resentment among spectators and its legitimacy is arguable if you feel that any game should be played with the object of winning. The circumstances still exist 40 years on and resolution is no nearer.

After bowling Middlesex out for 150, Hassett opened with McDonald and, after scoring a brisk 24, was out miscuing a drive from fast bowler Moss on the slow wicket and seeing his leg stump disappear. All the other recognised batsmen, except the unfortunate Ian Craig, got good practice, de Courcy top-scoring with 74. The innings closed at 416 around 4 p.m. on the last day and the county played out time, 4 wickets falling for 116, Hassett bowling a maiden over just before the end of proceedings.

The next Test was at Leeds, where the Headingley ground is much beloved of Australian cricketers — Don Bradman in particular. His record at Headingley shows 5 innings, 1 not out, 930 runs with an average of 232.5. The man's deeds make fiction seem commonplace.

For England, Lock, now fit, came in for Wardle, and Statham was in the twelve instead of Trueman, but became twelfth man. The Australian

## CRICKETING SWAN SONG — ENGLAND 1953

side was unchanged except that Benaud came back for Hill. Johnston was still unfit and his absence from the visitors' attack was of considerable importance. The match ended in rousing fashion with the Australians making a determined attempt to knock off the 177 runs needed for victory in just under two hours. They did not succeed, but the attempt made them a host of friends. England, in the last 45 minutes, was obliged to resort to bowling wide of leg stump — the architect of the plan, Hutton, the executor, Bailey. The tactics left a nasty aftertaste, but it was stated in the press that Warwick Armstrong had adopted something similar a generation before.

Whether or not this is so, in the Bailey/Hutton tactic, the bowler compounded his negative bowling by taking an unacceptable time to get through his 6-over spell. Surviving Australian players maintain that Bailey would follow through far up the wicket towards the batsman to receive or retrieve the ball. This lengthened the time span per over to about ten minutes. His 6 overs cost 9 runs and he obtained Hole's wicket. The umpires, Chester and Lee, made no effort to intervene in something that, if not against the laws of cricket, was certainly not in tune with the spirit of the game. If Armstrong did something similar the comment still applies — two wrongs do not make a right. A comparison of the attitudes of the sides engaged shows that, in the match, Australia made 413 runs in 407 minutes at the crease, England 442 runs in 972 minutes.

The pitch was green when play started and looked unappetising for batsmen when facing the pace of Lindwall, Miller, Davidson and Archer. For his part, Hassett would not have relished having Bedser to handle, plus Bailey. Accordingly Lindsay, on winning the toss, 'invited' England to bat. Hutton and Edrich were greeted by a mighty welcoming roar on Hutton's home patch, but when he departed second ball, yorked by Lindwall, a dreadful silence pervaded the ground. The Australians bowled well on this day, making full use of the grassy turf and the heavy atmosphere. England's other hero, Denis Compton, also fell for 0, caught at leg slip by Davidson off Lindwall. The England batting from here forward was funereal, Graveney alone seized with the realisation that some runs, as well as occupancy of the crease, are important in all forms of cricket, especially Tests. He was well caught by Benaud in the gully off Miller for 55. At the day's end after five hours, England had lost 7 wickets for 142 — a melancholy effort.

Next day, play began promptly and Evans gave Lindwall his 150th

Test wicket, lbw at 25. Simpson, returning after being injured the previous day, was given not out by umpire Chester when he appeared well short of his ground attempting a third run. Miller received Hassett's return and broke the wicket, and appeared very angry at Chester's decision. It mattered little, Simpson being caught at the wicket by Langley for 15. The innings closed shortly after at 167 made in six and a half hours. Lindwall took 5–54 in one of his many great performances — he'd bowled 35 overs with 10 maidens.

Hassett opened with Morris, the two taking the score to 27, both enjoying some luck as Bedser found the edges of both men's bats. Morris was out, Lock catching him at leg slip off the great bowler. Tony Lock was a first-class close-in fieldsman, specialising in the leg-slip position. Bedser had claimed Morris's wicket 17 times now, not so remarkable comsidering they were both openers. Lock now had his first encounter with the ball against the Australians, pushing deliveries through at a brisk pace and looking dangerous. Lock was a demonstrative appealer and quickly made his voice heard, accompanied by appropriate bodily contortions. The Australians thought his action suspect, but no English umpire called him. Later on, however, it seems Lock himself accepted the fact that his action was questionable and, to his credit, took steps to modify it. He continued to take plenty of wickets.

Harvey and Hassett, with fortune smiling on them, pushed the score up to 70 until Hassett, too, was caught by Lock, turning Bedser to leg. Miller failed but Hole and Harvey provided some attractive attacking cricket, carrying the score to 168 when Harvey was out for a patchy 71. Wickets fell regularly thereafter, but Ron Archer, batting at number nine, made a lively 31 and was not out when the innings closed at 266, a lead of 99. The magnificent Bedser took 6–95 and Bailey, with a damaged foot, 3–91.

Rain limited the third day's play to only one hour and forty-five minutes. Hutton and Edrich put on 57 for the first wicket, whereupon Hutton was caught at the wicket for 25 and Graveney quickly followed, bowled by Lindwall for 3. Edrich, a brave batsman, and his county teammate Compton, added 77 for the third wicket when Edrich, trying to drive Lindwall, got a thick edge which flew to de Courcy in the gully.

Bailey (38) and Laker (48) hung about long enough, it seemed, for England to be out of danger when the innings closed at 275. In the event, it proved just enough thanks to Trevor Bailey's delaying tactics with the ball, conceived by Hutton and disregarded by the umpires. I'm

◆ CRICKETING SWAN SONG — ENGLAND 1953 ◆

not aware whether Trevor Bailey has expressed regret for his behaviour that day, 28 July 1953, but I would regard it as unlikely. Peter May, now sadly no longer with us, was embarrassed by the tactics and frequently brought the matter up in a regretful way with Arthur Morris when they met in the years that followed. For the record, in the second innings, Hassett was out for 4, playing Lock on to the stumps.

So the Test drew to a close with a draw, Australia just 30 runs short of a win, with 6 wickets in hand. Lindsay Hassett, to his great credit, made no song and dance about the last day's incidents, nor did his vice-captain. The latter, Arthur Morris, is not a man to harbour grudges, although his private thoughts on the matter would be interesting.

The Australians arrived sleepless and tired for the return match at The Oval against Surrey. Hassett lost the toss but was heartened by the return of Bill Johnston, who turned in a good performance with 4–51. Rain restricted play on the first day with Fletcher and May well set. However, on the second morning, a refreshed Lindwall let himself go and, with Bill Johnston, brought the proceedings to a quick end at 8–209 when Surridge closed the innings. There followed some excellent batting against bowling which, without the resting Alec Bedser, was of only average quality. Morris and Hassett added 51 and then Hassett, with an incandescent Harvey, put on 117 for the third wicket in 70 minutes. Lindsay fell at 67 lofting a drive to mid-off where he was caught by Peter May off the bowling of Peter Loader. Harvey went on to 113, his ninth century of the tour which put him in touch with Bradman's thirteen in 1938. Ian Craig was run out when 15 and batting beautifully, and soon afterwards the rain pelted down. The match was drawn.

Lindsay did not play at Swansea against Glamorgan. The match was distinguished by some fine bowling by Johnston, 6–63, in the first innings and a glorious display by Harvey who made 180 — including a century — before lunch. There were 28 fours and 3 sixes in the innings. The county staved off defeat with 201 and 7–188 against Australia's 386.

At Birmingham against Warwickshire, Lindsay came in for some hostile barracking, batting for 165 minutes to make 21 to save a possible embarrassing defeat. The county captain, Dollery, closed his second innings to give Australia 170 minutes to score 166 runs for victory. The wicket was taking some spin and the county had the talents of Eric Hollies to exploit it. Hassett took the view that the task was impossible against a bowler of this quality and made an early decision to save the game rather than win or lose it. Had Australia lost, Lindsay would have been the first Australian captain to preside over his side's defeat by a county team. Whatever the rights or wrongs of it, opinions divided roughly between Englishmen who deplored the tactics and Australians who defended it. The county had led Australia by 89 on the first innings. In Australia's first innings, Lindsay top-scored with 60 in the side's 181, Hollies capturing 5–45 on a wicket already taking spin. The county closed its second innings at 3–76 and, despite criticism of his tactics, Lindsay's technique against the sharply spinning ball won praise from the critics. The match was drawn and the Australians left Birmingham for friendlier pastures.

At Manchester for the return match against the 'Red Rose' team, the Australians ended a series of draws with a 7-wicket win in a match marked by some of the most gracious weather they'd encountered. Morris was now in splendid form with 64 and 38, and Davidson displayed some spectacular driving in compiling 95 in less than three hours with 17 fours. Lindsay, who came in late, seemed to wish to cast care aside, but was quickly out — caught at the wicket in an ambitious attempt to cut Tattersall. Ring made 88 and the side totalled 372. Australian Ken Grieves again did well with 36 and 80, and the county, following on after totalling only 184 in the first innings, made 292 in the second. In both innings, the wickets were well shared among the Australian bowlers. The 106 required to win was reached with the loss of 3 wickets. Perhaps the most newsworthy detail was that Neil Harvey failed with 8, but was not out 9 in the second innings when the win had been achieved.

Lindsay gave the Essex match a miss and the visitors had a convincing innings win. De Courcy made 164 in an innings that entertained the spectators and made it difficult for the selectors to leave him out of the approaching Test match. His 164 was notched in 205 minutes with 18 fours and 4 sixes. Australia made 477 and then bowled the locals out for 129 and 136. Bailey made 11 and 9 and one imagines his dual dismissal gave general satisfaction among the Australians.

The fifth Test at Kennington Oval was to be extended to six days if required. The shadows of John Berry Hobbs (Sir Jack), Andy Sandham, Tom Richardson and others are almost tangible to those of an imaginative frame of mind. The ground itself is not particularly attractive, but has character chiefly attributable to the many great players who have graced it. It also usually provides a good batting wicket — Bill O'Reilly would have attested to that. Bill's analysis in the 1938 slaughter was 85–26–178–3, and he swore you could smell the fertiliser on the pitch as you walked through the pavilion gate. The 1953 pitch was nothing like that, albeit of benign appearance, and Lindsay was pleased to win the toss and bat on a humid August day. He opened with Morris and the pair put on 38 before Morris fell to Bedser, leg before for 16. Miller was leg before to Bailey for 1. Trueman added a new dimension to the England attack and had all batsmen playing a little late until they became accustomed to the extra pace.

Lindsay played very well, seeming to have that extra split second of time in which to play the ball. He and Harvey gained confidence taking the total on to 107, Hassett reaching 50 in 105 minutes. He was out to a diving catch by Evans from Bedser's bowling. Hooking at Trueman, Harvey mistimed the stroke and was well caught by Hutton running from square leg. At 4–107, the innings faltered badly until Lindwall and Davidson, with good attacking cricket, put on 47 for the eighth wicket when Davidson was out for 22. Lindwall carried on with Langley and lifted the total to 275, not as many as had been hoped for, but better than appeared likely at 7–160. Trueman had 4–86 and Bedser 3–88. Lindwall's 62 was the top score for Australia. Bill Johnston, with 9 not out, raised his tour average to 64 at this point.

Hutton and Edrich saw out an awkward few minutes until bad light ended the day's play with only 1 run on the board. Next morning, Lindwall had Edrich leg before to a full toss with the total 37. There followed some batting in the aristocratic mode by Hutton and May until, at 137, Bill Johnston defeated May with a slower ball. Compton was out of touch and fell to Lindwall for 16 and Graveney followed for 4. Hutton, to the surprise of everyone, was yorked by Johnston for a characteristic 82 and, at 5–170, the initiative passed to Australia. Evans and Bailey restored the position with a stand of 40 and, at stumps, England were 7–235 and honours were roughly even.

Lock went quickly next morning, but Bedser and Trueman helped Bailey (64) to a total of 306. Lindwall had 4–70 and the old hands doubted if England's lead of 31 would be of much significance. Nobody was prepared for the multiple disasters in store for Australia.

Arthur Morris recalls very well batting with Hassett in the second innings. He thought he was going along nicely with about 16 against his name, his partner about 7 or 8. Between overs, Lindsay called him to mid-pitch and, straight-faced as ever, enquired, 'When are you going to get a move on, Plod?' Morris says he was dumbfounded for a second, but then replied, 'Okay, Dasher. I'll do my best'. Whenever they corresponded in later years, it was 'Dear Plod' and 'Dear Dasher'. 'Dasher' as it happens, this day was leg before to Laker for 10 and 'Plod' followed soon after. Miller and Harvey quit the scene for 1 and 0 respectively and Australia were on the rack at 4–61, of which Morris had made 26. Hole played bravely for 17 on a wicket taking some spin, but it was left to Alan Davidson (21) and Ron Archer (49) to restore some pride. Lindwall, with Bill Johnston (again not out), took the score to 162 at 5.30 p.m. and that was that. Laker took 4–75, but the extra penetration, bite and sharp turn provided by Lock were new factors in the game — factors for which the batsmen were poorly prepared. England needed 132 to win.

There were 50 minutes remaining on this third afternoon. Hutton, playing fluently, and Edrich, pugnacious as always, looked odds-on to be there at the close until Hutton, foolishly and sadly, ran himself out attempting a second run on de Courcy's arm off a stroke to square leg. May and Edrich proceeded next morning in front of 25,000 lip-licking fans while Australia, both with the ball and in the field, made them fight every inch of the way. May was caught with deceptive ease by Davidson off Miller for 37 and Compton joined his Middlesex mate to steer England to victory in the Test, the rubber and the Ashes for the first time at home since 1926. With 11 runs to get, Hassett, Australia's secret weapon, brought himself in to the attack with Morris, the other previously hidden star, having a turn at the other end. Edrich pulled Arthur's fifth delivery to the fence at mid-wicket and it was all over.

Hutton and Hassett both addressed the rejoicing multitude, Lindsay saying that England had 'earned its victory from the first ball to the second-last over'. This drew gusts of applause and it was followed by another characteristic Hassett one-liner: 'It is now obvious to you that we have been playing under a disadvantage because of my injured right forearm'. This reference brought the house down, or would have done had the listeners been indoors. Hutton said Lindsay's captaincy had been 'flawless'.

The Australians had played well throughout the series. Their fielding had improved steadily until, by the last match, it was on a par with that of the 1948 team. Even Hassett, aged 40 and nicknamed 'the Panther', chased leather like a two-year-old. But in the seven years since the war, the wheel had turned considerably and would continue to turn for the next five years. Lindsay Hassett would watch this from the sidelines.

The end-of-the-tour games in England invariably bring with them a sense of anti-climax. At Taunton, the wooden spooners, Somerset, received a thrashing but managed to salvage a draw — Australia 486, Somerset 187 and 2–156. Hassett made his best score of the tour with 148, including 18 fours and 1 six, and Alan Davidson's 104 not out included an identical number of boundaries.

Lindsay missed the Lord's game against the 'Gentlemen of England', which Australia won by 8 wickets. In its second innings, Morris (126 not out) and Miller (67) administered an ungentlemanly thrashing in knocking off the 253 runs required in no time at all with the loss of 2 wickets.

At the lovely Canterbury ground in the equally lovely county of Kent, the Australians won by an innings and 163 runs. Kent, where the incomparable Woolley delighted crowds until he retired at the age of 51, had a lowly place in the County Championship, despite boasting the irrepressible Godfrey Evans, the coming champion Colin Cowdrey and one-time Test-match opener Arthur Fagg. Hassett's bogey man, Doug Wright, was the star bowler. Bill Johnston took 11 wickets in this match — 5–35 from 27 overs in Kent's first innings of 181 and 6–38 in the second effort — a measly 108. The Australians made 465, Hassett batted delightfully for 65 before Wright had him leg before, and Miller (68), Hole (78), Benaud (45) and Tallon (83 not out) all exacted a heavy toll. Wright's 2–106 bore no relation to his bowling, which was, as ever, probing and demanding. His talents were more appreciated by his opponents than the England selectors and, at age 39, one marvels that he had failed to gain selection in any England side in the summer now nearly over.

Lindsay scored another century against a fairly strong South of England Eleven at Hastings. Batting first, 'South' could muster only 198, of which Compton made 81 in two hours. The Australians made 564, McDonald (125) and de Courcy (118) joining Hassett (106). Doug Wright again claimed Hassett's wicket, his figures being 3–118 from 19 overs. 'South' made 203 in its second innings, with left-hander and future England opener Peter Richardson contributing 90. Johnston took 9 wickets in the match, as well as continuing his march to head the Australian tour averages.

Against Combined Services at Kingston-on-Thames, and without Hassett, Miller (262 not out) and de Courcy (204), pushed Australia to 4–592. Fred Trueman had 0–95 in this bonanza. Services made 161 and 170. What pleased the Australian players most was Ian Craig's undefeated 71 not out, his highest score of the tour.

T. N. Pearce, former Essex captain and England selector, put a strong Invitation Eleven together for the 'Festival' match at Scarborough on the Yorkshire coast. Pearce had inherited Leveson-Gower's mantle in arranging this traditional match, the festival aspect of which has not always been apparent to the casual observer, particularly when the Eleven has been stacked with Yorkshire players. The latter regard matches against t'Aussies with only slightly less antagonism than those against Lancashire. Only three Yorkshiremen, Hutton, Yardley and Wardle, appeared in this game. It was a great game, too, ending in the last over when Jack Hill struck a huge 6 over mid-wicket to win the match. Lindsay made 74 in his best style in the first innings, but Richie Benaud played a most amazing innings of 135 in 110 minutes with a world-record-equalling 11 sixes. His last 107 came in 50 minutes. Hutton made his 122nd first-class century in the fashion which even now puts him in a separate category — serene and scholarly, seemingly beyond human error, yet replete with the noblest strokes in the game. Neil Harvey, whose cataract of centuries had slackened in recent times, joined Trumper, Bradman and McCabe in making 2,000 runs on an England tour. Bill Johnston was not out in the first innings and did not bat in the second, leaving his tour average at 102. Australia won by 2 wickets — England 320 and 8–316, Australia 317 and 8–325.

There were two drawn games in Scotland at Paisley and Edinburgh, in the first of which Morris made 101. Lindsay played at Edinburgh and made 15. The young Scot, Chisholm, showed some class in both games, scoring 55 not out, 43 and 41.

In a wet summer, Hassett's 1953 Australians won 16 first-class matches, more than any side except Bradman's in 1948 and Armstrong's in 1921. Hassett himself was fourth in the tour averages with 1,236 runs at 44.14. In the Tests, however, he was number one: 10 innings for 365 runs at 36.5.

The figures tell only half the story. Lindsay proved by general consent the most popular captain to visit England, with scribes and cricketers running out of adjectives to describe him — genial, friendly, wry, humorous, inscrutable. His colleagues to a man would have walked through fire for him. His batting was precise and usually tailored to the conditions encountered, his fielding sprightly and his captaincy sound and thoughtful. There was general regret at his departure from the scene to which he'd contributed more than his share.

## CHAPTER 16
# MATCHING WITS WITH MENZIES

It would be fair to say that captaincy of the Australian cricket team is still the most prestigious sporting honour available in our country. Men such as Monty Noble, Jack Ryder, Bill Woodfull, Victor Richardson, Sir Donald Bradman, Lindsay Hassett, Richie Benaud and Mark Taylor have adorned the position. Some others have inherited the prestige but, at times, fallen short of the behaviour expected in the post. Lindsay Hassett, possibly most of all, was acclaimed, both at home and elsewhere, as filling the many and varied roles better than anyone. Among his admirers was Robert Gordon Menzies, Prime Minister of Australia 1939–1941 and 1949–1967.

The two shared a happy relationship which lasted throughout Lindsay's cricket career until 1978 when Sir Robert died. Tess Hassett was present on many occasions when the two were in conversation and said the quick wit of both men was an education. She added that, to the onlooker, the event was like a tennis match, the heads of those not engaged swivelling to and fro as they do in exciting rallies on the court.

Some of Sir Robert's private papers are now available, including telegrams and some letters exchanged by the two. I am grateful to the National Library in Canberra for making these letters available to me.

On 6 January 1953, apparently in response to a letter from the Prime Minister congratulating him on a recent century against South Australia, Lindsay wrote:

*I did not realise before this that all that was required to make a century was an official order from my worthy Prime Minister. I trust that the order was made in duplicate so that I can use the carbon copy over the coming weekend. With best wishes for 1953.*
*Respectfully, Lindsay Hassett*

On 31 January 1961, with Lindsay apparently on a reporting job in Adelaide, the Prime Minister telegraphed him:

*Would you be my guest for Prime Minister's XI match Feb 18 Canberra as my technical advisor.*
*Warm regards, RGM*

Lindsay and Ian Johnson were both guests at the Lodge for the game against the West Indies on 18 February 1961. The tone of Lindsay's telegram to the Prime Minister seems to suggest that there may have been a lively night at the Lodge. An undated message sent jointly by Hassett (technical advisor) and Johnson (business consultant) reads:

*The Prime Minister's Business Consultant and Technical Advisor have conferred and are concerned that, during this last weekend, the balance of glasses at the Lodge was disturbed. Since various balances are causing the Government so much concern at the moment, we feel that a small credit in glasses should be established in order to guard against future adverse trading. Consequently we have taken it upon ourselves to correct the deficiency and plan for the future in a practical manner.*
*Signed Lindsay Hassett (Technical Advisor) Ian Johnson (Business Consultant)*

In reply to the message, the Prime Minister telegraphed under date 21 February 1961:

*Your handsome message and more than compensatory gift greatly enjoyed by my wife and me. You gave us great pleasure. Please advise Business Consultant accordingly.*

Several years earlier, on 16 October 1956, Lindsay wrote to Mr Menzies:

*Dear Mr Menzies,*
*I hope I am not intruding too much on your time but I feel that this matter is of sufficient importance to transform both Mr Nasser and the Doc into complete insignificance if such transformation is necessary in both cases.*
   *I am starting a small company to manufacture cricket bats and would appreciate your direction as to whom I should contact with a view of [sic] obtaining a license [sic] to import the willow wefts from England. I feel that at the moment, a normal application to Sydney may be lost in the paper mountain.*
   *I realise that the license [sic] position is difficult but I am hopeful that my application will be favourably received as in this case, the proposed industry*

which is at present insufficiently catered for, would be built wholly on Australian labour. I intend to manufacture bats one inch wider for the use of Australian batsmen only.

I look forward to your advice and trust that I do not presume by this direct contact.

With best wishes,
Yours respectfully,
Lindsay Hassett.

'The Doc' referred to is Dr H. V. Evatt, one-time Deputy Prime Minister and Minister for Foreign Affairs in the wartime and early postwar governments. Both Evatt and Menzies were outstanding lawyers but, apart from a mutual love of cricket, they had nothing in common. The 'Nasser' referred to is Colonel Nasser of Egypt, who was causing Britain some inconvenience and Menzies had undertaken an unsuccessful mission to Cairo to get him onside again.

By letter dated 23 October 1956, Menzies replied:

*Many thanks for your letter of 16 October. I wish you all success with your venture and hope that when the new Hassett bats come into production there will be some corresponding effect upon Australian averages. If you would like to send your Import Licence application to me at Parliament House, Canberra, I shall see that it very quickly gets into the right hands in the Department of Trade. Although I would not like to offer you a guarantee that the application will be successful, I think at least I can assure you that it will get prompt attention.*

*Kindest regards,*
*Yours sincerely, Robert Gordon Menzies.*

On 30 October 1956, Lindsay wrote to Menzies on Sports Store letterhead:

*52 Swanston Street, Melbourne*
*Dear Mr Menzies,*
*I would like to thank you very much for your suggestions regarding my application for an Import Quota. I am enclosing herewith a letter for the Department of Trade.*

*At long last we seem to be getting some good news from the cricket front in India. Neil Harvey's and Jim Burke's centuries are about the only bright spots we have had for months. I still think that under normal conditions, our chaps could measure up with other international teams but they will have to learn a lot more of the technique on wickets that are taking spin.*

*Once again I would like to thank you for your trouble regarding this license [sic].*

*With best wishes to you and Dame Pattie,*
*Yours respectfully, Lindsay Hassett.*

Replying to this on 6 November 1956, Menzies wrote:

*My dear Lindsay,*
*I received your letter of 30 October and have already sent off your application to the Trade Department with the request that they take it into consideration as quickly as possible.*
*Best wishes for the success of your venture.*
*Yours sincerely,*
*Robert Gordon Menzies.*

The import licence was granted but the bat project did not prosper and folded up, though not before Lindsay had sent a specially selected bat for the use of Menzies' grandchild. Menzies wrote in acknowledgment:

*My Dear Lindsay,*
*I cannot tell you how delighted I am with the cricket bat. I shall guard it jealously until Alexander Robert is just a wee bit older. Perhaps you will see through this flimsy excuse of mine and realise that I just don't want to give it up!*

*Joking aside, it was an extremely kind thought on your part and in the years to come, it will be one of the young fellow's most prized possessions. I shall make myself responsible for imbuing him with the true idea of its worth.*
*Kindest regards,*
*Yours sincerely, Robert Gordon Menzies.*

On 27 June 1953, during Lindsay's last Test match series, at a dinner for the Australian tourists at the London Savoy hotel, the Prime Minister unburdened himself of 21 verses of doggerel, each one referring to a member of the Hassett team, plus a few other matters. I am indebted to Gideon Haigh for supplying the material and to Sir Robert's daughter, Mrs Heather Henderson, for allowing me to use it. The following is a selection of the best.

*Some folk think civil servants 'not the thing'!*
*But ah! They do not know our Douglas Ring.*
*Those who expect the ball to dip or break,*
*Find out, too late, from Jack, their great mistake.*

*When the wise men raise a reproving finger*
*At Colin Mac for edging the outswinger,*
*Mac glares at them, and thinks, for all I know,*
*He's back among the Campbells at Glencoe.*
[Colin McDonald's middle name was Campbell.]

*In team work, you'll agree the art*
*Is that the whole is greater than the part.*
*In cricket you'll agree the same*
*Is true when Graeme Hole is on his game.*

*When Langley keeps, it's as if a ship*
*Had moved, stern first, from its reluctant slip.*
*Lindsay's a wit, Lindsay has feet like lightning,*
*But all the critics thought his form was frightening.*
*But Lindsay knows, there comes another day*
*When those who came to mock remain to pray.*

*If Ronald Archer were no good at all,*
*Instead of adept with both bat and ball,*
*I still would cheer him both louder and faster,*
*For Queensland lately saved me from disaster.*
[Only in Queensland at the half Senate election of 9 May 1953 did the Coalition win more seats than Labor.]

*Oh, for a word of rare Cardusean fire,*
*Oh, for a song upon the poet's lyre,*
*Oh, that the bells should ring a noble peal*
*To hymn the glories of our sinister Neil.*

*I care not whether Keith gets runs or not*
*(That statement is, of course, the purest rot)*
*But what I swear is, that his off-drive yet*
*Is worth a lengthy paragraph in Debrett.*

*The clutching Tallon oft the Umpire hails*
*Before he's actually removed the bails*
*(I know that this is libellous, but stay*
*I could not get a rhyme another way).*

*The infant Craig reclining in the shade*
*Takes comfort from the history of McCabe.*
*The gloomy Hassett sulking in his tent,*
*Saying that shot was not quite what I meant.*

*The ancient Miller, too old now to bristle,*
*Nursing his something something something muscle.*
[Miller, nursing torn muscles, had not bowled in the first Test.]
*Lindwall with versatility inhuman,*
*Bowling his slows faster than Fred Trueman.*
*Benaud the bold, Benaud the giant killer,*
*Bowls like Doug Ring but gestures like Keith Miller.*

*Some people study kangaroos or fish,*
*The duck-billed platypus, or other birds.*
*Some practise late cuts as their dearest wish,*
*But Jim de Courcy concentrates on words.*
[Jim de Courcy was known for long silences and a general economy of speech.]

Lindsay was moved to reply to the Prime Minister in verse and the result, although briefer, revealed yet another side to the man's capacity and talents. The metre and rhyme would not disgrace Banjo Paterson or Gilbert and Sullivan. Here are the three verses unamended:

*With his iron grey hair and his pugnacious air,*
*His appearance tends to the sinister,*
*But there's no need to fear for he'll quaff down his beer*
*And he's merely our worthy Prime Minister.*

*When they play on the swards of the Oval or Lord's,*
*Though the state of Australia's distressing,*
*His time he'll employ at a pub called Savoy,*
*For external affairs are more pressing.*

> But we'll hide our hate of this terrible state,
> Though the blot on our conscience will stay;
> We've eaten and drunk and can now do a bunk,
> But he's got to bloody well pay.

To end this brief record of the very harmonious friendship between two disinguished Australians, what could be more appropriate than to recount the events of a sunny Canberra afternoon in 1959? Arthur Morris and Lindsay had been invited by Mr Menzies to play in the Prime Minister's Eleven against the visiting Englishmen. Arthur was still playing club cricket with Paddington in the Sydney Competition. He'd boldly invested in a new bat with which he was getting quite a few runs. On this Canberra day, opening for the PM's Eleven, he made 79 in his most fluent style, prompting the query from Dexter (Lord Ted), the English skipper, 'Who is this old bastard?'. Lindsay was to come in upon Arthur's dismissal and asked if anyone would lend him a bat. Generously, Arthur offered Lindsay his bat. Lindsay did not get many runs and Arthur, watching with Richie Benaud and Menzies, heard Menzies say, 'How typical of Lindsay — what a charming gesture — he really is the most wonderful man'. Arthur, who'd been chatting with Richie, turned to Menzies and asked, 'What happened, sir?'. Menzies replied, 'Lindsay, as generous as ever, has given his bat to a little boy in the crowd'. 'His bat!' Morris yelled, casting protocol to the wind. 'Like hell! It's my bloody bat!' To crown the incident, the youthful beneficiary later came to the dressing room and obtained all the players' signatures on the bat. When he'd signed, Lindsay whispered to the boy, 'And Mr Morris would certainly love to sign it for you!'.

Sadly, such incidents are now rare. Apart from the money involved, the participants view matters too seriously for flippancy, despite the interest shown by the present Prime Minister, John Howard, and recent incumbent, Bob Hawke, in the game. As another recent incumbent remarked, 'Life wasn't meant to be easy'.

## CHAPTER 17
# SOME THOUGHTS ON LINDSAY

In his book, *Clarrie Grimmett: the Bradman of Spin*, Ashley Mallett, an off spinner of note, states that Clarrie regarded Lindsay Hassett as one of the greatest batsmen he bowled against. Clarrie added, 'Hassett's footwork was almost perfect. He was also a great fighter.' Bill O'Reilly would have echoed these words of his bowling mate.

Lindsay told me that his brother Dick (a leg spinner of quality) used to string a couple of blankets across the backyard and toss his leg breaks up to his brother from behind the blankets. Lindsay couldn't see Dick's hand and wrist at the moment of delivery and he was obliged to study the direction of spin while the ball was in transit, so to speak. Later on, watching Bill O'Reilly bowl on tour in 1938, mainly in the nets, Lindsay noticed that whenever the bosie was bowled, O'Reilly tended to drop his left shoulder in the delivery stride. He also tossed the bosie a little higher. Working on the two clues and profiting from his five-hour innings against Bill in Melbourne in early 1938, Lindsay was able to give a good account of himself. Ray Robinson (the writer) said that Hassett would delight in taunting O'Reilly, a tactic carefully avoided by other players whose main concern was not to ruffle and aggravate the Tiger's already unconcealed hatred of all batsmen. Robinson added that Lindsay found the O'Reilly leg break more worrying than the high-bouncing bosie. O'Reilly could bowl his leg break at medium pace.

Lindsay's ten Test centuries were all scored from age 33 onwards. This is unique in Australian cricket. Bradman's total from that age forward is eight. Of Englishmen, Hobbs, Sutcliffe and Barrington are on a par with Lindsay. Although many thought he made his strokes very late, nobody was able to detect any technical flaw in his batting.

Peter May, a fine player and gentleman, wrote in 1985:

> Hassett v Bedser was a rich spectacle for the connoisseur. Elegance is not a word one associates with a batsman small in stature but somehow Lindsay had it. He was a beautiful cutter but is also remembered for his balanced driving, his timing and his gracefulness in all he did.

♦ SOME THOUGHTS ON LINDSAY ♦

Alec Bedser (now Sir Alec), probably bowled to Lindsay as often as any Englishman. Bedser was in all the postwar Anglo-Australian Tests from 1946 to 1953 in which Lindsay played, capturing his wicket ten times. He wrote:

> *[Lindsay] was a great and very fair opponent. He would not have allowed any of his team to adopt the so-called 'sledging' tactics which have applied today, apparently with the consent of the captains. He wanted the game played in a correct and sportsmanlike manner. He was a fine player, of course, and a knowledgable captain.*

Richie Benaud remembers batting with Lindsay at Edgbaston, Birmingham, in 1953. Eric Hollies, who played for Warwickshire, was almost unplayable on a dusty fourth-innings wicket and threatened to bowl the Australians to defeat on the eve of a Test match. Richie says the ball was turning two to three feet (60 to 80 cm) and he was glad when Lindsay told him to leave Hollies to him. Lindsay batted for two hours for 21 not out, giving a masterly exhibition on how to handle the viciously spitting Hollies leg breaks. His innings saved the match, but the ill-informed or parochial local spectators booed the two off the ground, kept it up on the short walk from dressing-room to bus and once on the bus until it passed through the Edgbaston gates. Lindsay maintained his calm just as he had whilst handling Hollies in the middle.

In South Africa in 1950, Lindsay occasionally indulged his penchant for causing embarrassment to people so long as it could be done without giving harm or distress. On the train from Johannesburg to Cape Town after playing the Transvaal, he set his sights on Arthur Mailey and Eric Rowan. Mailey, sometime leg spinner of renown, was reporting the tour for a Sydney paper; Rowan was skipper of the Transvaal Eleven. Mailey gave Rowan a 'roasting' over the tactics he'd used in the match just ended against the Australians. Lindsay boarded the train early, before it began its 950 km (590 mile) journey and rearranged the names on compartment doors so that Mailey and Rowan were 'billeted' together. This caused some embarrassment to the two occupants, who were unable either to alter the arrangements or pinpoint the culprit, if indeed they believed there'd been some mischief-making. Lindsay maintained his inscrutable demeanour, even sympathising with the pair — 950 kilometres is a long journey in the close confines of a train compartment, particularly if you are not on speaking terms with your companion.

Lindsay was a very good golfer with a handicap in the low single digits. Playing with Peter Thomson one day, he outdrove the five-times British Open champion by 18.3 metres (20 yards) on the first hole. 'Give in?' he enquired. Thomson, no doubt, found a suitable rejoinder to this cheeky remark from a diminutive amateur at the royal and ancient game.

On the surface, it appears strange that, of the Services team Lindsay led with distinction, only he and Keith Miller moved automatically to the national Australian side after the war. This is in sharp contrast to what transpired when the 1st AIF team returned home in 1919. Of that illustrious combination, the following were playing for Australia in Test cricket very soon after their return: Collins, Kelleway, Gregory, Taylor, Pellew and Oldfield. Macartney was an original member of the AIF team, too, but returned home early upon the death of his father. Perhaps the explanation lies in the fact that while the 1st AIF team had over 300,000 troops in France and England from whom to choose, the Services team had available only personnel serving in the United Kingdom or in the Middle East at the end of the war, plus those repatriated from prisoner-of-war camps. The bulk of Army personnel between 1942 and 1945 were located in the Pacific to counter the Japanese and were not available for selection. One thinks of Arthur Morris, Bill Brown and Ray Lindwall who, among others no doubt, fell into this category.

Neville Cardus was always an unashamed admirer of Lindsay Hassett. In addition to nominating him 'the finest back cutter since Stan McCabe', Neville wrote at the conclusion of the 1953 tour and of Hassett's career: 'Australia may have been led by subtler and more ruthless captains, never by any as truly a cricketer and sportsman as Hassett. He has lost a rubber and found, while doing so, thousands of friends here who wish him well.'

Cardus thought Lindsay had the twinkling eyes and mouth of a comedian. On another occasion he said that if Lindsay were batting on a snow-covered surface, he was so light on his feet that the prints he'd leave would almost be as light as those of a bird.

E. W. Swanton thought it would be hard to find a more charming opponent or colleague in any game than 'this whimsical little man'.

Late in his Test career and in the absence of a reliable opening batsman to partner Arthur Morris, Lindsay took on these duties. He had mixed success in this venture. In 1953, when there was no third opening batsman as there'd been in 1948 when Barnes and Brown were equally

♦ SOME THOUGHTS ON LINDSAY ♦

capable of supporting Morris, Lindsay's record was: second Test, 104 and 3; third Test, 26 and 8; fourth Test, 37 and 4; fifth Test, 53 and 10. This willingness to serve the side should be weighed when considering the slowness of many of his innings, his natural attacking instincts being curbed in the interests of his side.

Harold de Andrado of Colombo, a long-standing friend of Lindsay's (and indeed of several other Australian cricketers of the time), recalled an innings of 116 played by Lindsay in about an hour at Colombo when Bradman's 1938 side was en route to England. Bradman, who had a cold, did not play in the match, but Lindsay and Jack Badcock each scored 116 in partnership, out of a total of 367 made in about three hours. The locals were well satisfied.

On Lindsay's return with the Services team after the war, Harold de Andrado saw Hassett get a quick 50 and Keith Miller a 'dynamic' century. It was on this occasion that Lindsay first made the acquaintance of Ceylon 'arrack', the local whisky, presumably without any adverse results.

Harold de Andrado visited Australia in 1958–59 and saw us regain the Ashes. He considered Lindsay Hassett to be the most popular sporting figure in the world, one who could accept either victory or defeat with grace and equanimity. He thought Australia unlucky to lose the rubber in 1953 and believes the Hutton–Bailey negative bowling in the fourth Test to be responsible, the argument being that had Australia won that game, as appeared likely before England lowered the shutters, they would have held the Ashes irrespective of the result of the Oval Test. He thought the doyen of English umpires, Frank Chester, had a part in this Headingley episode by not intervening in the interests of fair play. Incidentally, although Bradman admired Chester's umpiring, many Australians did not. They found him arrogant and rude, attitudes to which Bill O'Reilly would attest as Chester responded to an O'Reilly appeal by turning his back and ignoring him. Bill O'Reilly was not easily ignored and had a few well-chosen words to say.

Mrs Elaine Barnett of Tamworth is the daughter of the Victorian left-hander, the late Len Darling, a good cricketer and a brave and kindly man. She remembers, as a child, living in Adelaide where the family settled when Len's cricketing days were over. At the Adelaide Test, which usually took place on the Australia Day long weekend in late January, Lindsay Hassett, Keith Miller and Arthur Morris, together with cricket scribes, Bill O'Reilly, Ray Robinson and others, would gather at the

Darling's Glenelg home. One of Elaine's favourite memories is of Lindsay getting on the phone in the small hours of the morning, picking numbers at random from the phone book and informing the surprised, incredulous and (one imagines) angry recipients that it was the captain of the Australian cricket team calling. This would impose strains on the sense of humour of some people, particularly those whose knowledge and regard for cricket were minimal.

Chris Hancock, daughter of Stan and Edna McCabe, was born in 1950. Her knowledge of Lindsay is fairly sketchy as she was so young. However, she clearly recalls several occasions when, late at night or early in the morning, her slumber would be interrupted by hammering on the door of the McCabes' Beauty Point home. Her father, with affection and exasperation evenly mixed, would say, 'It's that bloody Hassett' and stagger to the door to be greeted by Lindsay and whoever he'd been able to cajole into accompanying him, laden to the gunwales with vast quantities of ale and prawns. Stan would realise that further resistance was useless and make the best of the situation, which must sometimes have been a trial even to his gentle nature.

Lindsay was very fond of late hours and dragging people from their beds to keep him company. He loved singing and these nocturnal wassailings would inevitably be accompanied by ditties from his repertoire, in which all were expected to join. 'The Blackbird Song' and 'Bridle on the Wall' were regular ingredients of these musical extravaganzas. To protect themselves from the disturbances on tour, young team members, particularly, were warned to take extreme measures to foil the captain from getting into their bedrooms. Chairs and other items of furniture were frequently used to reinforce locks. But nobody could stay cross with Lindsay for long — he had the gift of quickly defusing any disagreeable consequences and his qualities made objections appear trivial.

Ron Archer, who toured with Hassett in 1953, gave a talk in the Newcastle City Hall upon his return home and I'm indebted to Kendall Smith for his recollections of the references made to Lindsay and, in particular, how he set about developing team spirit and 'bonding' on the voyage to England. Aboard was a group of, straitlaced female school teachers of mature years who were travelling first class and having a dampening effect upon the after-dinner enjoyment of the team in the lounge. Lindsay rose to the occasion after a few evenings of this boredom and, himself leading, the team following, he started a riotous

## SOME THOUGHTS ON LINDSAY

and ribald rendering of 'The Blackbird Song', quickly persuading (or coercing) these women into joining in, culminating with 'the girls' lustily belting out the grand finale: 'And down came a bloody great blackbird and pecked off her nose'. The ladies and the lads thought it was a great evening and after-dinner entertainment was not a problem during the rest of the voyage.

In his Testimonial match played at the MCG early in 1954, it was appropriate that Lindsay and Keith Miller should have both scored centuries and been together in a partnership of over 200, much to the delight of the crowd. In his report of the game, former State player Percy Beames wrote that despite the best efforts to ensure that Lindsay would come in soon after the lunch break, the dismissal of Les Favell, Neil Harvey and Colin McDonald in the first session necessitated Lindsay's entry just a few minutes before the luncheon adjournment. Beames says that, with players and spectators all applauding, Lindsay displayed nervousness, a condition completely foreign to him in the 20-plus years of cricket of all standards in many places. He was so nervous that he narrowly escaped being caught at backward point from a wild slash at a short ball wide of off stump. Surviving the awkward pre-lunch period, he rolled the years back in the afternoon, hooking, glancing and cutting Lindwall, Johnston and Archer with ease that made batting appear the simplest of enterprises. His century came up in 95 minutes with 10 fours. Richie Benaud was caned in the total of 415 ultimately reached by Lindsay's Eleven. Richie had 4–139 from 15 overs. The match yielded Lindsay £5,503.

It appears likely that Lindsay's sporting abilities extended to most ball games. He would have been eagerly recruited by some of the VFL teams had his interests lain in that area. He was Victorian Schoolboy Tennis Champion in 1931–32 and some regarded him as a better player than elder brother Harry, who was good enough to make the Australian Davis Cup squad. As to his golf, opinions vary as to the exact figure, but his handicap in his youth and middle years lay between 4 and 7.

The late John Arlott was to cricket broadcasting what Cardus was to cricket writing. In his book, *Gone to the Test Match*, written in 1949, he wrote admiringly and at some length of Lindsay Hassett. He thought Lindsay was equipped with a 'magnificent sense of timing and naturally perfect footwork'. He added that even when his team's needs demanded that he defend, he 'invested stonewalling with an elegance behind which amusement is always apparent'. For my part, I agree that amusement was always present, but Hassett's inscrutable demeanour would keep it under wraps for the most part.

Bob Simpson of more recent times never played against Lindsay. He did some commentating with him and delighted in his one-liners. Simpson wrote generously of Lindsay soon after his death in 1993: 'His contribution to cricket was fantastic. He was a link between eras after Bradman, and he was one of the finest batsmen and ambassadors Australia has ever had.'

In its 1996–97 handbook, the South Melbourne Club shows that two partnerships featuring Lindsay still stand as Club records. These are:

1946–47 6th wicket 153 (Hassett 143, Alderhaven 53 no)

1947–48 3rd wicket 217 (Hassett 101 no, Howard 111 no)

The Victorian Cricket Association has what is called its '200 Club'. Membership is achievable only by having played 200 games, including club, first-class and Test matches. Lindsay qualifies easily: South Melbourne 102, Colts 7, Victoria 73, Tests 43 — Total 225.

Another unique Hassett performance lies in the fact that no other player of any nationality has scored centuries in each innings of a match in which Bill O'Reilly was in the opposition. Apart from his 59 centuries and close to 17,000 first-class runs, Lindsay also took 170 catches. In his younger days, he was rated an outstanding outfieldsman. Later on he placed himself in closer proximity to the action in the mid wicket or cover position.

Keith Miller always thought Lindsay kept something of himself in reserve, but willingly acknowledges his great gifts of personality and ability to relate to all types of people in all situations. Despite his small size, he had what Keith terms 'presence', a description I take to mean that he attracted attention and respect from those with whom he came in contact. Keith also thinks Lindsay would have made a very good comedian after the style of Ronnie Corbett. As a captain, Miller thought him sound and orthodox. The flamboyant Miller regarded Richie Benaud as the best captain — Richie, particularly in his early days, modelled himself in some measure on Keith Miller.

Bill Johnston, left-hand bowler of many talents and close friend of Lindsay Hassett, first met him on the return of the Services side when Lindsay led Victoria against the MCC in late 1946. After being selected to play for Australia in the Tests against the Indians in the 1947–48 season, their friendship blossomed and became close on the tours of England in 1948 and, later, South Africa. Bill says that Lindsay pipped

## SOME THOUGHTS ON LINDSAY

Arthur Morris for the captaincy of the African tour by one vote in a split Cricket Board.

Bill considered Lindsay a very astute captain as well as a correct and capable batsman whose sense of humour was never far from the surface. Lindsay's marked facial resemblance to a well-known British jockey named Charles Smirke provided one outlet for this sense of humour. The similarity was close enough to lead an English punter, a complete stranger, to approach Lindsay in a London pub and ask him for his 'tip of the day', believing him to be Smirke and wanting to get a tip 'straight from the horse's mouth', as it were. Lindsay, straight-faced and obliging, answered, 'Number six in the fourth'. With encouragement from the team, he kept this up in a number of places. One hesitates to ask how the 'tips' fared!

Bill appreciated the Hassetts' concern for and help to, his wife, Judy, during Bill's absence on tour in the West Indies in 1955 when the Johnston baby was in early infancy. Later, Lindsay was a frequent visitor at the Johnston's Sandringham home on his way to his own residence in Beaumaris when returning from work in the city store.

Bill Johnston joins others in expressing amazement at his friend's ability to mix easily in any company. His liking for parties inevitably led him to organise group performances of 'The Blackbird Song' and other ditties. Bill was honoured when Lindsay asked him to accompany him to Buckingham Palace on the occasion of his investiture and is sorry not to have been able to visit Lindsay during his last illness.

Ted White toured England with Lindsay in Bradman's 1938 team and the two remained lifelong friends. Ted White was a medium-paced orthodox left-hand bowler of the type many thought would be useful in England, given normal damp English summer weather. Unfortunately, the summer of 1938 was a very dry one and Ted could not force his way into the Test side. He confirmed that Lindsay was on good terms with Bradman while some were inclined to form a 'disaffected group'. There were sectarian elements in this no doubt, although Lindsay and Stan McCabe were both Catholics who had good relationships with the captain.

Ted thought that in early 1940, when Lindsay set about O'Reilly in both innings of the Sydney Shield match, he was a better player than Bradman, an opinion that would be greeted with mixed responses. He bases his opinion on the way Lindsay handled Bill. Bradman batted against O'Reilly many times through the 1930s when the Tiger was in his prime and the pair probably broke even over the many encounters. By 1940, O'Reilly was 35 years old, still a wonderful bowler but perhaps a little less venomous than he'd been in the middle of the decade. It's an interesting opinion.

Comparing Lindsay (prewar) with Stan McCabe, Ted thought Stan a little more polished but Lindsay less impetuous and, as a result, rather more reliable. To see the pair batting together in their prime would have been a sight for connoisseurs.

Lindsay Hassett and Ted White served for a time together in the Army in the Middle East theatre in 1941–42. Ted was an officer, Lindsay an NCO of variable rank depending on how much mischief he'd been in. When feasible, they'd fit him out in officer's gear so that he could enter the officer's mess.

Bill Brown, a player of grace and style, and a model for young cricketers of the time, thinks Lindsay 'is one of the most interesting characters we have had in Australian cricket'. He believes that, added to outstanding ability as a player, Lindsay had a bubbling sense of humour which surfaced at significant and difficult times. After a lean trot in England in 1938, Brown sought Hassett's diagnosis of what he was doing wrong. Lindsay replied, 'Bill, I think you are trying too hard'. He then took Bill to a London pub where they talked cricket generally and batting in particular for more than two hours. As it transpired, Bill Brown scored a century in the next Test match and a double century in the one following. Bill had a warm regard for Lindsay, considers he was a great captain for his country, and believes his invaluable sense of humour endeared him to all his colleagues. Both Lindsay and Bill O'Reilly were great supports to Brown in the early postwar tour of New Zealand.

Arthur Morris played a lot of cricket with Lindsay and thought the world of him. Long experience had alerted him to Lindsay's penchant for late nights and his tendency to persuade others to join him. Richie Benaud, on his maiden tour in 1953, roomed with Arthur frequently. The latter warned him in great detail of the consequences were Richie to let Lindsay into the room in the early hours and told him not to open the door in any circumstances. Shocked and dismayed, Arthur was awakened at 1 a.m. one morning to find Lindsay in the room and all set to 'bat on'. 'Didn't I tell you not to let him in?' he asked Richie. Richie explained that he'd ignored persistent knocking until it ceased. Shortly afterwards, the telephone rang. Somebody who claimed to be at reception told Richie, 'There's somebody who wants to see you urgently and hasn't been able to rouse you'. Richie, still not aware of the lengths to which his captain would go, understandably answered when the knocking resumed. Opening the door, he found Hassett, immensely pleased with his stratagem and rearing to go.

Arthur recalls a day off in England, spent with Lindsay Hassett, that resulted in some happenings not uncommon when venturing out with the little man:

> During our tour of England in 1948, Lindsay and I had a match off. We went by train to Mildenhall where we were booked in at the Bull Inn.
>
> A man we met in the train compartment told us he was being picked up at the station and would give us a lift to the pub. We got in the old estate wagon, Lindsay getting in the back with our friend while I was stuck in the front with the driver, an old white-haired codger dressed in gardener's clothes, so I joined in the conversation in the back. When we arrived and they had left, we asked the publican who they were. 'Lord Sandhurst was driving and his son was in the back.'
>
> Next morning we were driven to the golf club on a road skirting a forest. After golf, with no transport available, we had to walk back quite a distance. Lindsay said, 'We'll take a shortcut. We'll go back through the forest'. An hour and a half later we were still in the forest and I knew we were lost when I sat on a fallen tree for the second time. It was with a certain amount of relief that we finally emerged to find the road, fortunately took the right turn and made it back to the Inn five minutes later.
>
> Well, it wasn't the first time Lindsay had led me astray nor was it the last. You would have thought I'd learned over the years, but, somehow or other, even when I sensed there would be trouble ahead, I was drawn to the company of the sometimes outlandish, impish, funny, loyal, delightful friend who was Lindsay Hassett.

At a function where Menzies was to speak, Lindsay thought it a good idea to visit the toilet before the Prime Minister rose. On his way out, the chairman announced the PM a bit ahead of schedule. Not wishing to appear rude, and in the absence of urgency, Lindsay halted in his tracks to listen, leaning on some loose partitioning and other hall equipment. Unfortunately, the equipment on which he was leaning collapsed in a cloud of dust and with considerable noise. Menzies glanced across to the scene of the disturbance, spotted a small dust-covered figure among the debris, said, 'Ah! There's Hassett,' and resumed his speech.

Stan Sismey, an RAAF Squadron Leader and wicket-keeper of the Services team, later played for New South Wales and was behind the stumps in the famous match of January 1940 when Lindsay took the bat out on Bill O'Reilly. He recalls that Lindsay showed little emotion, carrying out the demolition with clinical precision and sangfroid. Bill was fuming and conducting frequent conversations with his Maker. When it was over, the two were best of mates and had a beer or three together.

Stan Sismey was another who found umpire Chester a difficult man to deal with in the Victory Tests. Chester did not like Australians and made this very clear. All other English umpires were first class. Stan recalls that the Calcutta riots were worrying and the Australians were given armed escorts to and from Eden Gardens (see Chapter 1). In the game against Eastern Zone, Denis Compton was a 'guest' player in the home side. He was batting when the rioters invaded the ground. The leader addressed Compton: 'Mr Compton, you are a very good cricketer but you must go'. Miller used to greet Compton, his great friend, with this salutation when Denis came in to bat in later Test matches.

Stan said that the tension between Muslims and Hindus during the games in India was obvious and could be distracting, particularly when smoke bombs were thrown and mirrors flashed. Lindsay and all the team thought Merchant a magnificent player — 'The Ponsford of Indian cricket'. He contrasted with the elegant and aggressive Amarnath.

Stan McCabe died on the 25 August 1968, Lindsay Hassett's 55th birthday. Stan was only three years older than Lindsay and Lindsay admired him more than any other cricketer. At Stan's funeral, Lindsay, usually impassive, made no attempt to hide his grief. In their approach to cricket, the two had many similarities — both were urbane, both generous and fair to friend or foe, both widely loved on and off the cricket fields, here and abroad. Only in the length of their careers did they vary. McCabe's brief, unforgettable career lasted a bare ten years, his international career only eight. Lindsay's stretched to almost 20 years, including his memorable participation in the Victory Tests and matches that followed. Both men have left their mark.

## CHAPTER 18
# 'FADE-OUT'

Harold de Andrado, Lindsay's great admirer in Sri Lanka, was distressed to learn from Tess Hassett of Lindsay's passing. He had died peacefully in his sleep about six months after coronary bypass surgery at St Vincent's Hospital in Sydney. Tess said the surgery was successful but Lindsay had been in poor health generally in the period leading up to the operation. He'd not been fit enough to attend Bill O'Reilly's funeral in October 1992. Lindsay had been a practising Catholic and de Andrado arranged a memorial service for him in the Colombo Catholic Cathedral. It was quite an honour for a cricketer of another land, however famous, to be so respected in a country he'd passed through a few times many years previously.

There were plenty of accolades at home, heartfelt and sincere. Arthur Morris, Bill Johnston, Alan McGilvray, Sir Donald Bradman and Bob Simpson are just a few who had nothing but good to say about Lindsay's cricket and his character.

Lindsay died at home in Batehaven, a town on the New South Wales south coast that is a popular holiday and fishing resort. The Hassetts had two residences, both of which had delightful views across Denham's Beach and the bay that it circles. Tess Hassett still lives in the second of these, a villa they moved into in the early 1990s. Following Lindsay's death, she considered returning to Melbourne where the elder of her two daughters lives. However, she decided to remain at Batehaven — she has many friends in the area and finds life there congenial.

The Hassett family had left Beaumaris on Port Phillip Bay about 1975 and the choice of Batehaven, according to the South Coast local paper, was made by Lindsay following a visit during which he drove around the various peaceful spots in the area. The paper goes on to say that Lindsay and Tess 'fell in love' with the district and decided that this was where they wanted to spend the remaining years of their lives. Lindsay's brother, Ted Hassett disputed this and claimed that he talked Lindsay and Tess into it. Whatever the truth, it proved a happy choice, for the people of the area took the couple to their hearts and did their considerable best to make their lives there happy and fulfilling. This they continue to do for Tess.

The Clyde River estuary is a favoured area for anglers, among whom Lindsay Hassett was an enthusiastic member. He was an expert fisherman and a 'cordon bleu' barbecue chef. Golf, too, was frequently on the program. Lindsay enjoyed the company and fellowship of the game and the conviviality of an ale or two in the clubhouse afterwards. Most of his golf was played at the Catalina Club — one of the best courses on the South Coast. Among his many talents, Lindsay was blessed with 'a green thumb' and could grow anything. The gardens at the two Batehaven residences were eye-catching and Tess has maintained the quality of her present garden where plants and shrubs, annuals and perennials grow in rich profusion.

When questioned about cricket and cricketers, Lindsay avoided the controversial. He refused to be drawn into the Bradman debate that has simmered along for about 50 years. He was closer to Bradman than most and, like Arthur Morris, regarded him as a friend. Loyalty was always a quality that Lindsay gave, expected and received.

Lindsay Hasset so impressed the people of South Africa during the 1949–50 tour of the 'Union' that they propagated a special dahlia in his honour and dubbed it 'The Lindsay Hassett Dahlia'. It still flowers in early autumn in Batehaven and Tess Hassett sent a tuber to Dame Pattie Menzies.

Tess says that when Dick Whitington approached Lindsay with the suggestion that he write a book about him, Lindsay was not keen on the idea. However, Whitington went ahead and the book appeared in the late 1960s. Some of the stories attributed to Lindsay are incorrect, but otherwise, the book is an interesting account of 'life with Lindsay' during the Victory Tests and the games that followed.

Lindsay loved to sing and was especially glad when a member or two of his various teams shared his compulsive urge to burst into song. His action songs could reduce a roomful of dignitaries to helpless laughter. Tess sometimes viewed these performances with initial apprehension, but she was perceptive enough to see the pleasure they gave others, so accepted them and sometimes joined in. Baritones Harold Williams and Malcolm McEachern were not too proud to participate in the singalongs if they happened to be in the assembled company. Lindsay's favourite songs were those in which there was action.

Throughout his life, Lindsay remained loyal to Geelong in the Victorian Football League and Tess said a victory to 'the Cats' would make his cup run over. His favourite footballer was the great Geelong player, 'Polly' Farmer. Among cricket clubs, South Melbourne, where he'd started, always remained his favourite. Frank Rolland, his old head master at The Geelong College, held pride of place among all men.

Lindsay was reluctant to talk about the war. Losses of life in the smaller wars that followed World War II distressed him.

When the 1953 team was invited to Buckingham Palace to meet the Queen, Lindsay departed from usual practice and requested that Bill Ferguson, scorer and baggage master to cricket teams of several countries, accompany the players. When Lindsay received his MBE in 1956, guests noticed that Her Majesty chatted at some length to him. Perhaps she was arranging for a special performance of 'The Blackbird Song' at the Palace!

Lindsay wrote regularly for Melbourne newspapers and was more than capable of putting words together without the assistance of a 'ghost'.

Lindsay joined the Australian Broadcasting Commission (ABC) a few years after his retirement in 1953 and worked for about eighteen years, mainly alongside Alan McGilvray. Lindsay was the 'expert commentator'; Alan described the play. The two hit it off remarkably well, despite an unfortunate incident back in 1953. McGilvray, through his ghostwriter, describes this in detail but inaccurately in his book *The Game is Not the Same*. The facts of this incident, in a sharp rebuttal by Ian Johnson of the McGilvray account, are as follows.

Ian agrees that Moyes, the expert commentator with McGilvray at the time of the alleged incident, did suggest, and McGilvray concurred, that he (Ian Johnson) was being overbowled in South Africa's second innings of the first Test in Brisbane in late 1952. The inference was that the captain, Lindsay Hassett, wanted Ian in the 1953 team to tour England. Ian Johnson goes on to repudiate the suggestion made in McGilvray's book that a writ was issued against the ABC by the South Melbourne Cricket Club. As he was on the club's committee at the time, Ian would have known if this had happened.

McGilvray goes on to say that he and Moyes came to Johnson's home where the matter was resolved. This did not occur. The truth is that Johnson wrote to Moyes stating that the comments were pretty poor and not in line with Moyes' usual standard of sportsmanship. Ian Johnson cannot recall having received a reply. He adds that the matter was never taken to the ABC by himself, Lindsay Hassett or the South Melbourne

Club, nor does he recall ever discussing the matter with Lindsay. For the record, Ian Johnson bowled 30 overs in the innings in question, taking 3–52. He was not selected for the Ashes tour, but was recalled as captain in Australia in 1954–55, in the West Indies in 1955 and in England in 1956.

Alan McGilvray considered Lindsay a most perceptive cricket commentator, able to seize on many points in a game that others would miss.

Lindsay's commentating style, spoken in a surprisingly deep voice, avoided irrelevancies. He could be witty and was invariably sound and unbiased in his opinions.

Lindsay's period of cricket commentary took place in years when the broadcasting style of commentators was passing from the extremely formal type, which Bernard Kerr controlled in the early days, through to the much more relaxed style of present commentators. It seems likely, too, that the term 'Pyjama Game' to describe one-day cricket was a product of the Hassett brain. He agreed with O'Reilly in disliking the one-day or limited-over game and believed it had increased the poor behaviour of players on the field, which was anathema to Lindsay. The travelling involved, all of it in the warm months, cut into the time Lindsay could spend fishing and surfing in his beloved south-coast retreat.

It appears that the ABC in the mid 1970s terminated its association with Lindsay Hassett and he did, in fact, leave for a time. However, the ABC found it difficult to find a suitable replacement and had to ask Lindsay to return, which he did briefly. His partnership with McGilvray was highly successful, Alan stating that Lindsay was the best commentator since Victor Richardson.

Hugh Rodgers of Melbourne, a member of Melbourne Legacy, had worked with Ted Hassett on Yallourn open-cut mine. He had enormous respect for Ted, a brilliant engineer and a meticulous but fair boss. Hugh was present at Ted's 89th birthday party at which Lindsay proposed the old man's health — Lindsay would have been in his mid-seventies. In Lindsay's speech, he recalled Sam Loxton batting at Headingley in 1948. Sam had reached 93 on this occasion and was anxious to get his century in a hurry. In trying to hit Yardley for 6, he hit across the line and was bowled. Lindsay warned Ted of too much haste and said, 'When you reach 90, Ted, I suggest you take the following years in singles'.

♦ 'FADE-OUT' ♦

Lindsay was appointed a trustee of the Melbourne Cricket Ground Trust on 24 October 1966 when the chairman was the late Arthur Calwell. The MCG librarian, Mr Ross Peacock, says that Lindsay is rarely mentioned in the minutes but is on record as stating, on 25 November 1968, that he considered properly controlled advertising at one-day games would not present any dangers. Ross Peacock says that Lindsay's presence at Trust meetings was fairly irregular and virtually ceased when he and Tess moved to Bateman's Bay in the mid 1970s.

The Lindsay Hassett Club has about 4,000 members and provides first-class facilities so that members may book to view the various matches played on the ground. Funds raised are utilised for the benefit of young cricketers in Victoria. Membership is reasonably priced and a number of discounts and similar benefits are available. The club illustrates the high regard in which Lindsay Hassett is still held. The club's 'hard-core' members are the interested parents and teachers at The Geelong College, and from this nucleus the Club has grown to a very sizable body. Old Collegians figure prominently in the club and are kept in touch.

As noted earlier, Tess Hassett did not invariably follow Lindsay around to his various matches and speaking commitments. There were plenty of the latter, particularly following his retirement, at various clubs and charitable functions. He never charged any fee for these appearances.

Early in their marriage, on the first occasion that Tess met Bill O'Reilly, she asked, 'And, Mr O'Reilly, are you a batsman or a bowler?'. The Tiger was slightly taken aback by this enquiry and the colour was starting to rise in his face, in a manner familiar to cricketers, when Lindsay, assessing the situation, quickly intervened and defused it. As soon as possible after this faux pas, Lindsay took Tess aside and suggested that she avoid talking about cricket. She and the O'Reillys enjoyed a happy relationship over a long period and Tess was never slow in disputing matters with Bill when she considered herself to be in a sound debating position.

Tess shares Lindsay's affection for Stan McCabe and wife Edna and enjoyed warm friendships with the Ian Johnsons, Bill Johnstons, Millers and Morrises.

Lindsay's work in an accountant's office assisted him in handling the book-keeping of his expanding sports store business (until it was sold), as well as in their personal affairs. Tess left financial matters to him.

However, upon Lindsay's death, Tess had to acquaint herself with the fundamentals of book-keeping and keeping records of various transactions for taxation purposes. She is now competently handling the financial affairs of the body corporate of the villas in which she lives. She plays bridge regularly and has a wide circle of friends.

On one occasion, Tess took their daughter Margaret, as a toddler, to see Lindsay bat. Lindsay went out, watched by wife and daughter, who were seated close to the players' entrance-and-exit aisle. On this occasion, Lindsay made a speedy return, scoring only 5. He was applauded as he left the wicket, but as he approached and entered the pavilion gate, the clapping ceased. Amid the silence, Margaret's voice piped up: 'Why is Daddy coming back so soon?'. Lindsay heard it, as did quite a number of amused spectators.

Tess and Lindsay's two daughters have led fulfilling and successful lives. The elder, Margaret, is an arts graduate of Monash University and holds a diploma in library studies. She has worked as an editor for the CSIRO. Margaret is married to Professor Brian Scarlett, head of the philosophy department at Melbourne University, and they have two adult sons. Anna learnt Italian at school and graduated with a Bachelor of Arts from Melbourne University. Her marriage was tragically shortened by an accident in which her husband, Greg Daniel, was killed. Anna went on to secure an MBA degree from Perth University and a degree in Mandarin from Nanking. She is now Director of Human Services for Palmerston Council in Darwin.

As mentioned in Chapter 11, Anna was born close to the time of Lindsay's departure for South Africa in 1949. He was away for the best part of seven months on this tour, but Tess managed the two children with help from good neighbours in the Hampton district where they were living. Margaret was almost seven at that time.

Lindsay's qualities were such that despite lingering sectarianism in the cricket hierarchy, he could not be passed over as Australian captain, the first Catholic to be so appointed. He served his country in war and, more than anyone, ensured that cricket would regain its place in sport after that war. Humbug, meanness and falsity were completely foreign to him, but the authority concealed in that slight frame, together with his personality, were enough to persuade squadron leaders, majors and the like that he was the man to lead a combined services team. In exchange for the loyalty and affection he received, Lindsay gave of himself unreservedly and with a wry humour that disarmed people from all walks of life — dukes and duchesses, plumbers and taxi drivers alike. It's unlikely that the game will see his like again, for people of this quality are not often duplicated.

Jack Pollard, in his encyclopaedic book *Australian Cricket*, starts his review of Lindsay Hassett with some words and thoughts that sum up the character of an extraordinary man and I can think of no better way to close this book than by quoting them.

*He was the most underrated of all Australian captains, particularly early in his career when officials simply did not understand him. He was a marvellous blend of impish prankster, skilled batsman, clever tactician and sparkling speaker. He could deflate the pompous, encourage good fellowship and build confidence in his players as enthusiastically as he waltzed with a duchess or conducted a mass rendition of "The Desert Song" for a titled group of singers. In the art of making friends for Australian cricket there has been nobody like him. Bradman could not go out and joke with people like Hassett, it was not in his nature. Benaud was a little shy in groups he did not know; Chappell's behaviour had limited acceptance. Hassett was impeccable and witty when his team was on show, but he was never afraid to discipline a player who wavered socially.*

Lindsay found some recent trends in the game not to his taste. He believed in playing hard within the rules, but not to the exclusion of the occasional chivalrous gesture or bit of fun. Glaring at opponents, querying decisions and sledging were foreign to his nature. He thought the game was for enjoyment as well as for winning, opponents to be friendly enemies on the field and joint participants in relaxation off it. At home or abroad, at cricket, golf, fishing, gardening or arguing, he was equally comfortable — a genuine 'man for all seasons' or, as Tess has it 'one of a kind'.

# LINDSAY HASSETT

b. 28 August 1913

| Season | Mat | Inn | NO | HS | Runs | Aver | Cs | 1/2C |
|---|---|---|---|---|---|---|---|---|
| 1932–33 | 2 | 4 | - | 12 | 25 | 6.25 | - | - |
| 1935–36 | 4 | 7 | - | 73 | 212 | 30.29 | - | 2 |
| 1936–37 | 6 | 9 | 2 | 93 | 503 | 71.86 | - | 7 |
| 1937–38 | 11 | 15 | 2 | 127* | 693 | 53.31 | 1 | 5 |
| 1938 in England | 24 | 32 | 3 | 220* | 1,589 | 54.79 | 5 | 6 |
| 1938–39 | 9 | 15 | 2 | 211* | 967 | 74.38 | 5 | 4 |
| 1939–40 | 7 | 12 | - | 136 | 897 | 74.75 | 3 | 6 |
| 1940–41 | 4 | 8 | 1 | 113 | 384 | 54.86 | 1 | 2 |
| 1945 in England | 6 | 11 | - | 77 | 296 | 26.91 | - | 2 |
| 1945–46 India | 7 | 11 | 1 | 187 | 826 | 82.60 | 4 | 3 |
| 1945–46 | 5 | 9 | 1 | 92 | 312 | 39.00 | - | 3 |
| 1945–46 in NZ | 5 | 5 | - | 121 | 351 | 70.20 | 2 | 1 |
| 1946–47 | 13 | 18 | 1 | 200 | 1,213 | 71.35 | 5 | 3 |
| 1947–48 | 10 | 15 | 2 | 204 | 893 | 68.69 | 3 | 3 |
| 1948 in England | 22 | 27 | 6 | 200* | 1,563 | 74.43 | 7 | 4 |
| 1948–49 | 8 | 15 | 1 | 205 | 855 | 61.07 | 4 | 2 |
| 1949–50 in S Afr | 15 | 16 | 3 | 167 | 889 | 68.38 | 4 | 5 |
| 1950–51 | 14 | 25 | 3 | 232 | 1,423 | 64.68 | 4 | 5 |
| 1951–52 | 9 | 15 | 1 | 229 | 855 | 61.07 | 3 | 3 |
| 1952–53 | 13 | 21 | 1 | 163 | 779 | 38.95 | 2 | 3 |
| 1953 in England | 21 | 30 | 2 | 148 | 1,236 | 44.14 | 5 | 6 |
| 1953–54 | 1 | 2 | - | 126 | 129 | 64.50 | 1 | - |
| Totals | 216 | 322 | 32 | 232 | 16,890 | 58.24 | 59 | 75 |

**In Test Matches (by rubber)**

| | Mat | Inn | NO | HS | Runs | Aver | Cs | 1/2C |
|---|---|---|---|---|---|---|---|---|
| 1938 vs Eng | 4 | 8 | - | 56 | 199 | 24.88 | - | 1 |
| 1945–46 vs NZ | 1 | 1 | - | 19 | 19 | 19.00 | - | - |
| 1946–47 vs Eng | 5 | 7 | - | 128 | 332 | 47.43 | 1 | 1 |
| 1947–48 vs Ind | 4 | 4 | 1 | 198* | 332 | 110.67 | 1 | 1 |
| 1948 vs Eng | 5 | 8 | 1 | 137 | 310 | 44.29 | 1 | - |
| 1949–50 vs S Afr | 5 | 6 | - | 167 | 402 | 67.00 | 2 | 2 |
| 1950–51 vs Eng | 5 | 9 | - | 92 | 336 | 40.67 | - | 3 |
| 1951–52 vs WI | 4 | 8 | 1 | 132 | 402 | 57.42 | 2 | 1 |
| 1952–53 vs S Afr | 5 | 8 | - | 163 | 346 | 43.25 | 1 | 1 |
| 1953 vs Eng | 5 | 10 | - | 115 | 365 | 36.50 | 2 | 1 |
| Totals | 43 | 69 | 3 | 198* | 3,073 | 45.56 | 10 | 11 |

**In Test Matches (by country)**

| | Mat | Inn | NO | HS | Runs | Aver | Cs | 1/2C |
|---|---|---|---|---|---|---|---|---|
| vs England | 24 | 42 | 1 | 137 | 1,572 | 38.24 | 4 | 6 |
| vs Sth Africa | 10 | 14 | - | 167 | 748 | 53.24 | 3 | 3 |
| vs West Indies | 4 | 8 | 1 | 132 | 402 | 57.43 | 2 | 1 |
| vs India | 4 | 4 | 1 | 198* | 332 | 110.67 | 1 | 1 |
| vs New Zealand | 1 | 1 | - | 19 | 19 | 19.00 | - | - |

♦ STATISTICS ♦

## 1932–33 in Australia   2–4–0*–25–6.25                                      Team Total

| Victoria | vs S Australia (M) | lbw.b.Grimmett | 4 | 299 |
|---|---|---|---|---|
| | | c.Walker B.Lee | 9 | 120 |
| | vs Tasmania (R) | lbw.b.A.Coombs | 12 | 229 |
| | | c.Badcock B.Walsh | 0 | 4–24 |

## 1935–36 in Australia   4–7–0*–212–30.28

| Victoria | vs NSW (M) | c.Little b.MacGilvray | 12 | 392 |
|---|---|---|---|---|
| | | lbw.b.White | 4 | 210 |
| | vs NSW (S) | c.Little b.Hynes | 21 | 165 |
| | | c.MacGilvray b.White | 51 | 415 |
| Victoria | vs Queensland (B) | c.Tallon b.Cook | 49 | 446 |
| | vs S Australia (A) | c.Collins b.Wall | 73 | 201 |
| | | st.Walker b.Ward | 2 | 174 |

## 1936–37 in Australia   6–9–2*–503–71.86

| Victoria | vs Queensland (M) | c.Wyeth b.Amos | 5 | 309 |
|---|---|---|---|---|
| | vs NSW (M) | c.and b.McGilvray | 83 | 318 |
| | | not out | 71 | 3–308d |
| | vs Queensland (B) | c.Tallon b.Oxenham | 93 | 407 |
| | | not out | 56 | 5–129 |
| | vs NSW (S) | lbw.b.Hynes | 58 | 337 |
| | | c.Easton b.White | 68 | 340 |
| | vs MCC (M) | c.Ames b.Voce | 54 | 292 |
| | vs S Australia (A) | c.Walker b.Cotton | 15 | 213 |

## 1937–38 in Australia   11–15–2*–693–53.31

| Victoria | vs New Zealand (M) | c.Weir b.Parsloe | 36 | 141 |
|---|---|---|---|---|
| | | not out | 127 | 5–293 |
| Bradman XI | vs Richardson X1 (A) | c.Oldfield b.Grimmett | 13 | 184 |
| Victoria | vs Queensland (M) | c.Tallon b.Loxton | 90 | 6–416d |
| | vs NSW (M) | c. And b.O'Brien | 81 | 415 |
| | vs S Australia (M) | lbw.b.Grimmett | 17 | 364 |
| | vs Queensland (B) | c.Tallon b.Rushbrook | 32 | 396 |
| | vs NSW (S) | c.McCabe b.White | 57 | 123 |
| | vs S Australia (A) | c.Waite b.Williams | 7 | 195 |
| | | c.Ridings (sub) | | |
| | | b. Williams | 14 | 177 |
| McCabe's XI | vs Rigg's XI (S) | b.R.Gregory | 54 | 198 |
| | | c.Oldfield b.Jackson | 37 | 7–208 |
| 19th Aust | vs Tasmania (L) | b.James | 75 | 477 |
| | | not out | 24 | 4–172d |
| | vs W Australia (P) | c.J.Jeffreys b.Zimbulis | 29 | 7–208 |

## 1938 19th Australians in England   24–32–3*–1589–54.79

| Aust XI | vs Worcester | c.Howorth b.Perks | 43 | 541 |
|---|---|---|---|---|
| | vs Oxford Uni | b.Darwall–Smith | 146 | 7–679 |
| | vs Leicestershire | run out | 148 | 5–590 |
| | vs Cambridge Uni | not out | 220 | 5–708d |
| | vs MCC | c.Maxwell b.Compton | 57 | 502 |
| | vs Surrey | c.Squires b.Berry | 98 | 528 |
| | vs Middlesex | lbw.b.Sims | 27 | 132 |
| | vs Gloucestershire | c.Allen b.Sinfield | 29 | 164 |
| | vs Essex | b.Farnes | 26 | 145 |
| | | c.Dennis b.Farnes | 4 | 153 |

# LINDSAY HASSETT ♦ ONE OF A KIND

| | | | | |
|---|---|---|---|---|
| 1st Test | vs England (TB) | c.Hammond b.Wright | 1 | 411 |
| | | c.Compton b.Verity | 2 | 6–427 |
| Aust XI | vs Lancashire | b.Nutter | 118 | 301 |
| 2nd Test | vs England (L) | lbw.b.Wellard | 56 | 422 |
| | | b.Wright | 42 | 6–204 |
| Aust XI | vs Derbyshire | not out | 3 | 4–441d |
| | vs Yorkshire | lbw.b.Verity | 94 | 222 |
| | | lbw.b.Verity | 17 | 132 |
| 3rd Test | vs England (OT) | No play on any day because of rain. | | |
| Aust XI | vs Nottinghamshire | lbw–b.Voce | 2 | 243 |
| | | c.Wheat b.Hearne | 124 | 4–453 |
| 4th Test | vs England (Le) | c.Hammond b.Wright | 13 | 242 |
| | | c.Edrich b.Wright | 33 | 5–107 |
| Aust XI | vs Somerset | c.Gimblett b.Buse | 31 | 6–464 |
| | vs Glamorgan | not out | 26 | 3–61 |
| | vs Surrey | lbw.b.Bowes | 10 | 297 |
| 5th Test | vs England (O) | c.Compton b.Edrich | 42 | 201 |
| | | lbw.b.Gregory | 11 | 123 |
| Aust XI | vs Sussex | b.H.Hammond | 74 | 336 |
| | | c.J.Cornford b.Wood | 56 | 300 |
| | vs England XI | c.Worthington b.Amar Singh | 0 | 174 |
| | vs England XI | b.Todd | 18 | 390 |
| | | b.Wilkinson | 18 | 7–327d |

## 1938–39 in Australia 9–15–2*–967–74.38

| | | | | |
|---|---|---|---|---|
| Bradman XI | vs Rigg IX (M) | run out | 12 | 426 |
| Victoria | vs Queensland (M) | c.Dixon b.Ellis | 104 | 376 |
| | | c.and b.Dixon | 73 | 7–322 |
| | vs NSW (M) | c.Easton b.O'Reilly | 56 | 504 |
| | | lbw.b.O'Reilly | 0 | 6–179 |
| | vs S Australia (M) | not out | 211 | 499 |
| | | st.Walker b.Ward | 54 | 7–283d |
| | vs NSW (S) | lbw.b.Pepper | 82 | 259 |
| | | not out | 0 | 2–79 |
| | vs Queensland (B) | b.Christ | 139 | 348 |
| | | c.Guttormsen b.W.Tallon | 9 | 216 |
| | vs S Australia (A) | b.Ward | 102 | 321 |
| | vs W Australia (P) | lbw.b.Halcombe | 14 | 266 |
| | | st.Lovelock b.Jeffreys | 103 | 310 |
| | vs W Australia (P) | b.Eyres | 8 | 226 |

## 1939–40 in Australia 7–12–0*–897–74.75

| | | | | |
|---|---|---|---|---|
| Victoria | vs S Australia (A) | c.Grimmett b.Waite | 5 | 207 |
| | | c.Walker b.Cotton | 89 | 363 |
| | vs Queensland (M) | c.Tallon b.Dixon | 83 | 418 |
| | vs NSW (M) | c.Chipperfield b.Pepper | 33 | 280 |
| | | lbw.b.Pepper | 57 | 242 |
| | vs S Australia (M) | st.Walker b.Grimmett | 92 | 475 |
| | | c.and b.Ward | 66 | 313 |
| | vs Queensland (B) | c.Watt b.Stackpole | 17 | 9–435d |
| | vs NSW (S) | c.Pepper b.O'Reilly | 122 | 298 |
| | | c.Chipperfield b.Lush | 122 | 326 |
| Rest/Aust | vs NSW (S) | c.Mudge b.Cheetham | 136 | 289 |
| | | b.Pepper | 75 | 252 |

## 1940–41 in Australia 4–8–1*–384–54.86

| | | | | |
|---|---|---|---|---|
| Victoria | vs NSW (B) | c.McCool b.Trumper | 14 | 202 |

## ◆ STATISTICS ◆

| Victoria | vs S.Australia (M) | c.Saggers b.McCool<br>c.Waite b.Grimmett | 96<br>67 | 416<br>389 |
|---|---|---|---|---|

### 1945 Australian Services in England  6–11–0*–296–26.91

| Aust Serv | vs England (L) | b.Stephenson | 77 | 455 |
|---|---|---|---|---|
| | | c.Hammond b.Gover | 37 | 4–107d |
| | vs England (Sh) | b.Pollard | 5 | 147 |
| | | b.Pope | 32 | 288 |
| | vs England (L) | lbw.b.Pollard | 68 | 194 |
| | | c.Edrich b.Wright | 24 | 6–225 |
| | vs England (L) | c.Wright b.Pope | 20 | 388 |
| | | b.Pollard | 7 | 4–140 |
| | vs England (OT) | c.Pollard b.Pope | 6 | 173 |
| | | c.Griffith B.Pollard | 1 | 210 |
| | vs Leveson–Gower | c.and b.Robins | 19 | 506 |

### 1945–46 Australian Services in India/Ceylon  7–11–1*–826–82.60

| Aust Serv | vs North Zone | b.Chunilal | 73 | 351 |
|---|---|---|---|---|
| | vs Prince's XI | c.K.Nayudu b.Amir Elahi | 187 | 8–424d |
| | | not out | 124 | 5–304 |
| | vs India | lbw.b.Nayudu | 53 | 531 |
| | | b.Hazare | 11 | 1–31 |
| | vs East Zone | c.Mushtag Ali b.Choudhury | 25 | 107 |
| | | c.C.K.Nayudu b.C.S.Naydud | 125 | 304 |
| | vs India | c.Parthasarathi b.Mankad | 18 | 472 |
| | vs India | c.Hazare b.Sarwate | 143 | 339 |
| | | c.Mushtag Ali b.Sarwate | 10 | 275 |
| | vs Ceylon | b.Heyn | 57 | 306 |

### 1945–46 in Australia  5–9–1*–312–39.00

| Aust Serv | vs W.Australia (P) | b.Epstein | 2 | 301 |
|---|---|---|---|---|
| | vs S.Australia (A) | c.Michael b.Dooland | 1 | 314 |
| | | c.Klose b.Waite | 92 | 255 |
| | vs NSW (S) | b.Lindwall | 1 | 204 |
| | | c.Grieves b.Lindwall | 41 | 339 |
| | vs Queensland (B) | c.Dixon b.McCool | 67 | 296 |
| | | c.Ellis b.McCool | 41 | 8–227d |
| | vs Tasmania (H) | c.Murfett b.Morse | 59 | 459 |
| | | not out | 8 | 6–194d |

### 1945–46 Australia in New Zealand  5–5–0*–351–70.20

| Aust XI | vs Auckland | c.Emery b.Cleverley | 121 | 579 |
|---|---|---|---|---|
| | vs Canterbury | c.Butterfield b.O'Brien | 43 | 8–415d |
| | vs Otago | c.Groves b.Overton | 54 | 420 |
| | vs Wellington | b.Buchan | 114 | 415 |
| 1st Test | vs New Zealand (W) | c.Tindall b.Cowie | 19 | 8–199d |

### 1946–47 in Australia  13–18–1–1,213–71.35

| Victoria | vs MCC (M) | c.Bedser b.Ikin | 57 | 189 |
|---|---|---|---|---|
| | | c.Compton b.Wright | 57 | 204 |
| Aust XI | vs MCC (M) | c.Hutton b.Smith | 28 | 5–327 |
| Victoria | vs S.Australia (A) | b.Ridings | 114 | 548 |
| | | not out | 36 | 1–79 |

## LINDSAY HASSETT ♦ ONE OF A KIND

| | | | | |
|---|---|---|---|---|
| 1st Test | vs England (B) | c.Yardley b.Bedser | 128 | 645 |
| 2nd Test | vs England (S) | c.Compton b.Edrich | 34 | 8–659d |
| Victoria | vs NSW (M) | c.Lindwall b.Beath | 27 | 8–560d |
| 3rd Test | vs England (M) | c.Hammond b.Wright | 12 | 365 |
| | | b.Wright | 9 | 536 |
| Comb'd XI | vs MCC (H) | c.Evans b.Pollard | 35 | 374 |
| | | c.Fishlock b.Pollard | 11 | 241 |
| Victoria | vs Queensland (B) | c.Carrigan b.Raymer | 200 | 466 |
| | vs NSW (S) | c.Pettiford b.F.Johnston | 190 | 356 |
| 4th Test | vs England (A) | c.Hammond b.Wright | 78 | 487 |
| Victoria | vs England XI (M) | c.Fishlock b.Yardley | 126 | 327 |
| 5th Test | vs England (S) | c.Ikin b.Wright | 24 | 253 |
| | | c.Ikin b.Wright | 47 | 5–214 |

**1947–48 in Australia   10–15–2–893–68.69**

| | | | | |
|---|---|---|---|---|
| Victoria | vs Indian XI (M) | b.Rangachari | 1 | 273 |
| | | not out | 67 | 2–137 |
| | vs S.Australia (A) | c.Bradman b.Oswald | 118 | 440 |
| | | c.Noblet b.Craig | 0 | 182 |
| | vs Queensland (B) | lbw.b.L.Johnson | 204 | 436 |
| | | c.Mackay b.Cook | 2 | 3–70 |
| | vs NSW (S) | b.F.Johnston | 48 | 331 |
| 1st Test | vs India (B) | c.Gul Mahomed b.Mankad | 48 | 8–382d |
| 2nd Test | vs India (S) | c.Adhikari b.Hazare | 6 | 107 |
| Victoria | vs NSW (M) | st.Saggers b.Toshack | 24 | 130 |
| | | c.Miller b.Toshack | 75 | 474 |
| 3rd Test | vs India (M) | lbw.b.Mankad | 80 | 394 |
| 4th Test | vs India (A) | not out | 198 | 674 |
| Victoria | vs S.Australia (M) | b.Noblet | 0 | 218 |
| | | c.Klose b.Dooland | 22 | 280 |

**1948 20th Australians in England   22–27–6–1,563–74.43**

| | | | | |
|---|---|---|---|---|
| Aust XI | vs Worcestershire | c.Wyatt b.Jackson | 35 | 8–462d |
| | vs Yorkshire | b.Smailes | 0 | 101 |
| | | c.Sellers b.Smailes | 12 | 6–73 |
| | vs Surrey | b.Bedser | 110 | 632 |
| | vs Cambridge Uni | not out | 61 | 4–414d |
| | vs Oxford Uni | c.Robinson b.Whitcombe | 0 | 431 |
| | vs MCC | lbw.b.Young | 51 | 552 |
| | vs Nottinghamshire | b.Woodhead | 44 | 400 |
| | vs Hampshire | lbw.b.Knott | 26 | 117 |
| | | not out | 27 | 2–182 |
| 1st Test | vs England (TB) | b.Bedser | 137 | 509 |
| | | not out | 21 | 2–98 |
| Aust XI | vs Northamptonsh. | B.Nutter | 127 | 8–352d |
| 2nd Test | vs England (L) | b.Yardley | 47 | 350 |
| | | b.Yardley | 0 | 7–460d |
| Aust XI | vs Surrey | c.Holmes b.Watts | 139 | 389 |
| | vs Gloucestershire | st.Wilson b.Cook | 21 | 7–774d |
| 3rd Test | vs England (OT) | c.Washbrook b.Young | 38 | 221 |
| 4th Test | vs England (Le) | c.Crapp b.Pollard | 13 | 458 |
| | | c. and b.Compton | 17 | 3–404 |
| Aust XI | vs Glamorgan | not out | 71 | 3–215 |
| | vs Warwickshire | lbw.b.Hollies | 68 | 254 |
| 5th Test | vs England (O) | lbw.b.Young | 37 | 389 |
| Aust XI | vs Gentlemen/Eng | not out | 200 | 5–610d |
| | vs Somerset | c.Watts b.Redman | 103 | 5–560d |
| | vs South of Eng | c.Mallett b.Perks | 151 | 7–522d |
| | vs Leveson–Gower | not out | 7 | 8–489d |

◆ STATISTICS ◆

## 1948–49 in Australia   8–15–1*–855–61.07

| | | | | |
|---|---|---|---|---|
| Hasset XI | vs Bradman XI (M) | c.Tallon b.Loxton | 35 | 406 |
| | | st.Tallon b.Rng | 102 | 430 |
| Victoria | vs Queensland (M) | lbw.b.L.Jonhson | 104 | 436 |
| | | not out | 4 | 2–79 |
| | vs NSW (M) | c.Saggers b.Walker | 10 | 167 |
| | | c.Moss b.F.Johnston | 9 | 4–98 |
| | vs S.Australia (M) | c.Dooland b.McLean | 56 | 281 |
| | | c.Michael b.Ridings | 24 | 149 |
| | vs Queensland (B) | c.and b.Nolan | 205 | 456 |
| | vs NSW (S) | c.Saggers b.Miller | 6 | 165 |
| | | c.and b.Miller | 27 | 197 |
| | vs W.Australia (P) | c.Buttsworth b.Puckett | 40 | 364 |
| | | b.Dunn | 1 | 227 |
| Hassett XI | vs Morrix XI (S) | c.I.Johnson b.Ring | 73 | 204 |
| | | c.Morris b.I.Johnson | 159 | 437 |

## 1949–50 Australians in South Africa   15–16–3*–889–68.38

| | | | | |
|---|---|---|---|---|
| Aust XI | vs Natal | c.Dawson b.Markham | 44 | 275 |
| | vs N.E. Transvaal | c.Wiles b.Penning | 100 | 4–331d |
| | vs S.Rhodesia | not out | 66 | 398 |
| | vs S.African XI | b.Melle | 13 | 312 |
| | vs Orange Free St. | C.Wright b.Hawkins | 96 | 3–405d |
| | vs S.African XI | not out | 2 | 4–344 |
| 1st Test | vs Sth Africa (J) | b.Watkins | 112 | 413 |
| 2nd Test | vs Sth Africa (C) | c.and b.Mann | 57 | 7–526d |
| Aust XI | vs E.Province | c.Du Toit b.Liddle | 50 | 418 |
| | vs Border | not out | 106 | 4–425d |
| 3rd Test | vs Sth Africa (D) | lbw.b.Tayfield | 2 | 75 |
| | | lbw.b.Mann | 118 | 5–336 |
| 4th Test | vs Sth Africa (J) | b.McCarthy | 53 | 8–465d |
| Aust XI | vs Griqualand West | c.C.Helfrick b.McNamara | 2 | 9–355d |
| | vs Natal | c.and b.Tayfield | 8 | 312 |
| 5th Test | vs Sth Africa (PE) | c.McCarthy b.Mann | 167 | 7–549d |

## 1950–51 in Australia   14–25–3*–1,423–64.68

| | | | | |
|---|---|---|---|---|
| Victoria | vs England (M) | b.Bailey | 19 | 331 |
| | vs S.Australia (A) | st.Langley b.Hole | 113 | 264 |
| | | b.Hiern | 18 | 303 |
| | vs NSW (M) | c.Miller b.F Johnston | 179 | 374 |
| | | lbw.b.Benaud | 8 | 295 |
| 1st Test | vs England (B) | b.Bedser | 8 | 228 |
| | | lbw.b.Bailey | 3 | 7–32d |
| Victoria | vs Queensland (M) | c.and b.McCool | 127 | 322 |
| | | not out | 28 | 3–259 |
| 2nd Test | vs England (M) | b.Bailey | 52 | 194 |
| | | c.Bailey b.Brown | 19 | 181 |
| Victoria | vs S.Australia (M) | c.Hole b.Bowley | 69 | 271 |
| 3rd Test | vs England (S) | c.Bedser b.Brown | 70 | 426 |
| Victoria | vs Queensland (B) | c.Savage b.McCool | 29 | 388 |
| | | not out | 30 | 1–73 |
| | vs NSW (S) | b.Walker | 82 | 280 |
| | | b.F.Johnston | 27 | 298 |
| 4th Test | vs England (A) | c.Evans b.Wright | 43 | 371 |
| | | lbw b.Wright | 31 | 8–403d |
| Victoria | vs England XI (M) | c.Washbrook b.Close | 232 | 441 |

| | | | | |
|---|---|---|---|---|
| Victoria | vs W.Australia (M) | c.Close b.Washbrook | 36 | 234 |
| | | c. and b.Lovett | 47 | 8–182d |
| | | not out | 13 | 2–49 |
| 5th Test | vs England (M) | c.Hutton b.Brown | 92 | 217 |
| | | b.Wright | 48 | 197 |

### 1951–52 in Australia   9–15–1*–855–61.07

| | | | | |
|---|---|---|---|---|
| 1st Test | vs W.Indies (B) | b.Ramadhin | 6 | 226 |
| | | lbw.b.Ramadhin | 35 | 7–236 |
| Victoria | vs W.Indies (M) | lbw.b.Ramadhin | 12 | 195 |
| 2nd Test | vs W.Indies (S) | c.Christiani b.Jones | 132 | 517 |
| | | not out | 46 | 3–137 |
| Victoria | vs NSW (M) | c.Trueman b.Walker | 92 | 434 |
| | vs NSW (S) | c.Barnes b.Miller | 14 | 290 |
| | | c.Burke b.Davidson | 7 | 416 |
| 4th Test | vs W.Indies (M) | run out | 15 | 216 |
| | | lbw.b.Valentine | 102 | 9–260 |
| Victoria | vs W.Indies (M) | c.Jones b.Ferguson | 56 | 387 |
| | | b.Valentine | 43 | 7–236d |
| 5th Test | vs W.Indies (S) | c.Guillen b.Gomez | 2 | 116 |
| | | c.Worrell b.Valentine | 64 | 377 |
| Victoria | vs S.Australia (M) | b.Manning | 229 | 537 |

### 1952–53 in Australia   13–21–1–779–38.95

| | | | | |
|---|---|---|---|---|
| Victoria | vs S.Australia (A) | b.Thomas | 1 | 119 |
| | | lbw.b.Noblet | 91 | 325 |
| | vs NSW (M) | c.Davidson b.Miller | 4 | 347 |
| | | c.and b.Benaud | 31 | 185 |
| 1st Test | vs Sth Africa (B) | c.Waite b.Watkins | 55 | 280 |
| | | c.McGlew b.Melle | 17 | 277 |
| Victoria | vs Queensland (M) | c.Tallon b.Smith | 5 | 208 |
| | | not out | 47 | 1–142 |
| 2nd Test | vs Sth Africa (M) | c.Melle b.Mansell | 18 | 243 |
| | | lbw.b.Tayfield | 21 | 290 |
| Victoria | vs S.Australia (M) | b.Manning | 23 | 250 |
| | | c.Hole b.Wilson | 123 | 362 |
| | vs Queensland (B) | c.Smith b.Flynn | 51 | 365 |
| | | b.Smith | 13 | 3–88 |
| 3rd Test | vs Sth Africa (S) | c.Murray b.Funston | 2 | 443 |
| 4th Test | vs Sth Africa (A) | c.McGlew b.Mansell | 163 | 530 |
| Victoria | vs Sth Africa (M) | c.Mansell b.Fuller | 7 | 260 |
| 5th Test | vs Sth Africa (M) | run out | 40 | 520 |
| | | c.Endean b.Mansell | 30 | 209 |
| 21st Aust | vs Tasmania (H) | c.R.Davidson b.Hird | 11 | 510 |
| | vs Combined XI (L) | c.Cowley b.Hird | 26 | 469 |

### 1953 21st Australians in England   21–30–2*–1,236–44.14

| | | | | |
|---|---|---|---|---|
| Aust XI | vs Worcestershire | c.Ashman b.Whitehead | 2 | 7–542 |
| | vs Leicestershire | b.Palmer | 18 | 8–443d |
| | vs Minor Counties | lbw.b.Taylor | 32 | 289 |
| | vs Lancashire | c.Grieves b.M.Hilton | 34 | 298 |
| | vs Nottinghamshire | c.Dooland b.Goonesena | 62 | 6–290 |
| | vs Sussex | c.John Langridge b.Wood | 8 | 325 |
| | | not out | 108 | 1–259d |
| 1st Test | vs England (TB) | b.Bedser | 115 | 249 |
| | | c.Hutton b.Bedser | 5 | 123 |
| Aust XI | vs Derbyshire | c.Hamer b.Gladwin | 5 | 197 |

## STATISTICS

| | | | | |
|---|---|---|---|---|
| | | c.Kelly b.Gladwin | 0 | 146 |
| 2nd Test | vs England (L) | c.Bailey b.Bedser | 104 | 346 |
| | | c.Evans b.Statham | 3 | 368 |
| Aust XI | vs Gloucestershire | c.Milton b.Mortimer | 1 | 9–402d |
| 3rd Test | vs England (OT) | b.Bailey | 26 | 318 |
| | | c.Bailey b.Bedser | 8 | 8–35 |
| Aust XI | vs Middlesex | b.Moss | 24 | 416 |
| 4th Test | vs England (Le) | c.Lock b.Bedser | 37 | 266 |
| | | b.Lock | 4 | 4–147 |
| Aust XI | vs Surrey | c.May b.Loader | 67 | 9–327 |
| | vs Warwickshire | c.Hollies b.Pritchard | 60 | 181 |
| | | not out | 21 | 5–53 |
| | vs Lancashire | c.Wilson b.Tattersall | 11 | 372 |
| 5th Test | vs England (O) | c.Evans b.Bedser | 53 | 275 |
| | | lbw.b.Laker | 10 | 162 |
| Aust XI | vs Somerset | c.Smith b.Saeed | 148 | 486 |
| Aust XI | vs Kent | lbw.b.Wright | 65 | 8–465d |
| | vs South of Eng. | c.Compton b.Wright | 106 | 9–564d |
| | vs England XI | c.Yardley b.Bailey | 74 | 317 |
| | | c.Evans b.Bedser | 25 | 8–325 |

**1953–54 in Australia   1–2–0*–129–64.50**

| | | | | |
|---|---|---|---|---|
| Hassett XI | vs Morris XI (M) | c.Lindwall b.Benaud | 126 | 415 |
| | | b.Lindwall | 3 | 425 |

# AUTHOR'S NOTE

Having written about Stan McCabe, Bill O'Reilly and Arthur Morris, it seemed appropriate to do something on Lindsay Hassett. He had been most helpful to me concerning the three mentioned, by all of whom he was greatly admired. Stan and Bill had been close friends of Lindsay's throughout their cricketing careers and long afterwards. Arthur, who came on the scene later, blossomed under the eye of Bill O'Reilly, his club captain, and, later, Stan McCabe. Stan came to know Lindsay Hassett well in the immediate postwar years and the friendship endured until Stan quit the scene in 1968. In writing those earlier books, I'd chatted to Lindsay several times and fallen under the spell of his personality.

Although it was not possible to talk to Lindsay in detail about his own life and cricket, there was no shortage of people willing, indeed anxious, to provide information about him. Letters and phone calls came from various places at home and abroad, and the consensus was that Lindsay Hassett was one of our best-loved cricketers, a fine batsman and a captain whose varied gifts, both on and off the cricket field, made him something of a legend in his own time and an even greater one in his retirement years.

Lindsay's wife, Tess, was especially helpful and shares her husband's whimsical sense of humour and refusal to take life too seriously. Lindsay's daughters, Margaret and Anna, both contributed and many of Lindsay's contemporaries were eager to register their appreciation. Ian Johnson, lifelong friend and team-mate at club, state and national levels, wrote a splendid foreword for which I'm very grateful.

There was no shortage of testimonials from those who'd played with or against him. Apart from Ian, Bill Brown, Richie Benaud, Bill Johnston, Ted White and Alan Davidson all spoke with real affection of this 'man for all seasons', and Sir Alec Bedser added his voice for Englishmen.

The late Dick Whitington's book on Lindsay, written in the sixties, was a rich source of information about the Victory Tests and related games, while Stan Sismey, who knew all members of that famous combination, was always available for advice and guidance.

Colin Clowes, busy resident medico and cricket fanatic, produced his usual immaculate statistical summary and the New South Wales Cricket

Association and its librarian and staff were never too busy to lend a hand.

Ross Peacock of the MCG Library helped in similar fashion. Gideon Haigh supplied the Menzies/Hassett 'poetic dialogue' and Mrs Heather Henderson (née Menzies) gave permission to use it. The Legacy Club of Melbourne and Peter Danby, one of its members and an AIF colleague of Lindsay, both gave material assistance. Overseas, Mr Harold de Andrado of Sri Lanka added his thoughts of a fifty-year ffiendship.

Joan, my wife, typed her fourth cricket manuscript only to learn that this one had to be recorded on a computer disk. Undaunted, she quickly grasped the necessary knowledge, with assistance from computer-literate family members and friends, and nonchalantly did it all again.

The Geelong College was enthusastic about the project as was the Lindsay Hassett Club and old collegians and club members encouraged me at those low points inevitable occasionally in a work of this nature.

Ray Webster, another statistics man par excellence, frequently pointed me in the right direction, as did his friend, bookseller Roger Page of Melbourne.

I owe a considerable debt to Lindsay's surviving brothers, Vin (Geelong) and Dick (Melbourne) and the late Ted Hassett, with whom I spent a fascinating afternoon in September 1996. At 97, Ted's mind and imagination were as active and vivid as those of a person half his age and I regret that he slipped into the silence shortly after I saw him and before he could see the end result of this book.

It has been a privilege to write something of Lindsay Hassett, one whom Disraeli, had he known him, might have described as 'an Australian worthy'.

Photos in the book were kindly provided by Mrs Tess Hassett and Messrs Dick and Vin Hassett. The NSW Cricket Association, Ian Peter Danby and Mr Rick Smith also contributed. I am grateful to all for their interest and help.

# BIBLIOGRAPHY

Arlott, John, *Gone to the Test Match*, Longmans, Green & Co. Ltd, London, 1949

Barker, Ralph, *Ten Greal Bowlers*, Chatto & Windus, London, 1967

Bradman, Sir Donald, *Farewell to Cricket*, Pavilion Books Ltd, London, 1988

Brown, F. R., *Cricket Musketeer*, Nicholas Kaye, London, 1954

Cardus, Neville, *The Essential Cardus*, Jonathan Cape, London, 1949

Fingleton, Jack, *Brown and Company*, Collins, London, 1972

Harris, Bruce, *With England in Australia 1946–47*, Hutchinsons, London, 1947

Johnson, Ian, *Cricket at the Crossroads*, Cassell & Co., London, 1957

Moyes, A. G., *West Indies in Australia 1951–52*, Angus & Robertson, Sydney, 1952

Moyes, A. G., *The South Africans in Australia 1952–53*, Angus & Roberston, Sydney, 1953

Mallett, Ashley, *Clarrie Grimmett: The Bradman of Spin*, University of Queensland Press, 1993.

O'Reilly, W.J., *Cricket Conquest*, Werner Laurie, London, 1949

O'Reilly, W. J., *Tiger*, William Collins Pty Ltd, Sydney, 1985

*Oxford Companion to Australian Cricket*, Oxford University Press, Melbourne, 1996

Pollard, Jack, *Australian Cricket*, Angus & Robertson, Sydney, 1988

Swanton, E. W., *Sort of a Cricket Person*, Collins, Glasgow, 1972

Swanton, E. W., *Elusive Victory*, Hodder & Stoughton, London, 1951

Simpson, Bob, *Captain's Story*, Marlin Books, Richmond, Victoria, 1966

Sismey, S. G., *History of the 1945 Australian Services Cricket Team*, Private printing by the author (undated)

Valentine, Barry, *Cricket's Dawn that Died*, Breedon Books Publishing Co., Derby, 1991

*Wisden's Almanac*, 1949

Whitington, R. S., *The Lindsay Hassett Story*, Wren Publishing Pty Ltd, Melbourne, 1969

Webster, Ray, *First Class Cricket in Australia Vol. 1*, Ray Webster, Melbourne, 1991

Webster, Ray, *First Class Cricket in Australia Vol. 2*, Ray Webster, Melbourne, 1997

West, Peter, *The Fight for the Ashes 1953*, Australasian Publishing Co., Sydney, 1953

Woodward, Ian, *Cricket Not War*, S.M.K. Enterprises, Brighton East, Victoria, 1994

# INDEX

Adikhari, H.R., 87
Allen, G.O., 26, 160
Alley, W., 69
Amar Singh, 45
Amarnath, L., 66, 67, 87, 88, 90, 107, 108, 109
Ames, L.E.G., 27, 35, 45, 51, 56, 57
Amir Elahi, 87
Archer, K.A., 134, 137
Archer, R.G., 123, 156, 158, 159, 162, 171, 172, 176, 190, 191
Arlott, John, 57, 191
Armstrong, W.W. 25, 48, 171
Atkinson, D.E., 141
Australian Services Eleven, 56–69

Badcock, C.L., 29, 33, 34, 37, 41
Bailey, T.E., 51, 131, 132, 133, 134, 136, 138, 162, 166, 167, 169, 171, 172–3, 174, 175
Bannerman, Charles, 7
Barker, Ralph, 41
Barnes, S.G., 30, 33, 42, 44, 45, 69, 71, 76, 79, 81, 82, 85, 88, 107, 108, 111, 112, 113, 115, 116, 117, 118, 122, 142, 144, 149, 151, 160, 188
Barnett, B.A. (Ben), 30, 41, 42, 44, 154
Barnett, C.J., 35, 36, 40, 96
Barnett, Elaine, 189
Batehaven, 197–8
Barrington, K.F., 186
Bedser, A.V., 20, 51, 70, 77, 79, 81, 82, 83, 111, 113, 115, 116, 117, 118, 119, 131, 132, 133, 134, 135, 136, 137, 139, 160, 164–5, 167, 169, 170, 171, 172, 175, 186
Begbie, D.W., 127
Benaud, Richie, 131, 150, 152, 153, 155, 156, 158, 159, 162, 170, 177, 178, 185, 187, 191, 194, 203
Berry, Robert, 131
'Better Cricket', 70
Blackbird Song, 17, 190, 193
Board of Control, 33, 39, 76, 122, 142, 148
Border, A.R., 2, 6
Borwick, George, 79
Bowes, W.E. (Bill), 44, 50

Bradman, Sir Donald, 1, 2, 5, 6–7, 14, 16, 20, 26, 29, 31, 32, 34, 35, 37, 39, 40, 41, 42, 43, 44, 46, 69, 70–1, 72, 74–5, 76, 79, 80, 81, 82, 83, 85, 86, 87, 88, 89, 90, 107, 108, 110–11, 112, 113, 114, 115, 116, 117, 118, 119, 120, 122–23, 124, 137, 140, 148, 155, 160, 165, 167, 170, 193, 197, 198, 203
Bradman, Lady Jessie, 12
Brooks, Sir Dallas, 110
Brown, F.R., 50, 72, 130, 132, 133, 134, 135, 136, 137, 138, 160, 166, 167
Brown, W.A. (Bill), 26, 29, 34, 36, 38, 39, 40, 41, 44, 46, 55, 73, 76, 77, 84, 88, 89, 109, 111, 113, 115, 117, 120, 188, 194
'bumpers' (bouncers), 31, 85, 142, 144, 146, 154
Burke, J.W., 136, 137, 138, 142

Calvert, Clive, 52
Cardus, Neville, 1, 15–6, 26–7, 36, 37, 42, 43, 44, 49, 60, 63, 83, 166, 188
Carmody, D.K., 51, 52, 55, 58, 59, 60, 62, 67, 68
Carr, Donald, 60, 62
Casey, R.G. (Lord), 9
Chappell, Greg, 1, 2
Cheetham, Albert, 49, 54, 56, 58, 61
Cheetham, J.E., 127, 148, 152, 156–57
Cheshire, Group Captain Leonard, 19
Chester, Frank, 41, 42, 171, 172, 189, 196
Chipperfield, A.G., 29, 33
Christiani, R.J., 141, 146
Churchill, Sir Winston, 8, 55
Clay, J.C., 35
Close, D.B., 131, 134
Collins, H.L.. 4, 188
Compton, D.C.S. (Denis), 5, 34, 35, 36, 38, 40, 45, 51, 73–4, 79, 81, 82, 83, 85, 113, 114, 116, 117, 119, 130, 131, 132, 135, 136, 137, 138, 139, 162, 165, 167, 169, 171, 172, 175, 177, 196
Constantine, Leary (Lord), 22, 23, 65

Cowdrey, M.C.C. (Colin), 162, 167
Cowie, Jack, 76
Coxon, A., 115
Craig, Ian, 127, 153–54, 156, 157, 158, 161, 170, 173, 177–78
Cranston, Kenneth, 118
Crapp, Jack, 51, 101
Crisp, Bob, 61
Cristofani, R.S., 52, 54, 60, 61, 63, 64, 66, 69
Curtin, John, 54, 55, 56

Danby, Peter, 52
Darling, L.S., 189
Davidson, A.K. (Alan), 16, 158, 159, 161, 166, 171, 174, 176, 177
de Andrado, Harold, 189, 197
de Courcy, J., 158, 159, 162, 168, 169, 174, 176, 177
Dempster, C.S., 51
Dewes, J.G., 60, 61, 62, 131, 132
Dollery, H.E., 115, 116, 118
Donnelly, M.P., 65
Dooland, Bruce, 59, 76, 107
Draper, R.G., 127
Duleepsinghi, K.S., 66, 67
Dwyer, E.A. (Chappie), 14, 123, 128, 148

Edrich, W.J., 34, 35, 40, 42, 56, 57, 65, 77, 79, 80, 81, 82, 85, 112, 113, 114, 116, 118, 119, 168, 169, 172, 175, 176
Emmett, G.M., 117, 118, 168
Evans, T.G., 51, 77, 83, 92, 114, 116, 119, 131, 132, 134, 167, 169, 171, 175, 177
Evatt, Dr H.V., 65

Fagg, Arthur, 45, 177
Farnes, Kenneth, 34, 35, 36
Favell, Les, 191
Ferguson, W.A. (Bill), 199
Fingleton, Jack, 26, 29, 30, 34, 42, 43, 112, 139, 160
Fishlock, L.B., 62, 77
Fleetwood-Smith, L.O'B. (Chuck), 29, 33, 36, 37, 38, 41, 77, 85
Fletcher, K.W., 173
Freer, F.W., 81
Fry, C.B., 16

215

Fuller, E., 148, 156
Fullerton, G.M., 127, 128
Funston, K.J., 148, 150, 152, 154, 155

Geelong College, The, 2, 4, 21, 199, 201
Geelong Football Club, 198–99
Gibb, Paul, 51, 76
Gimblett, Harold, 51
Gladwin, C., 165
Goddard, John, 19, 141, 142, 144
Gomez, G.E., 141, 142, 143, 144, 146
Goonesena, C., 163
Gorman, Eugene, 54
Gover, A.R., 56, 58
Graveney, T.W., 165, 167, 168, 169, 171, 172, 175
Gregory, J.M., 188
Griffith, S.C., 56, 63
Grieves, Ken, 69, 163, 174
Grimmett, C.V., 26, 29, 59, 119, 124, 186
Guillen, S.C., 141
Gul, Mahomed, 87

Hamence, R., 76, 85, 111
Hammond, W.R, 7, 32, 35, 36, 38, 40, 43, 44, 56, 57, 58, 59, 60, 62, 63, 64, 65, 77, 79, 81, 82, 83, 84, 86, 167–68
Hancock, Christine, 190
Hampton, 158
Hardstaff, Joseph, 35, 41, 43, 46, 77, 83, 112, 113, 114
Harvey, R.N. (Neil), 2, 89, 90, 93, 95, 119, 123, 124, 126, 127, 128, 132, 134, 135, 137, 138, 139, 140, 145, 151, 152, 153, 155, 158, 161, 162, 163, 168, 169, 172, 173, 174, 176, 178
Harvey, Mervyn, 90
Hassett, Anna, 2, 12, 123, 158, 202

Hassett, Lindsay
*Personal details*
ability at other sports, 191, 198
accident at Dorchester Hotel, 71
appointed AIF Reception Group, 54
education, 2–3, 21–4, 201
enlists in AIF, 48
  Middle East, 49
  New Guinea, 51–3
family details, 12

marriage to Tess Davis, 50
meets Tess Davis, 12, 47
on pitch inspections, 72
overview, 1–2
personality
  as an entertainer, 17–8, 19, 73, 160, 190, 198
  as a practical joker, 5, 6, 14, 25, 39, 185, 189–90, 193
physique, 7, 31
receives MBE, 199
residences, 13, 110, 158, 197–8
sports stores, 12–13, 110
transferred to UK via USA, 54
works in accountant's office, 47, 110
works for 'Swiss Dye', 110

*General*
ABC commentator, 199–200
addresses crowd at the Oval, 176
appointed vice-captain, 1946–47, 78
arranges for Bill Johnston to top batting averages, 72–3
as bowler, 68 ,139, 176
attacked by NSW fast bowlers, 16–7
backyard cricket, 2–4
bats against Grimmett, 26
Bradman-Ikin incident in first test 1946, 78–9
century against West Indies while at The Geelong College, 23
comes of age as Test batsman (1938), 41
comparison with McCabe, 194
contrast in batting styles, 1, 7, 15–6, 188–89
cricket in A.I.F. in Middle East, 49
dismissed for 0 at Lord's, 100
encounters with Bill O'Reilly, 10–1, 27, 28, 71, 192, 195–96
encounters with D.V.P. Wright, 19, 38, 40, 83, 132, 177
first picked for Victoria, 26
friendship with R.G. Menzies, 179–85, 195
greeting at Southampton 1953, 160
opinion on one-day cricket, 200

opinions on Hassett, 186–97
'Plod and Dasher' at the Oval, 175–76
Pollard's summing up, 203
scores century against West Indies, 145
scores ten Test centuries, 186
sectarianism, 30, 202
South Melbourne Club, 15, 25, 192
subjected to jeering, 173–74
Testimonial Match, 191

*Cricketing details*
Australian Services Team formation, 54–5
  Victory Tests, 56–65
  India Tour 65–8
  Australian Tour 68–9

Sheffield Shield and other first-class matches in Australia, 26–7, 28–9, 48, 78, 84–5, 89, 90, 109, 122, 134, 135, 136, 138, 144, 146–47, 149, 156

Test cricket (including overseas tour matches)
  1938 v England in England, 31–46
  1946 v New Zealand in New Zealand, 76
  1946–7 v England in Australia, 76–86
  1947–48 v India in Australia, 87–90, 107–09
  1948 v England in England, 110–21
  1949–50 v South Africa in South Africa, 122–29
  1950–51 v England in Australia, 130–40
  1951–52 v West Indies in Australia, 141–47
  1952–53 v South Africa in Australia, 148–56
  1953 v England in England, 158–78

Hassett, Margaret, 12, 110, 158, 202
Hassett, Edward (Ted), 2, 3, 10, 197
Hassett, Edward Snr, 3, 27, 200
Hassett, Frances, 10
Hassett, Harry, 24

## ◆ INDEX ◆

Hassett, Richard, 2, 21, 27
Hassett, Vin, 2, 10, 21
Hassett, Tessa, 12, 13, 14, 47, 50, 53, 158, 197, 198, 201–02
Hassett's private army, 160
Hawke, (Lord), 36
Hazare, V.S., 66, 67, 87, 89, 107, 108–09
Herbert, Sir Alan, 160–61
Hill, J.C., 159, 161, 162, 163, 164, 166, 169, 178
Hilton, Malcolm, 163
Hobbs, Sir Jack, 4, 27, 34, 60, 90, 174, 186
Hole, G.B., 138, 139, 144, 146, 153, 156, 158, 164, 166, 169, 172, 176
Hollies, W.E., 120, 173, 174, 187
Holmes, E.R.T., 51, 58, 60
Howard, J.W., 185
Hurwood, Alec, 48, 50
Hutton, Sir Leonard,18, 24, 35, 36, 42, 43, 44, 46, 56, 57, 58, 59, 60, 61, 62, 64, 65, 77, 79, 82, 83, 85, 86, 112, 114, 116, 117, 118, 119, 125, 131, 132, 133, 134, 135, 137, 138, 139, 161, 165, 166, 167, 169, 171, 172, 175, 176, 178

Innes, A.R., 148, 156
Irani, J.K., 87
Ikin, J.T., 77, 79, 81, 85, 86
Iverson, Jack, 21, 24, 132, 135, 136, 137, 150

Jackson, A.A., 1, 16, 45
Jardine, D.R., 6, 160
Johnson, I.W. (Ian), 6, 8, 14, 15, 16–7, 18, 19, 25, 45, 55, 69, 70, 76, 80, 81, 90, 107, 108, 111, 112, 116, 118, 123, 125, 127, 133, 136, 144, 150, 159, 199
Johnson, K.O.E., 55, 68
Johnston, Fred, 88, 131
Johnston, W.A. (Bill), 8, 72–3, 88, 89, 90, 107, 111, 113, 115, 116, 117, 123, 124, 125, 127, 135, 142, 145, 155, 159, 163, 168, 173, 175, 176, 177, 178, 191, 192, 193, 197
Jones, P.E., 141

Kadar, A.H., 68
Keith, Headley, 148
Kelleway, C.E., 168
Kenyon, Donald, 164, 167, 168

Kippax, Alan, 1, 45, 122, 135
Kischenchand, H., 87, 107, 108
Laker, J.C., 63, 112, 113, 114, 117, 118, 119, 153, 168, 172, 176
Langridge, J., 77,
Langley, G.R.A., 123, 142, 150, 151, 159, 166, 172, 175
Larwood, Harold, 27, 39
Lee, P.K., 26
Lee, Frank, 171
Legacy Club of Melbourne, 52
Levison-Gower, H.D., 45, 65
Leyland, Maurice, 42, 43
Lindsay Hassett Club, 20, 201
Lindsay Hassett Dahlia, 198
Lindwall, R.R., 9, 16, 55, 76, 80, 81, 85, 86, 90, 107, 109, 111, 112, 114, 116, 117, 118, 120, 122, 123, 125, 126, 127, 128, 132, 133, 135, 138, 142, 143, 144, 146, 152, 154, 155, 159, 161, 162, 165, 169, 171–72, 175, 177, 188, 191
Loader, Peter , 173
Lock, G.A.R. (Tony), 5, 170, 172, 173, 176
Loxton, S.J.E. 109, 111, 117, 123, 127, 133, 136, 138, 200
Lush, J.G. (Ginty), 28, 29

Macartney, C.G., 1, 2, 4
Mailey, Arthur, 114, 160, 187
Mallyon, John, 54, 55
Mallett, Ashley, 186
Makad, Vinoo, 66, 67, 87, 88, 107, 109
Mansell, P.N.F., 148, 152, 157
Marshall, R.E., 141
Marylebone Cricket Club (MCC), 5
May, P.B.H., 162, 173, 175, 176, 186
Melbourne Cricket Ground Trust, 201
Melle, M.G., 127, 128, 148, 151
Menzies, Sir Robert, 179–85, 195
Meuleman, K., 76, 90, 123, 132
Merchant, V.M., 66, 67, 68, 87, 110, 196
Mitchell, Bruce, 124, 126
Miller, K.R., 16, 17, 47, 51, 54, 56, 57, 59, 61, 62, 64, 65, 69, 76, 78, 80, 82, 83, 85, 86, 90, 107, 111, 112, 115, 119, 120, 122, 124,

125, 126, 128, 132, 135, 138, 142, 143, 145, 146, 152, 154, 155, 159, 164, 166, 167, 168, 169, 171, 172, 175, 176, 177, 188, 189, 191, 192, 196
Modi, R.S., 67, 68, 87, 110
Moroney, Jack, 123, 125, 126, 127, 128, 132, 133, 134, 145
Morris, A.R., 13, 14, 16, 18, 20, 55, 73, 78, 79, 81, 82, 83, 85, 88, 107, 111, 113, 116, 117, 119, 120, 123, 125, 126, 127, 132, 133, 134, 137, 138, 144, 145, 150, 151, 152, 154, 156, 158, 161, 163, 164, 165, 167, 170, 175–76, 177, 178, 185, 188, 189, 192, 194, 195, 197, 198
Morris, Judith, 12
Mountbatten, Lord Louis, 87
Moyes, A.G. (Johnny), 144, 199
Murray, A.R., 148, 152
Mushtaq, Ali, 66, 67
McCabe, S.J., 1, 2, 7, 25, 26, 29, 30, 33, 37, 41, 42, 45, 46, 49, 50, 63, 70, 77, 110, 123, 135, 168, 190, 193, 194, 196, 201
McCabe, Edna, 12, 13
McCarthy, Cuan, 127
McCool, Colin, 55, 69, 76, 80, 82, 83, 85, 89–90, 111, 123, 142, 150
McCormick, E.L., 29, 30, 32–3, 35, 38
McDonald, A.W., 51,
McDonald, C.C., 146, 151, 154–55, 156, 159, 170, 177
McEachern, Malcolm, 198
McGlew, D.J., 148, 149, 152, 154
McGilvray, Alan, 13, 197, 199–200
McIntyre, A.J., 131
Mackay, K., 150
McLean, R.A., 148, 150, 152, 154, 156, 157

Nagle, Lisle, 48
Nayudu, C.K., 87, 88
Nel, Jack, 6
new ball rule, 84
Noblet, Geffrey, 123, 128, 144, 156
Norton, N.O., 148
Nourse, Dudley, 124, 126, 127, 128

Oldfield, W.A., 122, 160, 188
O'Neill, Norman, 16

217

O'Reilly, Molly, 12
O'Reilly, W.J. (Bill), 1, 8, 25, 26, 27, 28, 30, 33, 35, 36, 37, 38, 39, 40, 41, 43, 45, 46, 49, 69, 70, 71, 72, 73, 74, 76, 77, 107, 111, 113–14, 119, 121, 160, 174, 186, 189, 192, 193, 196, 200
Oxenham, R.K., 26, 29

Palmer, C.H., 14
Parkhouse, W.G., 131, 134, 137
Pawson, L., 96
Paynter, Eddie, 35, 36, 38, 45
Peacock, Ross, 201
Pearce, T.N., 178
Peebles, Ian, 18
Pellew, C.E., 188
Pepper, Cecil, 29, 54, 56, 57–8, 59, 60, 62, 64, 65, 67, 68, 69
Pettiford, Jack, 54, 62, 63, 67
Phadkar, D.G., 87, 88, 94
Phillipson, W.E., 63, 64
Pollard, Jack, 203
Pollard, Richard, 58, 59, 63, 65
Ponsford, W.H., 12, 20, 83
Pope, G.H., 35, 58, 59, 60, 62, 63
Price, Charlie, 54, 55, 56, 58, 60, 64

Rae, A.F., 141
Rai Singh, 88
Ramadhin, Sonny, 19, 141, 143, 145
Rangachari, C., 88, 89, 92
Ranjitsinjhi, K.S., 66
Rangnekar, K.M., 87
Redpath, Ian, 21, 24
Richardson, P.E., 177
Richardson, Tom, 174
Richardson, V.Y., 26, 67, 68, 200
Rickards, K.R., 145
Ridings, Phil, 148, 152
Ring, D.T., 111, 142, 143, 144, 145, 150–51, 153, 154, 156, 159, 161, 162, 166, 174
Robertson, J.D., 51, 56, 57, 58, 59, 60, 62
Robins, R.W.V., 5, 34, 51, 56, 58, 160
Robinson, Rayford, 49, 50
Robinson, R.A., 74, 186, 189
Rodgers, Hugh, 200
Rolland, Sir Frank, 2, 199
Roper, A.W., 51, 54, 55, 67, 69
Rowan, Athol, 124
Rowan, E.A.B., 124, 125, 126, 128, 187

Ryder, Jack, 20, 65–6, 123
Saggers, R.A., 60, 71, 95, 123
Sandham, Andrew, 174
Sandringham Club, 18, 158
Sarwate, C.T., 87, 107, 108
Schofield, George, 48, 50, 52, 110
Sen, P., 87
Sheehan, Paul, 21, 24
Sheppard, D.S., 131, 132, 137
Simpson, R.B. (Bob), 5, 192
Simpson, R.T. (Reg), 5, 24, 131, 135, 136, 137, 138, 139, 165, 168, 172
Sismey, S.G., 51, 54, 55, 56, 57, 58, 59, 60, 61, 62, 68, 79, 195–6
Smirke, Charles, 193
Smith, Kendall, 190
Smith, Peter, 77
South Melbourne Cricket Club, 15, 19, 25, 70, 192, 199–200
Stanford, R.M., 52, 55, 56, 57, 58, 61, 63
Statham, J.B., 86, 163, 166, 170
Stephenson, J.W.A., 56, 57, 58
Stollmeyer, J.B., 141, 143, 146
Strudwick, Herbert, 4
Sutcliffe, Billy, 166
Sutcliffe, Herbert, 4, 90, 186
Swanton, E.W., 5, 140, 188

Tallon, Donald, 29, 60, 76, 111, 115, 123, 142, 150, 151, 159, 165, 177
Tarrant, Frank, 65
Tate, Maurice, 4
Tattersall, Roy, 137, 164, 165
Tayfield, Hugh, 113, 126, 127, 128, 148, 150, 151, 152, 153, 154
Taylor, H.W., 148
Taylor, J.M., 4, 188
Taylor, Mark, 40
Thomson, Peter, 187
Toms, George, 14
Toshack, E.R.H., 76, 80, 83, 90, 107, 111, 115, 120, 123
Tribe, George, 161, 168
Trim, John, 141, 145
Trott, Harry, 25
Trueman, F.S., 86, 168, 170, 175, 177
Trumper, Victor, 1, 2, 63, 168
Turner, Dr Pauline, 21
Tyson, Frank, 86, 168

Ushers Hotel, 14

Valentine, Tom, 43, 46
Verity, Hedley, 35, 38, 39, 46

Victorian Cricket Association, 192
Victory Tests, 12, 55, 196 *see also* Australian Services Team
Viljoen, K., 148
Voce, W.A., 27, 39, 77, 81

Wade, W.W., 49, 124
Waite, J.H.B., 148, 151, 155, 156
Waite, M.G., 29, 42
Walcott, C.L., 19, 141, 142, 143, 146
Walker, C.W., 151
Walker, Alan, 16, 123
Wall, T.W., 26
Ward, Frank, 26, 29, 34, 37, 45, 77
Wardle, J.H., 164, 165, 166, 167, 178
Warne, Shane, 29
Warner, Sir Pelham ('Plum'), 51, 57, 65
Warr, J.J., 131, 135, 136, 137
Washbrook, Cyril, 5, 8, 24, 51, 56, 57, 59, 63, 64, 65, 72, 77, 79, 83, 112, 114, 117, 118, 131, 132, 137, 139
Watkins, J.C., 127, 148, 155, 156
Watson, William, 166, 167
Weekes, E. de C., 141, 142, 143, 145
White, E.C.S. (Ted), 29, 48, 49, 50, 193, 194
White, Luke, 60, 62
Whitington, R.S., 8, 9, 47, 54, 55, 56, 57, 59, 62, 63, 67, 198
Williams, Graham, 55, 56, 57, 64
Williams, Harold, 198
*Wisden's Almanac*, 121
Wood, Arthur, 43–4
Woodfull, W.M., 20, 25, 60
Woolley, F.E., 7, 42, 45
Workman, J.A., 51, 55, 56, 59, 62, 63
Worrall, Sir Frank, 141, 142, 147
Wright, D.V.P. (Doug), 19-20, 35, 37, 38, 40, 41, 56, 61, 62, 77, 80, 81, 82, 85, 86, 115, 117, 119, 131, 132, 133, 135, 137, 139, 177
Wright, Matthew, 22, 23
Wyatt, R.E.S., 34, 46, 51
Wynne, O.E., 127

Yardley, N.W.D., 81, 82, 83, 113, 114, 116, 118, 119, 178
Young, J.A., 96, 115, 117, 118